AMERICAN VALUES

OPPOSING VIEWPOINTS®

Other Books of Related Interest in the Opposing
Viewpoints Series:

AMERICAN
VALUES
OPPOSING VIEWPOINTS®

David Bender & Bruno Leone, *Series Editors*

Charles P. Cozic, *Book Editor*

Greenhaven Press, Inc., San Diego, CA

Greenhaven Press, Inc.
PO Box 289009
San Diego, CA 92198-9009

Library of Congress Cataloging-in-Publication Data

American Values : opposing viewpoints / Charles P. Cozic, book editor.
    p.   cm. — (Opposing viewpoints series)
  Includes bibliographical references and index.
  ISBN 1-56510-242-8 (lib. : alk. paper) — ISBN 1-56510-241-X (pbk. : alk. paper).
  1. Life. 2. Values. 3. United States—Moral conditions.
I. Cozic, Charles P., 1957–   . II. Series: Opposing viewpoints series (Unnumbered)
BD435.A56   1995
170'.973—dc20   94-41912
                                                            CIP
                                                            AC

"Congress shall make no law . . . abridging the freedom of speech, or of the press."

First Amendment to the U.S. Constitution

The basic foundation of our democracy is the First Amendment guarantee of freedom of expression. The Opposing Viewpoints Series is dedicated to the concept of this basic freedom and the idea that it is more important to practice it than to enshrine it.

Contents

Why Consider Opposing Viewpoints?

"The only way in which a human being can make some approach to knowing the whole of a subject is by hearing what can be said about it by persons of every variety of opinion and studying all modes in which it can be looked at by every character of mind. No wise man ever acquired his wisdom in any mode but this."

John Stuart Mill

In our media-intensive culture it is not difficult to find differing opinions. Thousands of newspapers and magazines and dozens of radio and television talk shows resound with differing points of view. The difficulty lies in deciding which opinion to agree with and which "experts" seem the most credible. The more inundated we become with differing opinions and claims, the more essential it is to hone critical reading and thinking skills to evaluate these ideas. Opposing Viewpoints books address this problem directly by presenting stimulating debates that can be used to enhance and teach these skills. The varied opinions contained in each book examine many different aspects of a single issue. While examining these conveniently edited opposing views, readers can develop critical thinking skills such as the ability to compare and contrast authors' credibility, facts, argumentation styles, use of persuasive techniques, and other stylistic tools. In short, the Opposing Viewpoints Series is an ideal way to attain the higher-level thinking and reading skills so essential in a culture of diverse and contradictory opinions.

In addition to providing a tool for critical thinking, Opposing Viewpoints books challenge readers to question their own strongly held opinions and assumptions. Most people form their opinions on the basis of upbringing, peer pressure, and personal, cultural, or professional bias. By reading carefully balanced opposing views, readers must directly confront new ideas as well as the opinions of those with whom they disagree. This is not to simplistically argue that everyone who reads opposing views will—or should—change his or her opinion. Instead, the series enhances readers' depth of understanding of their own views by encouraging confrontation with opposing ideas. Careful examination of others' views can lead to the readers' understanding of the logical inconsistencies in their own opinions, perspective on why they hold an opinion, and the consideration of the possibility that their opinion requires further evaluation.

Evaluating Other Opinions

To ensure that this type of examination occurs, Opposing Viewpoints books present all types of opinions. Prominent spokespeople on different sides of each issue as well as well-known professionals from many disciplines challenge the reader. An additional goal of the series is to provide a forum for other, less known, or even unpopular viewpoints. The opinion of an ordinary person who has had to make the decision to cut off life support from a terminally ill relative, for example, may be just as valuable and provide just as much insight as a medical ethicist's professional opinion. The editors have two additional purposes in including these less known views. One, the editors encourage readers to respect others' opinions—even when not enhanced by professional credibility. It is only by reading or listening to and objectively evaluating others' ideas that one can determine whether they are worthy of consideration. Two, the inclusion of such viewpoints encourages the important critical thinking skill of objectively evaluating an author's credentials and bias. This evaluation will illuminate an author's reasons for taking a particular stance on an issue and will aid in readers' evaluation of the author's ideas.

As series editors of the Opposing Viewpoints Series, it is our hope that these books will give readers a deeper understanding of the issues debated and an appreciation of the complexity of even seemingly simple issues when good and honest people disagree. This awareness is particularly important in a democratic society such as ours in which people enter into public debate to determine the common good. Those with whom one disagrees should not be regarded as enemies but rather as people whose views deserve careful examination and may shed light on one's own.

Thomas Jefferson once said that "difference of opinion leads to inquiry, and inquiry to truth." Jefferson, a broadly educated man, argued that "if a nation expects to be ignorant and free . . . it expects what never was and never will be." As individuals and as a nation, it is imperative that we consider the opinions of others and examine them with skill and discernment. The Opposing Viewpoints Series is intended to help readers achieve this goal.

David L. Bender & Bruno Leone,
Series Editors

Introduction

"We have to reach deep inside to the values, the spirit, the soul, and the truth of human nature [to] take us where we need to go."

—Bill Clinton, 1993

Among a large segment of America, there seems to be a pervasive sense of anxiety and pessimism about the present and the future and a longing for "the good old days." This pessimism is not new in America. In 1948, according to a Roper Organization poll, twice as many Americans expected "the next few years" to bring "worse times" than "better times." In 1963, a Gallup poll found 59 percent of Americans dissatisfied with the level of "honesty and standards of behavior of people in the country today."

Perhaps related to such pessimism is the idea that America's values have deteriorated. The set of beliefs—often interrelated —coming under the banner of "values" is a large one: traditional values such as freedom, family values such as love and self-sacrifice, ethical or moral values such as honesty, and many more.

Among such diverse types of values, there are those that are considered to be so commonly shared among Americans that they are defined as traditional values. These include, but are not limited to, liberty, democracy, and constitutional rights; humanitarian values such as charity; and individualism and enterprise. It is incumbent upon Americans, many argue, to live up to these traditional values through their actions. In the words of Stanford University public service professor John W. Gardner: "The identifying of values is a light, preliminary exercise before the real and heroic task, which is to make the values live—in our behavior and customs and laws."

Many Americans believe this task has not been met and that important traditional values—at least in terms of how people practice them—have decayed. As some observers see it, Americans suffer from an ethical or moral failure, neglecting responsible behavior and values such as honesty. According to conservative scholar William J. Bennett, "During the last quarter-century, the American people increasingly have abandoned time-honored moral codes." The source of moral decay, many contend, is the

13

fraying of social bonds. As Gardner notes, "Unfortunately for our nation, the soil in which shared values are rooted and nurtured—the family and community—is being blown away in the dust storm of contemporary life." The result, Bennett explains, is evident in a myriad of social ills such as rampant crime, family disintegration, and values-deficient schools.

But others argue that traditional values remain as vital and durable today as when praised by the nation's founders two hundred years ago. Such strength may simply be less apparent when the mood of many Americans is one of pessimism. In the words of public opinion expert Everett Carll Ladd: "Many citizens these days evince considerable concern and dissatisfaction. Yet a large structure of national self-images, expectations, norms, and values remains in place, largely undisturbed." Former United Technologies CEO Harry J. Gray agrees: "Change is a constant in society, but the really important things have *not* changed. I refer to the traditional values—the simple, basic truths—all of us believe in." Gray asserts that such truths as individualism, liberty, and patriotism "are ingrained in our character" and are responsible for America's overall success.

There is much confidence that the American character, or spirit—brimming with imagination, motivation, and talent—can reinforce traditional values. Although Gardner and Gray disagree about whether these values have withered, they agree that motivation is an inherent trait Americans can summon forth to strengthen basic values that society thrives on. To many Americans, nothing less than national ideals themselves are at stake. In Gardner's words, "The capacity of the American people for motivated action is not to be doubted. The great ideas still beckon —freedom, equality, and justice."

The traditional values passed from one generation to the next and the assimilation of values by immigrants have sustained ideals such as democracy and freedom. But at the same time, shifts in social attitudes and beliefs have generated concern about America's values. The authors of this revised edition of *American Values: Opposing Viewpoints* examine the state of traditional and other values in the following chapters: What Values Should America Uphold? How Are American Values Changing? Is America in Decline? How Important Are Family Values? How Do Religious Values Influence America? How Does Materialism Affect America? Values, these authors would stress, are guiding principles that Americans should devote much attention to. In the words of William J. Bennett, "Behavior follows attitude, and attitude follows belief."

What Values Should America Uphold?

AMERICAN
VALUES

Chapter Preface

Individualism is the term that many people believe best defines American culture and society. The ability to exercise free will and individual choice permeates society and is the foundation of cherished freedoms—including the freedom of speech, religious liberty, and the right to associate, vote, and work without government interference. In the words of news commentator George F. Will, "America has been well-served by the individualism of its political philosophy and economic practice. Liberty and prosperity are individualism's fruits."

But critics warn that an overemphasis on individualism—rampant individualism—is destroying the sense of community in America. According to George Washington University professor Amitai Etzioni, a leader of the expanding communitarian movement, "We have tilted too far in the direction of letting people do their own thing and have concerned ourselves too little with our social responsibilities." Will echoes Etzioni's apprehension and notes that from 1964 to 1995, participation in parent-teacher associations suffered a decline from twelve million to seven million, as did volunteering for service organizations such as the Boy Scouts and the Red Cross.

Many Americans desire stronger communities and more responsible conduct, but at the same time they value the freedom to act individually and in their own self-interest. A tempered individualism, one less far-reaching and insistent than that of the past, may become an ideal pursued by Americans who value both the individual will and the communal spirit. The authors in this chapter debate whether individualism, communitarianism, or other values are best for America.

16

"The three pillars of modern conservatism are religion, nationalism and economic growth."

Conservatism Is Ideal for America

Irving Kristol

Irving Kristol is one of America's most renowned conservative writers. In the following viewpoint, Kristol argues that conservatism is poised to replace liberalism and secular humanism as America's dominant ideology. The failure of liberal programs, Kristol asserts, demands that pressing concerns such as crime and the budget deficit be addressed from a conservative view of human nature and responsibility. He contends that the crisis provoked by liberalism must be countered by the reaffirmation of conservatism's three pillars—religion, nationalism, and economic growth. Kristol predicts that religious conservatives—growing in number and influence—will become the core of conservatism. Kristol, a distinguished fellow at the American Enterprise Institute in Washington, D.C., publishes the *National Interest* and coedits the *Public Interest* quarterly journals.

As you read, consider the following questions:

1. In Kristol's opinion, why is religion the most important component of conservatism?
2. What does Kristol mean by the politics of "unmet needs"?
3. Why are religious people important to the Republican Party, according to the author?

Irving Kristol, "The Coming 'Conservative Century,'" *The Wall Street Journal*, February 1, 1993. Reprinted with permission of *The Wall Street Journal*, ©1993 Dow Jones & Company, Inc. All rights reserved.

The beginning of political wisdom in the 1990s is the recognition that liberalism today is at the end of its intellectual tether. The fact that it can win elections is irrelevant. Conservatives continued to win elections during "the liberal century" (1870-1970); but, once in office, they revealed themselves to be impotent to enact a sustained conservative agenda. The tide of public opinion was too strong against them.

That tide has now turned. It is liberal administrations today, in all the Western democracies, that find themselves relatively impotent when in office. Just as conservative administrations used to nibble away at liberal reforms previously enacted, so liberals in office today do their share of nibbling at the occasional conservative reform that has taken root. More often, they find themselves nibbling away at the liberal reforms of their predecessors, reforms that threaten fiscal insolvency as well as political fragmentation.

The Sterility of Secular Humanism

The liberal consensus, as expressed in the media, is that, with the election of Bill Clinton, conservatism in America is in disarray, is groping for some center of equilibrium, and that only a "moderate" Republican coalition, one that disengages itself from the religious right, can create an American majority. This may be true in the shorter term, as defined by the next presidential election or two, but in the longer term that consensus is false. The religious conservatives are already too numerous to be shunted aside, and their numbers are growing, as is their influence. They are going to be the very core of an emerging American conservatism.

For the past century the rise of liberalism has been wedded to the rise of secularism in all areas of American life. In the decades ahead, the decline of secularism will signify the decline of liberalism as well. Already on the far-left fringes of liberalism itself, artists and philosophers are welcoming the collapse of a "secular humanism" that they find sterile and oppressive. They can offer nothing with which to replace this liberal-secular humanism. But others can, and will. Today, it is the religious who have a sense that the tide has turned and that the wave of the future is moving in their direction.

The three pillars of modern conservatism are religion, nationalism and economic growth. Of these, religion is easily the most important because it is the only power that, in the longer term, can shape people's characters and regulate their motivation. In economics, secular incentives (i.e., materialist incentives) can be effective. But in the really troubled areas of modern life, where social policy is at work, the welfare state has given birth to a long train of calamities. Perverse economic incentives can encourage a corrupting dependency, and liberalism has, in the name of compassion, created a network of such perverse incentives. But it does not follow that modifying such incentives will have a dramatic effect.

The reason is simple: It is not possible to motivate people to do the right thing, and avoid doing the wrong thing, unless people are told, from childhood on, what the right things and the wrong things are. This explains why so many of our newer immigrants, from traditional families, ignore these tempting, corrupting incentives and instead move on to productive law-abiding lives. Even then, some do not pay heed. But most do, most of the time.

The New Citizenship

Out of the ashes of George Bush's defeat in 1992 has come a bold new strategy for American conservatism. The strategy, called the "new citizenship," builds on the scholarship of Robert Nisbet, Michael Novak, Peter Berger, Richard John Neuhaus, and other leading conservative thinkers. Its goal is the reconstruction of civil society, the return of America to the self-governing republic described by Alexis de Tocqueville and envisioned by the Founding Fathers. Its social vision contrasts sharply with the similar-sounding but profoundly different rhetoric of "national community" espoused by President Clinton.

Michael Joyce, president of the Bradley Foundation, has been the principal architect of this new strategy. . . .

Americans [according to Joyce] are "sick and tired of being treated as helpless, pathetic victims of social forces that are beyond their understanding or control . . . of being treated as passive clients by arrogant, paternalistic social scientists, therapists, professionals, and bureaucrats." Under the "new citizenship" strategy, conservatives would empower families to take back their schools and neighborhoods, to make key decisions about education and health care and the character of their communities.

William A. Schambra, *Policy Review*, Summer 1994.

The most extraordinary social phenomenon of the liberal century has been the totally unexpected increase in criminality. The first obligation of government always has been to ensure the security of the person. Liberalism does not believe this—it represents "too punitive" a conception of the governmental mission. Instead, liberalism believes that if you diminish income inequalities and provide cradle-to-birth income security and ample provision of medical care, then the criminal impulse will wither away. In the face of increasing criminality, therefore, liberalism responds with ever more fanciful and ever more desperate "therapeutic" programs, all of which are ineffectual.

As with crime, so with all the other social pathologies that now infest our liberal society and its welfare state. The "joy of sex" has been compromised by an infusion of sexual anxiety, as venereal diseases ranging from the fatal to the noxious proliferate. It has also produced a large and growing population of unwed mothers and their babies. The liberal answer to this human disaster is either to deny that it is any kind of disaster—"just a new kind of family," the social workers chirp—or to create more programs of "sex education." But it is such secular, nonjudgmental education—an education bereft of moral guidance—that has helped create this problem in the first place.

Back in 1897, John Dewey defined the essence of the liberal credo: "The practical problem of modern society is the maintenance of the spiritual values of civilization, through the medium of the insight and decision of the individual."

A noble idea but ultimately a self-contradictory one. You do not preserve spiritual values by turning them over to a rampant spiritual individualism. That experiment has been tried, and it has failed—though any admission of failure is not something we can expect.

On the contrary: What we are witnessing and living through is a prolonged spasm of liberal fanaticism—a redoubling of liberal effort as liberal program after liberal program fails. With each failure, the credibility of government is diminished and cynicism about politics increases. Does anyone really believe that the Clinton administration will significantly reduce, or that a Bush administration would have significantly reduced, the budget deficit?

Human Nature: A Different View

The plain truth is that if we are ever going to cope with the deficit, and the social programs that inflate it, we are going to have to begin with a very different view of human nature and human responsibility in relation to such issues as criminality, sexuality, welfare dependency, even medical insurance. Only to the degree that such a new—actually very old—way of looking at ourselves and our fellow citizens emerges can a public opinion be shaped that will candidly confront the fiscal crisis of the welfare state. Presidential calls for "sacrifice," meaning a willingness to pay higher taxes, are a liberal cop-out. Why don't we hear something about self-control and self-reliance? It's the traditional spiritual values that we as individuals need, not newly invented, trendy ones.

We hear it said constantly and with pseudo-solemnity that this

20

fiscal crisis results from the people demanding benefits that they are then unwilling to pay for. Were this so, the inference would be that such a corrupt people are incapable of democratic self-government and are in need of an elite to do the job for them. Liberals, despite their populist rhetoric, have been discreetly drawing this inference for many years now. Much of our overblown welfare state was created by liberal political entrepreneurs, not in response to an evident popular demand. Liberals may scornfully dismiss "supply-side" economics, but they are profoundly committed to "supply-side" politics—the politics of "unmet needs," a category that is constantly expanding. Also expanding, of course, are the official bureaucracies and those "helping" professions that cope with those "needs."

To counter the crisis that liberalism is provoking in our society, conservatism has to rediscover and reaffirm its attachment to its three traditional pillars. A reaffirmation of the goal of economic growth should not be difficult. It is becoming even more widely appreciated that economic growth is crucially dependent on the ability of "economic activists" to invest and innovate. Just as political activists, spurred by political ambition, are at the heart of liberal public policy, so economic activists, spurred by economic ambition, are at the heart of conservative economic policy. It is they who promote the growth that pacifies egalitarian and redistributional appetites. There is still an influential segment of "old conservatives" who do not understand that a pro-entrepreneurial emphasis in economic policy is not simply a "pro-business" policy. But they are gradually fading away.

Similarly, an affirmation of the national spirit is practically inevitable, as the liberal internationalism that has defined American foreign policy since the days of Woodrow Wilson continues to unravel. The U.S. will surely want to, and will need to, remain an active world power, but this activity will not be within the confines prescribed by the United Nations or NATO [North Atlantic Treaty Organization] or whatever. In this post-Cold War era, those organizations are on their way to becoming moribund. Nor are we about to engage in some kind of benign humanitarian imperialism—except in very special circumstances, decided case by case. A renascent nationalism will be accompanied by a renascent neo-realism in foreign policy. This is something that most conservatives have long wished for.

Embracing the Religious

Coping with a religious revival, however, is something that conservatives and the Republican Party are not yet prepared to do. Religious people always create problems since their ardor tends to outrun the limits of politics in a constitutional democracy. But if the Republican Party is to survive, it must work at

21

accommodating these people. In a sense, the influx of the religious into American politics is analogous to the influx of European immigrants into our urban centers between 1870 and 1914. They created many problems, but the Democrats welcomed them while the Republicans shunned them. That was the origin of the "natural" Democratic majority.

The Democrats are never going to be able to welcome the religious, but if the Republicans keep them at arm's length instead of embracing them, and shaping their political thinking, a third party and a restructuring of American politics are certain. One way or another, in the decades ahead they will not be denied.

"Liberals have traditionally been concerned with liberty, rights, justice, and equality—in short, the ideals of 'liberal democracy.'"

Liberalism Is Ideal for America

Gary Doore

In the 1980s, a resurgence of conservatism swept America as Ronald Reagan and other conservatives capitalized on public disenchantment with liberal politics. In the following viewpoint, Gary Doore argues that this shift in the public mood has forced many liberals to become more conservative. Doore argues that the public does not comprehend how severely democracy has eroded under Reagan-style conservatism, leading to authoritarianism in government and the workplace. Doore maintains that liberals in power should reassert liberal ideals to democratize American political and business systems. Doore holds a doctorate in the philosophy of religion from Oxford University and is a freelance writer in San Diego.

As you read, consider the following questions:

1. What does the term "imperial presidency" mean, according to Arthur Schlesinger, as cited by the author?
2. How did the Reagan administration censor information, according to Doore?
3. How can greater democracy help businesses, in the author's opinion?

"Democratizing the United States" by Gary Doore first appeared in the May/June 1993 issue of *The Humanist* and is reprinted by permission of The American Humanist Association, ©1993.

Liberals have traditionally been concerned with liberty, rights, justice, and equality—in short, the ideals of "liberal democracy." True, the original liberals, beginning with Adam Smith's generation, interpreted democratic ideals as applying only to white men who owned a certain amount of property. But a truly egalitarian democracy was implicit in their rhetoric from the start, though it was only gradually implemented by later generations. Thus, liberalism has become *more* liberal with age—so much so that its original tenets are now regarded as extreme conservatism. Laissez-faire, for instance, was one of the main planks of the eighteenth-century "liberal" economic platform.

Since about 1980, however, the trend toward an increasingly liberal liberalism has been reversed. Democratic candidates who 20 years ago would have been called moderate liberals are now called "too liberal to win." This reflects a general shift to the right in American politics, under the impact of a sick economy whose symptoms were blamed—rightly or wrongly—on liberal economics. Double-digit inflation and sky-high interest rates in the late 1970s were widely seen as discrediting the Keynesian principles of deficit finance that liberal economists had prescribed for decades as the remedy for recession. "Tax-and-spend liberals" then became the chief devils in the old-time conservative religion preached by Ronald Reagan and his supply-side deacons, led by Milton Friedman (ironically, a disciple of Adam Smith, one of the original "liberals").

A Rightward Trend

The debacle of liberal economics in turn cast doubt on liberalism in general, so that the term *liberal* itself became a kind of political slur, and successfully pinning it on one's opponent increasingly became a way to win elections. To cope with the harsh new political climate, the Democratic Party was forced to become more "centrist," which is to say less liberal. If this rightward trend continues, the moderate Democrats of tomorrow will resemble today's conservative Republicans, whereas the latter will then be the equivalent of today's ultraconservatives.

Bill Clinton's election represents a victory for the new Democratic centrism. Clinton has distanced himself from many of the liberal economic and fiscal policies advocated by old-style Democrats because voters were clearly disenchanted with those policies. But during the Reagan-Bush era, much of the public also became disenchanted with liberal *political* ideals as well. This was reflected in widespread support for (or at least acquiescence in) more than a decade of regressive policies in such areas as equal opportunity, civil rights, social welfare, and environmental protection. The [Reagan and Bush] administrations were also notable for an erosion of First Amendment rights, for more government secrecy, censorship, and repression, and for an increasing centralization of power in the executive branch—in short, a drift toward authoritarianism and away from democratic ideals.

If the Clinton administration wants to maintain the support of its more liberal constituencies, it must help to restore the good name of liberalism by reaffirming those ideals of liberal democracy that were trampled under by the Reagan and Bush administrations. At the same time, it must remain true to its pledge to discard those elements of old-style liberal economics that proved to be counterproductive. There are, however, a few obstacles in the way.

Unfortunately, most Americans do not yet fully realize how reactionary the Reagan and Bush administrations were—and the press, for the most part, is now interested in other things. Thus, the illusion is fostered that the past two administrations represented nothing out of the ordinary. Twelve years of reactionary propaganda and daily exposure, via the media, to the regressive-thinking-in-action of top government officials produced in much of the public a passive acceptance of illiberal, anti-democratic attitudes. And since Clinton seems so anxious not to offend public opinion—even when it is misguided—there is a real danger that he will fail to use the power and influence of his office to help rehabilitate liberal democratic ideals.

Strong, Assertive Liberalism

A strong, assertive liberalism is a prerequisite for the changes that are needed in America, as well as for the renewal of a linked or adjacent democratic left.

This country needs a democratic left—a movement that will speak about the democratization of society, that will seek to control business and to stimulate investment and innovation for the general good, that will create a basis for majority electoral coalitions. The social basis for such a left already exists—in the unions and in women's movements, in movements for ecology, for the rights of minorities and immigrants. A desire for such a movement isn't hard to detect, either—among educated young people, for instance, who wish to pursue careers devoted to social progress, egalitarianism, the sharing of privileges.

Dissent, Fall 1991.

One of the worst illusions fostered by the political rhetoric of both parties is that America already is a fully democratic society, with little room for further democratization. We hold up our own nation as a model for others to emulate; we condemn governments that we judge to be "undemocratic." This rhetoric of democracy is obligatory in politicians because it makes voters feel good about themselves and their country. But it obscures the fact that there is plenty of room for more *actual* democracy in American life.

For instance, most people spend about half of their waking hours in workplaces that are run according to authoritarian—not democratic—principles. Employees in the typical corporation have absolutely no voice in the crucial decisions that affect them most directly and profoundly—decisions such as what to produce, where to produce it, and how to produce it (not to mention how much to pay those who produce it). Like authoritarian states, most corporations are based upon centralized power, bureaucratic hierarchy, anti-democratic controls, and an absence of individual initiative and autonomy. It is therefore not surprising that the millions of Americans who work for large corporations—and the majority do—develop the psychological traits needed to survive under authoritarian rule: obedience, conformity, subservience, and fear of responsibility.

Such conditioning in turn affects a people's political behavior. True democracy depends upon the existence of many independent, self-disciplined, and innovative citizens who are willing to accept responsibility for their own decisions. But the psychological traits developed from years of "fitting in" (and, thus, keeping one's job) in a corporate hierarchy are just the opposite. Although voting every year or two may technically make us a political democracy, a noticeable *lack* of democracy in the workplace is a far more basic fact of life for most people.

Not coincidentally, perhaps, there has been an erosion of democratic ideals in government during this century parallel to the growth of large corporations. This erosion has been most visible since the end of World War II, accelerating during the Reagan-Bush era. The increase of presidential power mentioned earlier is one of its chief manifestations.

The Imperial Presidency

Historian Arthur Schlesinger coined the term *imperial presidency* to refer to the increased authority of modern presidents. Ronald Reagan and George Bush may have contributed more to the growth of executive-branch power than any of their predecessors. For example, even as Reagan was professing to favor less centralization, he was strengthening his own control over the budget and calling for more extensive CIA activities inside the country (with less congressional surveillance)—both of which increased central authority. At the same time, he used "invisible government" to extend his power beyond its official limits. Iran-contra [secret operations by Reagan administration officials in the mid-1980s to sell weapons to Iran and funnel the profits to Nicaraguan *contra* rebels] was just the tip of the iceberg.

One of the most potent methods of invisible government is the president's authority to determine foreign and domestic policy through secret National Security Directives [NSDs]. Such directives cover a virtually unlimited field of action, shaping policy which may be radically different from that stated publicly by the White House and which may involve interference with First Amendment rights, initiation of activities leading to war, the subversion of democratically elected foreign governments, or the commitment of billions of dollars in loan guarantees—all without congressional approval or even knowledge.

The Reagan administration wrote more than 320 NSDs on everything from the future of Micronesia to ways of keeping the government going after a nuclear holocaust. The Bush administration, as of early 1992, had written more than 100 NSDs on subjects ranging from the drug wars to nuclear weaponry to aid to Saddam Hussein. Not one of these directives has been declassified or released to Congress. The Bush administration even refused to release the *unclassified* NSDs!

Reagan also involved the government in systematic censorship activities. Federal employees, for example, were required to sign a form that allowed them to be prosecuted for divulging not only classified information but that which is "nonclassified but classifiable"—a deliberately vague, Catch-22 category that allowed most would-be whistleblowers to be harassed. Under Reagan, foreign nationals were denied entry into the United States because of their political and ideological beliefs, among them Nobel Prize–winning author Gabriel Garcia Marquez, playwright Dario Fo, author Carlos Fuentes, actress Franca Rame, novelist Doris Lessing, and NATO [North Atlantic Treaty Organization] Deputy Supreme Commander Nino Pasti.

The Reagan administration even placed an embargo on magazines and newspapers from Cuba, North Vietnam, and Albania and confiscated certain Iranian books purchased by television journalists abroad—not because these materials contained government secrets but because they were believed to contain information the administration did not want Americans to know. The trend toward a system of official censorship is clear.

Presidential Power and Social Upheaval

Although Clinton will no doubt be judged by future historians on his ability to reform the health-care system and reduce the federal deficit, he will just as surely be judged on the strength of his commitment to democratization and decentralization—not only in foreign nations but in the United States as well.

27

Unfortunately, there are strong forces working against greater democracy and decentralization at the federal level. For one thing, an increase of presidential power is facilitated by the gridlock, partisan bickering, and corruption of Congress. As congressional legislators lose the public's respect, the stature and authority of the executive branch naturally grow. Unless Congress can get its act together soon, the imperial presidency is likely to become even more imperial under Clinton.

For another thing, central authority tends to increase in times of great social upheaval. In republican Rome, for example, Augustus was delegated vast powers by the Roman senate to restore order during a chaotic period of rioting, looting, and political corruption. Similarly, at the end of medieval feudalism, most of Europe was plunged into a period of anarchy, civil war, and peasant rebellions, followed immediately by a concentration of power in the hands of absolute monarchs.

The 1992 uprising in Los Angeles may be a harbinger of more civil disturbances to come. Certainly the continuing deterioration of the inner cities does not bode well for domestic tranquility. If so, there will be great pressure on the president to deal with any future unrest through executive orders and directives that impose draconian measures. A power-hungry president might use such a situation to persuade Congress to legislate a permanent increase of executive-branch authority. Therefore, a major test for the Clinton administration will be whether or not it can reverse the decay of the inner cities, thus defusing the potential for further violence, before authoritarian tactics become necessary. Given the size of the federal deficit, finding the money to do so will be difficult.

Workplace Democracy

But even if Clinton finds it impossible to "deimperialize" the presidency, he can still help to bring about greater democracy and decentralization in the workplace. Studies indicate that almost any move toward a more democratic and egalitarian structure increases effectiveness, innovation, and productivity. Since this is exactly what American businesses need for success, the administration can simultaneously achieve its goal of making America more competitive *and* help to fulfill the promise of American democratic ideals by providing incentives to businesses committed to greater worker involvement, ownership, and control.

It is time we stopped talking about democracy and started practicing it where we spend our most productive hours: at work. This, in turn, will help create among average citizens those psychological traits that will make further democratization of the political system possible.

"What must be done in America today is to restore *individualism, not re-evaluate it or* modify it. . . . It is the core, the genesis, the foundation of all freedom."

Individualism Strengthens America

Nelson Hultberg

One of America's trademarks is the concept of individualism—a belief in individual rights and dignity inherent in such principles as capitalism, democracy, and religious liberty. In the following viewpoint, Nelson Hultberg calls for the restoration of individualism, which he credits as the impetus for America's freedom and prosperity. Hultberg contends that there has long been a common belief that individualism—in particular, the idea of laissez-faire capitalism—is a relic of the past, unsuitable for modern society. Hultberg maintains, however, that the world's recent social and economic transformations, such as the demise of the Soviet Union, show that what are actually inadequate are socialism and welfarism. Hultberg is a freelance writer in San Antonio, Texas.

As you read, consider the following questions:

1. What are early American examples of individualism, according to Hultberg?
2. On what basis does Hultberg argue that economies suffer under socialism?
3. How did the idea of individual liberty affect the medieval era, according to the author?

From "Is Individualism Dead?" by Nelson Hultberg, *The Freeman*, June 1994. Reprinted with permission of the Foundation for Economic Education, Irvington-on-Hudson, New York.

Whatever you can do or dream you can, begin it.
For boldness has genius, power and magic in it.
—Goethe

Study any account of the growth of America and one fact always jumps out at you—the heroic self-determination of the men and women who shaped the events of our history. Throughout those sprawling colonial years, to the trying times of the Revolution, and beyond to the boom towns of the West, the railroad age, Thomas Edison, Henry Ford, and the roaring twenties, there is observable in the people of these eras an unrelenting sense of self-reliance and willingness to take risks.

It is not a history of government social agendas, with their inevitable concomitants of futility and despair. It is a history of adventurous, self-assured individuals in pursuit of great accomplishments, of personal daring and discovery. The dominant figures that built this country were not leveling bureaucrats, but dynamic entrepreneurs, pioneers, scientists, inventors, immigrants—bold individuals with "genius, power, and magic" in them, willing to rise or fall on their own merits and the strength of their faith in a just Providence.

Seeking Freedom

They fought a war with a ragged little army against a mighty empire, and won. They wrote a Constitution for all the ages, and crossed a vast and death-dealing frontier with nothing but covered wagons and their own personal stamina. New inventions, miracles of production, and an astonishing wealth sprang from their unbounded ambition. They turned useless prairies into golden wheatfields, wagons into powerful locomotives, and a savage wilderness into a network of commerce and trade.

To such restless enterprising people, there was little on earth that was impossible. All they wanted was to be free, to keep what they produced, and to seek their destiny beyond the next horizon. They would work out their own security. "Just let us be free," they insisted.

It was thus that a whole new philosophy came to be, through the first stirrings of these brave men and women. It was the philosophy of *individualism*, and it stood in direct contrast to the accepted beliefs of Europe, which taught men to seek security and subordinate themselves to the dictates of the monarch, or the feudal lords, or whoever had the power of the state and church behind them. This new American philosophy declared that men were their own rulers, that they were responsible for their own lives and possessed the power within them to overcome any obstacle. It was a philosophy that exploded across a whole continent. It transformed the world and turned life into an active

30

force for good.

For a century and a quarter, Americans adhered to individualism, and as a result, their prosperity grew to unparalleled heights.

Abandoning Principles

Beginning around the turn of the century, though, a great many Americans began to abandon the individualistic principles that had served them so well. By the start of the 1930s, the primitive concept of *statism*, dominant throughout the monarchist age in Europe, began to re-emerge under the guise of "social progressivism." As a result, bureaucracy grew, life became less meaningful, peace became the exception, and that vital spirit of individualism faded in face of the burgeoning welfare state.

Individualism and Business

The more the corporate world endorses a theory which subordinates individuals to groups, the more society as a whole will be encouraged to subordinate both corporations and entrepreneurs to vaguely defined community interests that may benefit no one and actually be injurious to the businesses involved.

Some social critics, such as Amitai Etzioni, Michael Lerner, and, most famously, Ralph Nader, have proposed that corporations ought to be subjected to public control for the common good. If such constraints were widely accepted, corporate executives would swiftly find that business had taken a turn for the worse. Besides being the social theory that is most conducive to individual human well-being, individualism is the social theory that best serves the business world, corporate as well as entrepreneurial.

Aeon J. Skoble, *The Freeman*, July 1994.

"The individual means less and less, mass and collectivity more and more—and so the net of servitude which hems in personal development becomes ever denser, more closely meshed, and inescapable," wrote Wilhelm Röpke, some 40 years ago in his great classic, *A Humane Economy*. He saw all too clearly the horrible changes that were sweeping over the Western world as a result of collectivism and bureaucratism.

The fundamental question we face now is: Can the philosophy of individualism survive, or is it to wither away under the ever swelling shadow of a monster government and the womb-to-tomb security its social engineers are forcing upon us? Must we passively accept being wards of the state, or do we still possess enough of the spirit that founded America to recapture our basic rights? Do we still value freedom, or is it really state regimentation that we seek down deep in some craven corner of our souls?

If a free America is to be preserved then the first and greatest enemy of freedom must be contested. And that is the notion that freedom is no longer possible in a modern world, that individualism as a philosophy of life is a relic of the past. We hear it everywhere. In fact, we're bombarded by such pronouncements from the time we first go to school. "Individualism was a good thing in its day," we're told, "but it's no longer workable." A growing flood of socioeconomic studies pours forth from the nation's universities proclaiming to Americans that, while a free market is certainly productive, the underlying fundamentals of laissez-faire capitalism were nefariously unsound. Thus we must move toward a more "public spirited," a more "nationally planned" social structure.

Such appeals speak soothingly to us, with benign and futuristic phrases: "new social vistas," "the upcoming challenges of America's third century," "the necessity to build a modern era of co-operation between the greatness of government and the productivity of the business world." It all sounds very progressive, very necessary. The world is changing, and therefore America must change also. A laissez-faire economy is just not applicable to modern times. "We cannot afford the anarchy of the capitalist system," explain the experts. "Individualism may have worked fine in a frontier society, but not in a modern technological society." And we obediently clasp such fateful declarations to our bosom without so much as an afterthought.

The Failure of Socialism

Should it not be obvious by now, though, in light of the world's present catastrophic economic convulsions, that it is actually the other way around—that it is actually *socialism* and *welfarism* that cannot work in a modern technological society? Witness the all-encompassing collapse of socialist principles in the USSR and Eastern Europe as viable means of societal organization. Witness the "democratic socialism" that has kept India starving for decades, with its people subjected to endless turmoil, demoralizing uncertainty and ruthless power grabs. Witness the pathetic stagnancy of Sweden this past century, into a somnolent nation of collectivist poltroons, now staggering under the debilitating taxation and bureaucratic servitude that their "state welfarism" has generated.

During the past 80 years, every nation in the civilized world, that has adopted either socialism or welfarism as its form of political-economic organization, has incurred deterioration and chaos in every conceivable area of life. Inflation has plagued their economies, distorting their marketplaces and eroding the value of their currencies. A silent and sickly moroseness has settled over the lives of their young (for who can find pleasure in living when the state determines the limits of one's dreams?). Real prosperity has diminished. True freedom is gone. Joy and exuberance and the zest that life should hold for all is non-existent.

In the more primitive parts of the Third World, the record is even worse. Barbarism and tyranny, of a sort that Americans can scarcely fathom, are commonplace. Poverty lingers. Illiteracy, disease, inhumanity, and regimentation overwhelm everyone visiting such "collectivist paradises."

No Incentives

Why has this happened? As predicted long ago by [economist] Ludwig von Mises, socialist systems cannot calculate prices because they obliterate the entrepreneur, and thus they have no means to *rationally* determine supply and demand. Thus they have no power to produce either a quantity or quality of productive goods. Because they are devoid of the incentives that result from private property, socialist countries can bring forth only shabbiness and squalor—for their subjects will produce only enough to keep themselves out of trouble. So the great collectivist "ideal" of the political left, that was to transform the world into a technological Eden where all men can live in harmony without worrying about such grubby pursuits as earning a living, has not materialized. In fact precisely the opposite has come about.

With the dramatic collapse of the Soviet Union in 1991 and the fading of Communist Party control over Eastern Europe, the ideology of *socialism* was dealt, in many Western eyes, a devastating death blow. But a closer look reveals that socialism is merely reforming its basic goals into a more salable ideological framework.

Incredibly the purveyors of forced collectivity in Europe and America still cling to their dream of merging Eastern socialism and Western capitalism into an authoritarian World Welfare State, where *equality of conditions* for everyone is implemented. Still they proclaim that mankind must continue on to build the collectivist ideal; it just has to be along more "democratic lines." Still they proclaim that free markets and coercive bureaucracies must merge, that with just a little more *time*, a little more *taxation*, a little more *regulation*, humanity will one day realize the collectivist paradise. What is needed is not the extreme version of Marxism, but a more moderate "middle way" in the manner of Sweden. But to consider individualist capitalism is impossible. People must relinquish the direction of their lives to oligarchic bureaucrats and professorial elites, who are so much more "qualified" to determine how we are to live. When all this has come to pass, mankind will surely have found the egalitarian kingdom.

Even in [the] face of collectivism's squalor and despair, most pundits of the West still believe this failed ideology retains some semblance of idealism, needing only a few "theoretical adjustments."

But collectivism's ineptitude does not lie in the depravity of its rulers, or the absence of purchasing power, or lack of time to prove itself. It lies in the overwhelming irrationality of its basic conception of life. Men are not meant to live in subservience to the commands of the state. They are meant to live as the Founding Fathers of America decreed: as free and responsible beings, with obedience to neither King nor mass opinion, but to "the laws of Nature and of Nature's God."

For those who wish to prosper and find their way toward a meaningful existence that gives back a richness of reward for one's efforts, there is only one vehicle with which to bring about such values: *the philosophy of individualism and its marketplace of liberty.* The whole history of the past 800 years in the West stands as testament to such a truth.

The Birth of Liberty

The idea of individual liberty was philosophically born with the signing of the Magna Charta in 1215, and then painstakingly built upon and honed and strengthened over the centuries by such great men as Erasmus, John Locke, Edmund Burke, Adam Smith, Alexis de Tocqueville, and Frederic Bastiat. It was never thoroughly grasped, and never perfectly practiced, and many times lost altogether, but it lifted men from the Dark Ages to medieval commerce, and out of the era of monarchies to the New World. There it brought into being a radical new social structure of *personal independence* for all people, forming in 1776 the foundation for a system of living that was to become the envy of the entire globe, luring wave after wave of immigrants to our shores.

Such a system produced unprecedented freedom and human dignity. But intimidated by the false theories of Karl Marx and his intellectual progeny, such a system has been for many decades now under severe attack in our colleges and our legislatures.

What has been taking place in America throughout the past eighty years—the bureaucratization of the marketplace and the centralization of power in Washington—is not at all the glorious march toward "justice and equality" that has been portrayed. It's a virulent and purposeful assault upon the most cherished philosophical premises of our lives. Every value, so dear to the preservation of our freedom, is being steadily eroded by the technocratic sweep of twentieth-century statism and its ideological frenzies of regimenting all men into a massive welfare-state utopia.

"In all fields," writes Wilhelm Röpke, "mass and concentration are the mark of modern society; they smother the area of individual responsibility, life, and thought. . . . The small circles— from the family on up—with their human warmth and natural solidarity, are giving way before . . . the amorphous conglomeration of people in huge cities and industrial centers, before rootlessness and mass organizations, before the anonymous bureaucracy of giant concerns and eventually, of government itself, which holds this crumbling society together through the coercive machinery of the welfare state, the police, and the tax screw. This is what was ailing modern society even before the Second World War, and since then the illness has become more acute and quite unmistakable. It is a desperate disease calling for the desperate cure of *decentralization*. . . . People need to be taken out of the mass and given roots again."

If such compulsive centralization of our society is to be checked and America's unique brand of freedom to be saved, then it will take a genuine restoration of the philosophy that our forefathers so boldly forged with blood and sinew throughout the early years of this nation. If the political brilliance that the Founding Fathers gave to us is not truly revived in America, then freedom as we know it will not remain; and in its place will come the New Orwellians [after author George Orwell] of Technocracy, brandishing convoluted laws and regulations.

The educationists and editorialists who dominate today's university and media scene, and so glibly report in their manifold outpourings that we must "re-evaluate and modify the antiquated principles of individualism," that we must strive to make our government "more creative in the solving of modern-day problems," are so consumed with myopic scientism and programmatic avidity, that they can no longer grasp the principles necessary for the living of life in heroic form.

To "re-evaluate individualism" is to question the moral legitimacy of freedom itself, and the natural right of all men to personally direct the furtherance of their own lives. To say we must "legislatively modify individualism," is to say we must "forcefully modify humans," which is to make men into mechanized cogs.

What must be done in America today is to *restore* individualism, not re-evaluate it or modify it. Individualism cannot be "modernized." It cannot be made "relative to our time." It transcends time. It is a set of principles that are unalterable. It is the core, the genesis, the foundation of all freedom, all prosperity, all dignity, all life. Without it as our guide, our future will be bleak and despotic for sure.

"A strong case can be made that it is precisely the bonding together of community members that enables us to remain independent of the state."

Communitarianism Strengthens America

Amitai Etzioni

Communitarianism, according to Amitai Etzioni and its other proponents, seeks "balances between individuals and groups, rights and responsibilities, and among the institutions of state, market, and civil society." In the following viewpoint, Etzioni asserts that communitarianism can be instrumental in helping America rediscover the "moral voice of the community." Etzioni argues that individual conscience alone is not enough to nourish moral conduct, and that the concept of individualism is not inconsistent with the idea of people's encouraging mutual moral conduct. Etzioni is a professor at George Washington University in Washington, D.C., and editor of the quarterly journal *The Responsive Community*.

As you read, consider the following questions:

1. How does Etzioni contrast the way humans and animals respond to their impulses?
2. What difference does Etzioni note between communitarianism and conformism?
3. In the author's opinion, how is communitarianism vital to resisting state coercion?

Amitai Etzioni, "Restoring Our Moral Voice." Reprinted with permission of the author and *The Public Interest* No. 116, Summer 1994, pp. 107-13, ©1994 by National Affairs, Inc.

Audiences that are quite enthusiastic about the communitarian message, which I carry these days to all who will listen, cringe when I turn to discuss the moral voice. One of my best friends took me aside and gently advised me to speak of "concern" rather than morality, warning that otherwise I would "sound like the Moral Majority." During most call-in radio shows in which I participate, sooner or later some caller exclaims that "nobody should tell us what to do." *Time* magazine, in an otherwise highly favorable cover story on communitarian thinking, warned against busybodies "humorlessly imposing on others arbitrary (meaning their own) standards of behavior, health and thought." Studies of an American suburb by sociologist M. P. Baumgartner found a disturbing unwillingness of people to make moral claims on one another. Most people did not feel it was their place to express their convictions when someone did something that was wrong.

At the same time, the overwhelming majority of Americans, public opinion polls show, recognize that our moral fabric has worn rather thin. A typical finding is that while school teachers in the forties listed as their top problems talking out of turn, making noise, cutting in line, and littering, they now list drug abuse, alcohol abuse, pregnancy, and suicide. Wanton taking of life, often for a few bucks to buy a vial of crack or to gain a pair of sneakers, is much more common than it is in other civilized societies or than it used to be in America. Countless teenagers bring infants into the world to satisfy their ego needs, with little attention to the long term consequences for the children, themselves, or society.

How We Lost Our Moral Voice

How can people recognize the enormous moral deficit we face and at the same time be so reluctant to lay moral claims on one another? One reason is that they see immorality not in their friends and neighborhoods but practically everyplace else. (In the same vein, they find members of Congress in general to be corrupt but often re-elect "their" representative because he or she is "O.K.," just as they complain frequently about physicians but find their own doctor above reproach.) This phenomenon may be referred to as moral myopia; a phenomenon for which there seems to be no ready cure.

In addition, many Americans seem to have internalized the writings of Dale Carnegie on how to win friends and influence people: you are supposed to work hard at flattering the other person and never chastise anyone. Otherwise, generations of Americans have been told by their parents, you may lose a "friend" and set back your "networking." A study found that when college co-eds were asked whether or not they would tell their best friend if, in their eyes, the person the friend had chosen to wed was utterly unsuitable, most said they would refrain. They would prefer that she go ahead and hurt herself rather than endanger the friendship. Also, Daniel Patrick Moynihan has argued convincingly in his Winter 1993 article in the *American Scholar*, "Defining Deviancy Down," that people have been so bombarded with evidence of social ills that they have developed moral calluses, which make them relatively inured to immorality.

What Communitarians Are Saying

It's a good time to be a communitarian. Not only is the philosophy *au courant* in the press and in academia, but even our president [Bill Clinton] got his job partially by invoking communitarian ideals (more responsibilities, fewer rights) and pushing for communitarian public policies (national service, campaign finance reform, welfare reform). And if that president hasn't lived up to those promises, no matter: One of his advisors (William Galston) is a leading communitarian, so there's still room for hope.

Now that they have the national ear, just what is it that communitarians have to say? Americans, they argue, have become obsessed with rights, and neglectful of responsibilities. They want to be represented by juries, but not to serve on them. They want a government that caters to their every need, but collects little in taxes. They want marital freedom, but neglect the consequences—the children—of these unions. And so on.

Joshua Abramowitz, *The Public Interest*, Fall 1993.

When Americans do contemplate moral reform, many are rather asociological: they believe that our problem is primarily one of individual conscience. If youngsters could be taught again to tell right from wrong by their families and schools, if churches could reach them again, our moral and social order would be on the mend. They focus on what is only one, albeit important, component of the moral equation: the inner voice.

In the process many Americans disregard the crucial role of the community in reinforcing the individual's moral commitments. To document the importance of the community, I must turn to the question: what constitutes a moral person?

Impulses and Judgments

I build here on the writings of Harry Frankfurt, Albert Hirschman, and others who have argued that humans differ from animals in that, while both species experience impulses, humans have the capacity to pass judgments on their impulses. I choose my words carefully: it is not suggested that humans can "control" their impulses, but that they can defer responding to them long enough to evaluate the behavior toward which they feel inclined. Once this evaluation takes place, sometimes the judgments win, sometimes the impulses. If the judgments always took precedence, we would be saintly; if the impulses always won, we would be psychopaths or animals. The human fate is a constant struggle between the noble and the debased parts of human nature. While I reach this conclusion from social science findings and observations, I am often challenged by those who exclaim "Why, this is what religion taught us!" or as one heckler cried out, "What about the rest of the catechism?" As I see it, while some may find it surprising that religions contain social truths, I see no reason to doubt that the distillation of centuries of human experience by those entrusted with moral education has resulted in some empirically solid, sociologically valid observations.

It is to the struggle between judgments and impulses that the moral voice of the community speaks. The never-ending struggle within the human soul over which course to follow is not limited to intra-individual dialogues between impulses that tempt us to disregard our marital vows, to be deceitful, or to be selfish, and the values we previously internalized, which warn us against yielding to these temptations. In making our moral choices (to be precise, our choices between moral and immoral conduct rather than among moral claims) we are influenced by the approbation and censure of others, especially of those with whom we have close relations—family members, friends, neighbors; in short, our communities. It may not flatter our view of ourselves, but human nature is such that if these community voices speak in unison and with clarity (without being shrill), we are much more likely to follow our inner judgments than if these voices are silent, conflicted, or speaking too softly. Hence, the pivotal importance of a community's voice in raising the moral level of its members.

Not a Case of Conformism

I need to respond to various challenges to this line of argumentation, beyond the general unarticulated uneasiness it seems to evoke in a generation that has largely lost its moral voice. Some argue that the reliance on community points to conformism, to "other-directed" individuals who seek merely to satisfy whatever pleases their community. This is not the vision evoked here. The community voice as depicted here is not the only voice that lays claims on individuals as to the course they ought to follow, but rather is a voice that speaks in addition to the inner one. When the community's voice and the inner voice are in harmony, this is not a case of conformism, of one "party" yielding to the other, but one of two tributaries flowing into the same channel (e.g., if I firmly believe that it is wrong to leave my children unattended and so do my neighbors, and I stay home, this is hardly an instance of conformism). If these two voices conflict, I must pass judgment not only vis-à-vis my impulses (should I yield or follow the dictates of my conscience?) but also pass judgment on whether or not I shall heed my fellow community members, or follow my own lead. In short, the very existence of a community moral voice does not necessarily spell conformism. Conformism occurs only if and when one automatically or routinely sets aside personal judgments to grant supremacy to the community. That happens when personal voices are weak—far from a necessary condition for the existence of a community voice. To put it differently, while conformism is a danger so is the absence of the reinforcing effects of the communal voice. The antidote to conformism is not to undermine the community's voice but to seek to ensure that the personal one is also firmly instilled.

Above all, it must be noted that while the moral voice urges and counsels us, it is unable to force us. Whatever friends, neighbors, ministers, or community leaders say, the ultimate judgment call is up to the individual. (True, in some limited situations, as when a community ostracizes or hounds someone, the pressure can be quite intense, but this rarely happens in modern-day communities because individuals are able to move to other communities when they are unduly pressured, and because they often are members of two or more communities—say of residence and of work—and hence are able psychologically to draw on one community to ward off excessive pressure from the other.)

Shared Values

Others argue that the community voice is largely lost because of American pluralism. Individuals are subject to the voices of numerous communities, each pulling in a different direction and thus neutralizing the others. Or the cacophony is so high that no clear voice can be heard. The notion that no community is right and all claims have equal standing, championed by multiculturalists, further diminishes the claim of the moral voice. The fact is that there is no way to return to the days of simple, homogeneous communities. In any case, these communities were often rather oppressive. The contemporary solution, if not salvation, lies in seeking and developing an evolving framework of shared values—one which all subcultures will be expected to endorse and support without losing their distinct identities. Thus, Muslim Americans can be free to follow the dictates of their religion, cherish their music and cuisine, and be proud of select parts of their history (no group should be encouraged to embrace all of its history). But at the same time they (and all other communities that make up the American society) need to accept the dignity of the individual, the basic value of liberty, the democratic form of government, and other such core values. On these matters we should expect and encourage all communities to speak in one voice.

Freedom from the State

Other critics argue that the essence of individual freedom is every person following his own course and social institutions leaving us alone. (More technically, economists write about the primacy of our preferences and scoff at intellectuals and ideologues who want to impose their "tastes" on others.) In honoring this pivotal value of a free society, one must be careful not to confuse allusions to freedom from the state's control with freedom from the moral urgings of our fellow community members. One can be as opposed to state intervention and regulation as a diehard libertarian and still see a great deal of merit in people encouraging one another to do what is right. (Technically speaking, the reference here is not to frustrating people and preventing them from acting on their preferences, which is what the coercive state does, but rather appealing to their better selves to change or reorder their preferences.)

Indeed, a strong case can be made that it is precisely the bonding together of community members that enables us to remain independent of the state. The anchoring of individuals in viable families, webs of friendships, communities of faith, and neighborhoods—in short, in communities—best sustains their ability to resist the pressures of the state. The absence of these social foundations opens isolated individuals to totalitarian pressures. (This, of course, is a point Tocqueville makes in *Democracy in America*.)

Getting Our Voice Back

In my discussions with students and others about the moral voice, I have borrowed a leaf from Joel Feinberg's seminal work *Offense to Others*. In his book, Feinberg asks us to imagine we are riding on a full bus that we cannot readily leave. He then presents a series of hypothetical scenes that would cause offense, such as someone playing loud music, scratching a metallic surface, handling what looks like a real grenade, engaging in sexual behavior, and so on.

I am interested not so much in the question of what members of the community find tolerable versus unbearable, but what will make them speak up. Hence I asked students and colleagues, "Imagine you are in a supermarket and a mother beats the daylights out of a three-year-old child—would you speak

41

up?" (I say "mother" because I learned that if I just say "some-one" most of my respondents state that they would not react be-cause they would fear that the other person might clobber them.) Practically everyone I asked responded that they would not speak up. They would at most try to "distract" the mother, "find out what the child really did," and so on. However, when I asked "imagine you are resting on the shore of a pristine lake; a picnicking family, about to depart, leaves behind a trail of trash—would you suggest they clean up after themselves?" Here again, many demurred but a fair number were willing to con-sider saying something.

A New Consensus

Possibly, my informal sample is skewed. However, it seems to me something else is at work: we have had a consensus-building grand dialogue about the environment. While there are still sharp disagreements about numerous details (for instance, about the relative standing of spotted owls vs. loggers), there is a basic consensus that we must be mindful of the environment and not trash it. However, we have had neither a grand dialogue nor a new consensus about the way to treat children. This would sug-gest one more reason our moral voice is so feeble and reluctant: too many of us, too often, are no longer sure what to say.

A return to a firm moral voice will require a major town hall meeting of sorts, the kind we have when Americans spend bil-lions of hours in bowling alleys, next to water coolers, and on call-in shows. We need to form a new consensus, such as the kind we have about the environment, civil rights, and excessive general regulation, and are now beginning to have about gay rights. This time we need to agree with one another that the common good requires that we speak up and enunciate commu-nal values. To reiterate, heeding such consensus should never be automatic; we need to examine the values the community urges upon us to determine whether or not they square with our conscience and the basic values we sense no person or com-munity has a right to violate. However, we must also focus on the other side of the coin: it is not enough that individuals at-tempt to tell right from wrong, as crucial as that is. We must also be willing to encourage others to attend to values we as a community share.

"A society that abandons personal responsibility will lose its moral sense. And it is the urban poor whose lives are being destroyed the most by this."

Minorities and the Poor Should Value Personal Responsibility

Clarence Thomas

Clarence Thomas was appointed an associate justice of the U.S. Supreme Court in 1991. In the following viewpoint, Thomas maintains that a lack of personal responsibility among many Americans contributes to crime and other antisocial behavior. Thomas explains that in a democratic society, social obligations demand that people abide by laws and that government enforce those laws. Thomas argues that failure to mete out sufficient punishment for wrongful behavior cheats those who abide by the law, negates the law's threat of force, and sanctions harmful conduct. He asserts that the combined lack of personal responsibility and just punishment has devastated minorities and the poor, especially in urban areas.

As you read, consider the following questions:

1. According to Thomas, what message does the punishment of criminals send to society?
2. What examples does Thomas use of wrongful conduct that could escape punishment?
3. What warning does the author voice regarding rehabilitation of criminals?

From "The Rights Revolution and America's Urban Poor," a speech delivered by Clarence Thomas to the Federalist Society and the Manhattan Institute, May 1994. (Full text available in *Vital Speeches of the Day*, June 15, 1994.) Reprinted with the author's permission.

I am convinced that there can be no freedom and opportunity for many in our society if our criminal law loses sight of the importance of individual responsibility. Indeed, in my mind, the principal reason for a criminal justice system is to hold people accountable for the consequences of their actions. Put simply, it is to hold people's feet to the fire when they do something harmful to individuals or society as a whole.

The Importance of Accountability

Why is holding people accountable for harmful behavior important to us? Three reasons strike me as especially convincing: persuasion or deterrence, respect for the individual who violates the law, and payment of a debt to society.

Let's begin with the most practical reason for why we hold people accountable. The law cannot persuade where it cannot punish. Alexander Hamilton made this very point when he observed, "It is essential to the idea of a law that it be attended with a sanction . . . a punishment for disobedience." Most of us, I am sure, are regularly faced with the deterrent effect of the law, the incentive not to engage in conduct that might harm others. To be sure, we choose to honor speed limits because such behavior might well save our own lives. But we just as surely follow the rules because of the legal consequences of speeding—harsh fines and possible loss of our licenses. In a similar vein, a company might refrain from polluting a neighboring river to avoid harming others who rely on its clean water for drinking and recreation. Clearly, though, stiff fines give the company a tangible incentive to avoid such harmful conduct. As Saint Thomas Aquinas said, "It is not always through the perfect goodness of virtue that one obeys the law, but sometimes it is through fear of punishment."

Some underscore a different aspect of human nature in explaining why holding people responsible for their actions is central to our criminal justice system. Unlike any other living creature in the world, humans are moral, rational, and thinking beings. We, therefore, expect one another to be able to distinguish between right and wrong and to act accordingly. Thus, when society punishes someone for breaking the law—when it holds him accountable for the consequences of his acts—we are recognizing that only mankind is capable of being moral or rational. We are, in short, acknowledging the human dignity of our fellow man. Indeed, people thrive in our society because of the expectations we all have regarding the capacity of the human will to do good. But to disregard this potential—to ignore the fact that someone has harmed others by breaking the law—treats our fellow man as beings that are incapable of determining right from wrong and controlling their behavior. Ultimately, our hopes for the future of society can be no brighter than the expectations we have regarding the conduct of its individual citizens.

There are others who believe that the principal reason we hold people responsible for the consequences of their actions is because of our mutual political or social obligations in a civilized, democratic society. In accepting and benefitting from the wonderful opportunities of our free society, we each consent or agree to be bound by the rules and expect government to enforce them. When someone breaks the law a fundamental trust has been violated. In effect, the lawbreaker is telling all of us that there can be no mutual expectation that society's rules will be followed and thereby protect all of us. On this view, we punish the criminal because he owes a debt to society for violating our trust. To do otherwise would cheat those who abide by law, and dilute the threat of force that the law is supposed to convey. And, if our government failed to remedy wrongs by holding people responsible for their acts, we would be faced with the prospect of vigilante justice and all the evils that accompany it.

What Social Justice Means

If social justice means anything at all, it is a system of governance where laws are written solely to prevent people from violating the persons of others or their right to acquire, keep and dispose of property in any way, so long as they don't violate anyone else's right to do the same. In other words, laws should be written to prevent force and fraud.

Walter Williams, *The Washington Times*, December 27, 1992.

For these and other reasons, then, I think most everyone agrees that we have a criminal justice system in order to hold people accountable. If properly administered, it stands to reason that the criminal law should help to ensure a greater degree of personal responsibility in our society. Put differently, the criminal law serves a signalling function when we hold people accountable for their harmful acts. Punishing people is an expression of society's resolve that certain behavior will not be tolerated either because it hurts others, is counterproductive, or is offensive to the sensibilities of our culture. In the absence of such a signal—if government does not punish harmful conduct—we send a dangerous message to society. In effect, we fall prey to the law of unintended consequences—we end up sanctioning harmful behavior. What are we telling students who are trying hard to do well in school and to avoid drugs, or the upstanding public housing tenant who respects others' property and well-being, when our law fails to express outrage at those who do wrong?

One must wonder, though, whether our criminal law is carrying out this signalling function. Why are so many of our streets rife with drug bazaars and other criminal enterprises? Why are so many of our schools devoid of the discipline that is necessary for a healthy learning environment and instead plagued by lawlessness? Why is there unprecedented fear of violence—or just a plain unwillingness to cultivate neighborhood unity and spirit— among so many of our fellow citizens?

The Rights Revolution

One reason, I believe, is that the rights revolution [the legal revolution in creating and expanding individual rights that began in the 1960s] worked a fundamental transformation in our criminal law. The very same ideas that prompted the judicial revolution in due process rights for the poor and that circumscribed the authority of local communities to set standards for decorum and civility on the streets or in the public schools also made it far more difficult for the criminal justice system to hold people responsible for the consequences of their harmful acts. I want to focus on one particular force behind the rights revolution that in my view had the most profound effect on the direction of the criminal law: namely, the idea that our society had failed to safeguard the interests of minorities, the poor, and other groups; and, as a consequence, was, in fact, primarily at fault for their plight.

Much of the judicial revolution in individual rights was justified on the ground that the dignity and well-being of large segments of our population—minorities, women, the poor—were consistently ignored by our social and political institutions. As the victims of centuries of discrimination and oppression, blacks and other minorities could not enjoy the full benefits and opportunities that society had to offer. So too were the poor viewed as victims—uncontrollable forces contributed to their poverty, and yet, their "stake" in welfare and other public benefits was not insulated from unregulated state power in the same way as the property interests of the more fortunate in society.

These concerns greatly influenced our courts in requiring that government hold hearings or comply with other procedural requirements before terminating public benefits received by minorities and the poorest of Americans. The view was that these entitlements were worth protecting because they aid the poor and underrepresented in achieving security and well-being.

Procedural protections also were viewed as necessary to ensure that government interference with public benefits was not arbitrary and unfair. Because minority and disadvantaged students are the most frequent objects of school discipline, for example, advocates of greater constitutional protections insisted that the absence of stringent procedural requirements for suspension could lead to racial discrimination and other forms of unequal treatment. Much the same arguments were made regarding limits on the power to evict tenants from public housing and to enforce broad vagrancy or antipanhandling laws—government discretion had to be curbed in order to ensure that minorities or unpopular groups were not singled out for unfair and discriminatory treatment.

The Myth of Victimhood

We can see, then, how the intellectual currents of the legal revolution in individual rights affected the management of community institutions such as schools and the civility of our streets, parks, and other common spaces. But how did the ideas underlying this revolution affect the functioning of the criminal justice system?

Many began questioning whether the poor and minorities could be blamed for the crimes they committed. Our legal institutions and popular culture began identifying those accused of wrongdoing as victims of upbringing and circumstance. The point was made that human actions and choices, like events in the natural world, are often caused by factors outside of one's control. No longer was an individual identified as the cause of a harmful act. Rather, societal conditions or the actions of institutions and others in society became the responsible causes of harm. These external causes might be poverty, poor education, a faltering family structure, systemic racism or other forms of bigotry, and spousal or child abuse, just to name a few. The consequence of this new way of thinking about accountability and responsibility—or the lack thereof—was that a large part of our society could escape being held accountable for the consequences of harmful conduct. The law punishes only those who are responsible for their actions, and in a world of countless uncontrollable causes of aggression or lawlessness, few will have to account for their behavior.

As a further extension of these ideas, some began challenging society's moral authority to hold many of our less fortunate citizens responsible for their harmful acts. Punishment is an expression of society's disapproval or reprobation. In other words, punishment is a way of directing society's moral indignation toward persons responsible for violating its rules. Critics insisted, though, that an individual's harmful conduct is not the only relevant factor in determining whether punishment is morally justified. The individual's conduct must be judged in relation to how society has acted toward that individual in the past. In this regard, many began appearing hesitant to hold responsible those individuals whose conduct might be explained as a response to societal injustice. How can we hold the poor responsible for their actions, some asked, when our society does little to remedy the social conditions of the ill-educated and unemployed in our urban areas? In a similar vein, others questioned how we could tell blacks in our inner cities to face the consequences for breaking the law when the very legal system and society which will judge their conduct perpetuated years of racism and unequal treatment under the law.

Boundless Excuses

Once our legal system accepted the general premise that social conditions and upbringing could be excuses for harmful conduct, the range of causes that might prevent society from holding anyone accountable for his actions became potentially limitless. Do we punish the drunk driver who has a family history of alcoholism? A bigoted employer reared in the segregationist environment, who was taught that blacks are inferior? The fraudulent and manipulative businessman who was raised in a poor family and who had never experienced the good life? The abusive father or husband who was the object of similar mistreatment as a child? A thief or drug pusher who was raised in a dysfunctional family and who received a poor education? A violent gang member, rioter, or murderer who attributes his rage, aggression, and lack of respect for authority to a racist society that has oppressed him since birth? Which of these individuals, if any, should be excused for their conduct? Can we really distinguish among them in a principled way?

An effective criminal justice system—one that holds people accountable for harmful conduct—simply cannot be sustained under conditions where there are boundless excuses for violent behavior and no moral authority for the state to punish. If people know that they are not going to be held accountable because of a myriad of excuses, how will our society be able to influence behavior and provide incentives to follow the law? How can we teach future generations right from wrong if the idea of criminal responsibility is riddled with exceptions and our governing institutions and courts lack the moral self-confidence? A society that does not hold someone accountable for harmful behavior can be viewed as condoning—or even worse, endorsing—such conduct. In the long run, a society that abandons personal responsibility will lose its moral sense. And it is the urban poor whose lives are being destroyed the most by this loss of moral sense.

This is not surprising. A system that does not hold individuals accountable for their harmful acts treats them as less than full citizens. In such a world, people are reduced to the status of children, or even worse, treated as though they are animals without a soul. There may be a hard lesson here: in the face of injustice on the part of society, it is natural and easy to demand recompense or a dispensation from conventional norms. But all too often, doing so involves the individual accepting diminished responsibility for his future. Does the acceptance of diminished responsibility assure that the human spirit will not rise above the tragedies of one's existence? When we demand something from our oppressors—more lenient standards of conduct, for example—are we merely going from a state of slavery to a more deceptive, but equally destructive, state of dependence?

Rehabilitating Criminals

It also bears noting that contemporary efforts to rehabilitate criminals will never work in a system that often neglects to assign blame to individuals for their harmful acts. How can we encourage criminals not to return to crime if our justice system fosters the idea that it is the society that has perpetuated racism and poverty—not the individual who engaged in harmful conduct—that is to blame for aggression and crime, and thus, in greatest need of rehabilitation and reform.

Let me close by observing that the transformation of the criminal justice system has had and will continue to have its greatest impact in our urban areas. It is there that modern excuses for criminal behavior abound—poverty, substandard education, faltering families, unemployment, a lack of respect for authority because of deep feelings of oppression.

I have no doubt that the rights revolution had a noble purpose: to stop society from treating blacks, the poor, and others—many of whom today occupy our urban areas—as if they were invisible, not worthy of attention. But the revolution missed a larger point by merely changing their status from invisible to victimized. Minorities and the poor are humans—capable of dignity as well as shame, folly as well as success. We should be treated as such.

"The poor suffer not from their own deficient natures, but from a lack of good jobs; from segregation and governmental neglect."

Minorities and the Poor Do Not Lack a Sense of Personal Responsibility

David Futrelle

The "underclass" is a modern term used to describe such populations as minorities, the poor, and criminals—particularly those in inner cities. In the following viewpoint, David Futrelle argues that conservatives scapegoat the so-called underclass by attacking their lack of personal responsibility. Futrelle contends that "personal responsibility" is a red herring that distracts attention from the real problems of minorities and the poor: segregation, governmental neglect, and the lack of good jobs and schools. Such conditions, Futrelle asserts, deprive people of their dignity. Futrelle is the assistant managing editor of *In These Times*, a biweekly, politically left magazine.

As you read, consider the following questions:

1. How does Futrelle compare conservatives' and liberals' responses to questions of values and personal responsibility?
2. What are the myths surrounding the underclass and welfare, in the author's opinion?
3. How did Hillary Clinton change the meaning of Michael Lerner's invocation of caring and community, according to Futrelle?

Abridged from David Futrelle, "Surplus Values," *In These Times*, November 29, 1993. Reprinted with permission.

Conservatives talk about values with a certain assurance. When Dan Quayle attacked Murphy Brown's "lifestyle choice," with a straight face and a sonorous tone, he did so in the name of "family, hard work, integrity and personal responsibility." When in the heat of the culture war Rep. William Dannemeyer (R-CA) attacked "obscene" art, he did so, he said, to protect "the Judeo-Christian ethic" from "Hollywood, homosexuals, abortionists, family planners, the sexually promiscuous, failed spouses, failed parents, failed kids" and all other such outgrowths of secular humanism. And when Rush Limbaugh assails the left (and the liberals he takes to be the left) he does so in the name of "those corny old traditional values."

Those on the left are more circumspect in their moralizing. And there are good reasons for the left to look upon talk of values with suspicion. Talk of morality is divisive; it often has been (and still is) used to stigmatize those who deviate (for good reason or bad) from the confines of convention. Too often, talk of morality and responsibility takes the form of veiled accusation: I am responsible, you are not; I am moral, you are immoral. Such accusations are an affront to the liberal value of tolerance. . . .

Liberals on Values

Many liberals respond with a guilty defensiveness when the subject of "values" comes up. When prominent citizens announce that our society is coming apart at the seams, we can hardly disagree. Yet while we agree with the diagnosis, we look upon the individualistic, symbolic solutions of the moralistic right with a certain dismay. We don't want to stigmatize anyone, to make, say, gays and women the scapegoats for family "decay." And we can hardly, all by ourselves, "rush about revitalizing the family and renewing respect for the law," as historian Robert Wiebe has observed. We're stuck in a bind. "If we respond, we have difficulty knowing where to begin," Wiebe notes. "Yet if we shrug and hide, we invite society to go bankrupt around us."

Given such a distressing possibility, it is hardly a surprise that some liberals (and a few vaguely on the left) have attempted to recapture the language of morality—and, in particular, the language of responsibility—from the right. Some have done so with a notable opportunism—like Bill Clinton, whose appeals to "personal responsibility" during the 1992 campaign seemed less an attempt to infuse morality into the political realm as a coded message to white voters that he would be tough with the "underclass."

Others have attempted to work the language of responsibility into a broader, and explicitly progressive, morality. Michael Lerner, the editor of the Jewish left-liberal journal *Tikkun*, argues that progressives need to overcome their resistance to talking the language of moral values. "It is pure self-delusion to think that moral values can be kept out of politics," he writes. Indeed, "values [have] already . . . entered the public sphere." During the Reagan-Bush years, in fact, "right-wing values were triumphing because liberals refused to enter the debate." Denouncing the Reaganite excesses of individualism and greed, Lerner calls for liberals to "challenge the ethos of selfishness and replace it with an ethos of caring, social responsibility, trust and mutual aid."

Social vs. Individual Responsibility

This notion of *social* responsibility is, at least in theory, a challenge to the traditional American notion of *individual* responsibility. Yet liberals have not had a notable success in pushing the debate on responsibility to the left, away from individualism and toward the notion of "mutual aid." In attempting both to adapt to and to challenge the ideological constructs of the right, liberals have found themselves listing considerably (and increasingly) to the right. The notions of social or corporate responsibility—however laudable as ideas—have degenerated into public relations ploys on the part of businesses eager to convince customers that their products and procedures are ecologically and socially "responsible." And when liberals speak, as they increasingly do, of individual responsibility, it is often impossible to distinguish their version from that of the right. . . .

Much of the contemporary discussion of "responsibility"—among the right and even among many liberals—has a distinctly Victorian ring, combining an old-style moralism (and an equally old-fashioned faith in upward mobility) with the latest in psychological jargon. Discussions of responsibility today, just as they did in Victorian times, tend to turn quickly to the subject of the allegedly "irresponsible" poor.

The Underclass

Well-fed experts on the "underclass" laud each other in the pages of prominent magazines for their supposed courage in restating what has now, once again, become the conventional wisdom: those who are poor are somehow deficient, dysfunctional, different, "undeserving"—in short, irresponsible.

This argument, as historian Jacqueline Jones has suggested, "serves a larger political purpose, for it encourages some people to believe that the poor positively revel in their own misery, that they shun stable marriages and steady employment almost as a matter of perverse principle. According to this view, the poor live in a different country, living a life that is as incomprehensible as it is self-destructive."

We can read, in any number of recent books and articles, exquisite explorations of the supposed "pathologies" of the poor, relying on long-distance psychoanalysis of their "dysfunctions" and "dependency." Taking refuge in a reductive misreading of psychology, the poverty experts present draconian welfare "reforms" as tough love for childlike welfare "dependents." The problem with the poor, in this model, is that we give them too much money; we coddle them and make them weak. If we were to cut off their benefits, they would be able to learn discipline and good character; thus cured of the psychic wounds of "dependency," they too could climb (or claw) their way to the top.

Gamble/*Florida Times-Union* ©1992. Used with permission.

The political implications of the underclass model are apparent enough. *The New Republic*, for example, in its editorial response to the L.A. riots, fell into the classic language of blame-the-victim neoliberalism. "The black underclass perpetuates racial division in this country," the editors confidently announced. "It has helped weaken the American city, speeding up white flight to the suburbs and decreasing the level of black-white geographic contact. When black-white mixing does occur, the powerful image of the black underclass . . . has served to stigmatize the vast majority of middle-class blacks, and to powerfully perpetuate the racism of whites." The editors, warming up to the task, called sternly for politicians to "break underclass culture," to "break through this culture of idleness, poverty, illegitimacy, and crime" by tearing down the welfare system, "the critical sustaining element in the life of the underclass."

This approach has its own internal logic; if you buy its central assumptions these draconian policy suggestions make a certain sense. But since much of the conventional wisdom about the underclass is based less on facts than myths, the stern moralism of *The New Republic* editors (like that of most of those who pontificate most confidently on the subject) is at best irrelevant to the problems of the poor, and in many ways actively harmful.

In reality, the poor suffer not from their own deficient natures, but from a lack of good jobs; from segregation and governmental neglect; from an educational system riddled with savage inequalities. Indeed, poverty today is less the result of "idleness" or "illegitimacy" than of poor wages. In contemporary America, Jones observes, "much of the widening gap between the rich and the poor result[s] not from the growing ranks of the unemployed, but from the worsening relative position of two-parent families that [cannot] earn a living wage."

Who Are the Underclass?

Few who have adopted the term "underclass"—as a generic reference for the demonized urban black poor—have gone to the trouble of defining the term with any precision. Not surprisingly, there is no real consensus over what, if anything, the term denotes. Some define virtually *all* urban poor people as part of the underclass; others reserve the term for the "deviant" minority of drug sellers, criminals and so on. Journalist Ken Auletta, whose 1982 book *The Underclass* popularized the term, defines the group by its "behavioral deficiencies," as a collection of misfits "operating outside the generally accepted boundaries of society . . . set apart by their 'deviant' or antisocial behavior, by their bad habits, not just their poverty." Academic Isabel Sawhill offers a simpler, if somewhat inexact, definition: the underclass consists of "people who engage in bad behavior or a set of bad behaviors."

Aside from the obvious candidates for "bad behavior"—drug dealing, mugging and the like—it has been the putatively deviant family structure of the underclass that has received the most attention from the think-tankers. We have been assured, over and over again for the last decade or so, that black fathers are "irresponsible" deserters, that similarly "irresponsible" black single mothers produce children at whim (or to increase their AFDC [Aid to Families with Dependent Children] allotment), and that the instability of the black family has led to the social instability of the urban core.

In fact, many of the commonly asserted (and accepted) "facts" about the underclass are at best misleading, and at worst deliberate distortions. Most poor people are white, and poverty is as much rural as urban. Many among the urban poor fit few of the stereotypical characteristics ascribed to the underclass, such as single motherhood and persistent (if not willful) unemployment. As historian Stephanie Coontz points out, the majority of "the persistently poor urban black population . . . have one or more of the characteristics usually associated with the 'deserving poor': they are elderly, seriously disabled, or employed for a substantial portion of the year."

Black single mothers have been singled out for special opprobrium, denounced as opportunistic welfare chiselers producing babies for profit. In fact, though the percentage of black households headed by single women is high, and growing, the birthrates for black teenagers, far from spiraling out of control, have actually been *dropping* for the last few decades. And, though poverty pundits are convinced that AFDC payments are a major incentive to out-of-wedlock births, there is no real evidence of this; some researchers have found what appears to be an opposite effect. States with meager welfare benefits (like Mississippi) have high rates of illegitimate births, while those with relatively more generous benefits have lower rates. In fact, as sociologist Mark Rank reports, "welfare mothers" tend to have low fertility rates during the times when they are receiving benefits.

The common remedy proposed by the poverty pundits is simple discipline. In his notorious 1967 report on the "negro family," Daniel Patrick Moynihan suggested that the "utterly masculine world" of military service would provide black men an escape route of sorts from the "disorganized and matrifocal family life in which so many negro youths come of age . . . a world run by strong men of unquestioned authority, where discipline, if harsh, is nonetheless orderly and predictable." Aside from the punitive condescension of Moynihan's language—not to mention his sexism—there are a few technical problems with his solution to underclass pathology: studies have shown that military families have higher rates of divorce, drug abuse and family violence than other families.

The "Curative" of Work

More generally, poverty pundits turn to work as the salve for underclass indiscipline. Any kind of work will do. Sawhill, for example, sees the unwillingness of the urban poor "to take a low-paid job" as a key example of underclass pathology. *New Republic* senior editor Mickey Kaus, in his book *The End of Equality*, suggests that we simply get rid of welfare, replacing the "underclass culture's life support system" with the offer of sub-minimum wage jobs for all who are "able" and willing to work—including single mothers with children. Those who *aren't* willing to work will just have to survive without money, relying on soup kitchens and homeless shelters; their children will end up in orphanages. (Kaus assures us, like some latter-day Herbert Hoover, that "nobody would starve.")

What Kaus forgets is that work (if it is of a sufficiently menial sort, as so much of it is) can be as destructive to dignity as idleness. It is true that the central problem of the underclass is the lack of jobs—that the inner cities have been left stranded, over the last several decades, as jobs have fled to the suburbs. But not *any* job will do. Kaus, like many among the more comfortable members of society, may find satisfaction and fulfillment in his work; single mothers flipping burgers at McDonald's may not be quite so fulfilled. When "underclass" youths denounce the low pay of the degrading jobs available to them as "chump change"—the poverty pundits never tire of repeating this phrase, for them the ultimate indication of a willful indolence—they are, in fact, in their own way, asserting a certain dignity.

Hope or Desperation

This nation must make a basic decision. Poverty is neither inevitable nor irremediable. People are not born violent or useless. Children need not be homeless. Schools need not fail. Young men and women need not be without jobs and hope. No country in Europe warehouses its poor in such desperate circumstance. No other industrial country accepts such staggering inequality. . . .

We must decide. We can bear the costs of hope or pay the costs of neglect. We need a plan to rebuild our cities, to invest in people, to provide opportunity. It will be costly and take years. But we will either provide hope or suffer the far greater costs of desperation. We can provide Head Start, health care, day care on the front side of life or spend far more on welfare and jail-care on the backside.

Jesse Jackson, *Los Angeles Times*, May 2, 1992.

It goes without saying that such an impulse, unless channelled in a properly political way, may simply lead (as it does too often today) to a self-defeating nihilism—to drugs, gangs and crime, to all the familiar curses of the poor. Such behavior is rightly condemned. But the impulse behind such behavior does not itself flow from nihilism; in the refusal to accept the confines of the status quo we should see, rather, the potential for hope.

The conservatives are right about one thing: we on the left need to speak more, and more explicitly, about dignity. Glenn C. Loury, the black neocon, is right when he argues that "the pride and self-respect valued by aspiring peoples throughout the world cannot be the gift of outsiders," and that "neither the guilt nor the pity of one's oppressor is a sufficient basis upon which to construct a sense of self-worth."

But Loury is wrong to argue that anyone—black, white, or whatever—should simply ignore the effects of past (and present) discrimination, and even more wrong to assume that "if we are to be a truly free people, we must accept responsibility for our fate even when it does not lie wholly in our hands." Why? It is not improper for someone who has faced injustice to demand redress; such a demand hardly reflects a poor sense of self-worth or an abdication of responsibility. . . .

Missing the Idea of Social Responsibility

Michael Lerner has attempted (in the pages of *Tikkun* and elsewhere) to promote a vague and vacuous ideological concoction of social and moral responsibility he calls the "Politics of Meaning." The goals of Lerner's movement are certainly ambitious enough: he hopes that "over the course of the next two decades" he will be able to insinuate his "values-oriented, psychologically and spiritually sensitive approach" into "every area of contemporary thought and activity." It's not clear, though, that anyone would notice if he did; there's precious little meaning to the Politics of Meaning. Lerner's philosophy—an attempt to "deeply address the human needs for love, connection, meaning and purpose in a humane way"—manages to be both trivial and pretentious at once, as if one could provide "meaning" to life by simply repeating the word like a mantra.

Like his rhetoric, Lerner's specific policy recommendations lean heavily on the power of symbolism, and range from the meaningless (he asks Clinton to "create a new public discourse of caring, social responsibility, idealism and commitment to ethical, spiritual and ecological sensitivity") to the silly (he suggests that every congressional district hold a yearly contest to determine the 20 families that have "produced children who were, by age 18, the most loving, caring, honest, responsible and supportive people in their communities"). Lerner supports workfare [welfare reform that encourages or mandates recipients to work], and though he declares himself against "alienated labor," he derides those who "talk about workers' rights without talking about their responsibilities as well." When faced with the specter of "irresponsible" workers, Lerner (uncharacteristically) turns stern: "The economy is not a bottomless cookie jar for us to reach in and remove goodies whenever we want." Most of us figured that out a long time ago, thank you.

But if Lerner has had his problems with the philosophy, he's had a notable success with the promotion: in April 1993, Hillary Rodham Clinton delivered a speech drawing heavily on Lerner's rhetorical invocations of caring and community. But there was an interesting slip that took place during the transit of Lerner's ideas from the page to Hillary's lips: Lerner called, you may recall, for "an ethos of caring and social responsibility." Hillary called, instead, for "a new ethos of individual responsibility and caring."

It wasn't just the order of the phrases that Hillary reversed; she changed the adjective as well—and by extension the political meaning of her call for meaning. There's a world of difference between those two adjectives—*social* and *individual*—though Lerner (like most liberals) appears not to understand (or even to have noticed) the crucial shift.

This is a perfect example of why the liberal invocation of responsibility has been so unsuccessful. Unable to distinguish between individual and social responsibility (or unable to recognize that the difference is important), those on the left hope that vague talk of values will be enough to offset the moralistic onslaught on the right. Unless liberals (and, more properly, those on the left) are able to articulate a vision of social responsibility that goes beyond cliché, and to talk about personal dignity without giving in to the illusions of *laissez-faire* individualism, all the newly popular talk about responsibility will merely help to grease the further slide of liberalism to the right. *That* would be irresponsible.

Periodical Bibliography

The following articles have been selected to supplement the diverse views presented in this chapter.

Mona Charen — "Liberal Thinking Has Put Our Civilization at Risk," *Conservative Chronicle*, August 24, 1994. Available from PO Box 11297, Des Moines, IA 50340-1297.

Ruth Conniff — "An Interview with Katha Pollitt," *The Progressive*, December 1994.

Michael D'Antonio — "I or We?" *Mother Jones*, May/June 1994.

Bruce Frohnen — "Has Conservatism Lost Its Mind?" *Policy Review*, Winter 1994.

Greg Guma — "Old Tactics, New Game," *Toward Freedom*, October/November 1994.

John Paul II — "The Person: Subject and Community," *Crisis*, May 1994. Available from PO Box 1006, Notre Dame, IN 46556.

Morton A. Kaplan — "Why Conservative or Liberal?" *Society*, January/February 1994.

Jack Kemp — "The Reagan Revolution Marches On," *Human Events*, November 4, 1994. Available from 422 First St. SE, Washington, DC 20003.

Judith Mirkinson — "Building a Culture of Resistance," *Forward Motion*, Summer 1994. Available from PO Box 311, Van Brunt Station, Brooklyn, NY 11215.

Murray N. Rothbard — "Life in the Old Right," *Chronicles*, August 1994. Available from PO Box 800, Mount Morris, IL 61054.

Philip Selznick — "Foundations of Communitarian Liberalism," *The Responsive Community*, Fall 1994. Available from Circulation Dept., 2020 Pennsylvania Ave. NW, Suite 282, Washington, DC 20006.

Joseph Sobran — "UnDemocratic America," *The Wanderer*, December 8, 1994. Available from 201 Ohio St., St. Paul, MN 55107.

Thomas Sowell — "A Road to Hell Paved with Good Intentions," *Forbes*, January 17, 1994.

Tikkun	"Roundtable: The Politics of Meaning," September/October 1993.
Scott Tucker	"The Good Fight: The Case for Socialism in the Twenty-First Century," *The Humanist*, March/April 1994.
Michael Walzer	"Multiculturalism and Individualism," *Dissent*, Spring 1994.

2 CHAPTER

How Are American Values Changing?

AMERICAN
VALUES

Chapter Preface

America's public schools are often viewed as barometers of social change, reflecting changes in the values of society at large. For example, in August 1994, the Irving, Texas, school board passed a "Resolution Authorizing the Teaching of Traditional Moral Values" in its district's twenty-seven schools, stating in part:

> It is recognized that traditional moral values such as determining right from wrong . . . accountability, self-discipline, sexual abstinence, self-restraint . . . and respect for and value of human life and property are common to all established societies, and are clearly reflective of Irving as a community.

According to syndicated columnist Cal Thomas, this passage "shows how far schools and the nation have moved from what once was considered vital foundational principles. Didn't this list used to be so widely held it rarely had to be expressed?" Thomas contends that the Irving board's sanctioning of the teaching of moral principles—including its abstinence-based AIDS curriculum and ban on condom distribution—should be adopted elsewhere to thwart what he considers the steady erosion of moral values in public schools.

Whether they agree or disagree with Thomas's diagnosis, many parents, educators, and others criticize school boards that solely stress traditional values or teach children to "just say no." In the words of Stanford law professor Deborah L. Rhode: "No significant progress can occur as long as Americans view the issue in terms of individual rather than societal responsibilities and insist on policies that reflect traditional family values rather than contemporary adolescent needs."

Children's values and behavior will continue to be an important indicator of social change. The viewpoints in the following chapter debate whether—and how—American values are changing.

"The death of the work ethic in America is a direct result of the loss of a spiritual center in our society."

America Has Lost Its Work Ethic

Charles Colson and Jack Eckerd

Charles Colson, who was a special counsel to President Richard M. Nixon, was convicted for obstructing justice in the Watergate scandal, which involved a variety of illegal activities—including burglary, wiretapping, and sabotage—designed to secure Nixon's reelection in 1972. He is the founder of Christian Fellowship, a Christian outreach group in Washington, D.C. Jack Eckerd is the founder and former CEO of Eckerd Drug, a drugstore chain. In the following viewpoint, adapted from their book *Why America Doesn't Work*, Colson and Eckerd argue that the early American ethic of hard work centered on religious faith has eroded. The primary cause, they maintain, has been the loss of spirituality resulting from the nation's technological progress and the ideas of such intellectuals as Charles Darwin and Sigmund Freud.

As you read, consider the following questions:

1. What was the focus of the Puritans' hard work, according to Colson and Eckerd?
2. According to the authors, what effect did nineteenth-century intellectuals have on religion?
3. How can the work ethic be restored, in the authors' opinion?

"Why Has Hard Work Fallen on Hard Times?" by Charles Colson and Jack Eckerd. Adapted from *Christianity Today*, February 10, 1992. © 1995. Reprinted by permission of Prison Fellowship, PO Box 17500, Washington, DC 20041-0500.

Something is wrong.

Americans are not working much, and they are not working well. Our rate of production as a country is in trouble because of it. But that's not all. Pollster Lou Harris found some years ago that 63 percent of American workers believed that people don't work as hard as they did ten years ago: 78 percent said people are taking less pride in their work; 69 percent thought workmanship is inferior; and 73 percent believed workers are less motivated.

What has happened to the industry and productivity that made this country the marvel of the industrialized world?

America's Work Ethic

Americans have largely forgotten the place of thrift, industry, diligence, and perseverance—ideals summed up by the words *work ethic*. From the sturdy Scottish Protestants to the Italian Catholics and enterprising Jewish immigrants, from the tiny country churches to the synagogues to the grand cathedrals of the cities, America was built by a religious people. And one of the basic beliefs they brought with them was that, in the words of writer Arthur Burns, "their work mattered to God."

They understood that work is much more than just a need to keep busy or bring home a paycheck. Meaningful work is a fundamental dimension of human existence. Set within us from the beginning, this purposeful nature drives us to work hard, to be productive, to create, and to accumulate the results of our labor. Work is thus a moral imperative, which is the source of *ethic* in *work ethic*—probably one of the most misunderstood terms in the English language.

The *work ethic*—commonly called the *Protestant work ethic*—is largely credited by many with industrializing the West and fueling America's incredible economic growth. For many people, however, it conjures up simple notions about hard work or images of black-robed Puritans who preached about God as the Great Taskmaster, cracking his whip over poor humanity. . . .

Praising God Through Work

The most precious cargo carried with the shiploads of immigrants who set sail for the New World seeking religious freedom and economic opportunity was their view of work. Primarily Puritans and Quakers, they came, as historian David Rodgers notes, "as laborers for their Lord, straighteners of crooked places, engaged in a task filled with hardship, deprivation and toil."

Contrary to what is often supposed, the much-maligned Puritans did not seek wealth as the ultimate reward; neither did they make the mistake of some moderns and worship work itself. They worshiped God *through* their work, which enabled them to treat success with equanimity and failure without regret.

The virtue of work thereby became as deeply ingrained in American culture as democracy. Over succeeding generations this ethic produced a thriving society and later fueled vast increases in invention, productivity, and wealth.

In the midnineteenth century, however, the ethic began to erode, partly because of the very society it helped to create. In the view of writer Sherwood Wirt, this loss was directly connected with the rise of a technical civilization: "The calling lost its vertical bearings in the incessant whirr of machinery and the grime of the mill town. . . . As the modern world awoke to its material strength and shook off the disciplines of the Puritan way of life, it found that the doctrine of the secular calling had become unnecessary. . . . Vocation became simply 'occupation.'"

The result was a hollowed-out version of the work ethic. God was no longer the sacred object of human labors; instead, labor itself became the shrine. So deeply ingrained was the work ethic in the American psyche, however, that it continued to preserve the essential virtues of honest work, thrift, investment, savings, respect of property, and charity toward others.

However, challenges also came from the intellectual front. In the eighteenth century, the Enlightenment, viewed as the dawn of human reason, radically reinterpreted the forces of nature, the organization of society, and the character of morality. Then, in the nineteenth century, Charles Darwin dispensed with the need for God to understand human origins and the order of creation; Sigmund Freud explained religion as a purely human construction; and Friedrich Nietzsche and Karl Marx argued that man was now free to be master of his own universe.

Although philosophers and intellectuals debated them, these ideas did not really penetrate the popular consciousness. That changed with the sixties. The right to "do your own thing" meant all barriers had to fall, and political radicalism burst forth on campuses all across America. These revolutionaries were not just trying to reform curricula or protest Vietnam; they were organizing a wholesale assault on all "bourgeois, middle-class values." And nothing came under more intense assault than the work ethic. One writer of the 1960s spoke glowingly of the vision "of a practical culture in which man is free from labor, free to begin at last the historic task of constructing truly human relationships."

The popular culture and student radicalism succeeded in making *work* a dirty word—something one did only if one must pay for pleasure. Work was no longer ennobling; it was utilitarian— simply a means to an end.

Back to Our Roots

How do we get America back to our work-ethic roots?

There is no one answer, no simple solution. But the problem is not going to be cured by technological, psychological, or governmental solutions, important though some of these are. The death of the work ethic in America is a direct result of the loss of a spiritual center in our society.

This has implications, first of all, for the home. As [former] Secretary of Health and Human Services Louis Sullivan said, the first department of education is the family. Parents need to instill in their children the values of hard work, doing one's best, and knowing the value of a hard-earned dollar. If we are going to restore the work ethic, we must teach our children that there is virtue and dignity in work. They must learn the importance of individual responsibility.

Apart from the family, no institution can play a more vital and basic role in moral education and in restoring the work ethic than the church. All those characteristics we associate with the work ethic—dedication, excellence, thrift, pride in what we do, industry, and an ennobling view of work—find their deepest roots in Scripture and through the centuries have been defined and articulated by the church. Today the call to recover the traditional virtues of the work ethic should ring forth from our pulpits, but the church, along with the culture at large, needs to be re-educated in those virtues.

From School Boards to Boardrooms

We should also work to change our schools. Nothing less than a massive overhaul of our educational system will do. We should start banging on the doors of our school boards, go to their meetings, maybe even run for the school board. We can examine the curriculum and ask about tests and standards and what values are being taught—or not being taught. The people who teach in our schools must be held to the same standard of excellence that we expect of our children.

No matter how many structures we fix, however, restoring the work ethic in our society boils down to one thing: We must restore it in the hearts and minds of individuals. It is through the individual—the factory worker, the floor manager, the CEO, the secretary, the volunteer, the fast-food server—that the work ethic becomes a reality on the floor of the shop, at the desk in the office, or in the boardroom.

"Americans work astonishingly hard, compared with both our own recent past and most of our trade competitors."

America Has Not Lost Its Work Ethic

Michael Kinsley

Michael Kinsley is a senior editor of the *New Republic* magazine and appears on the television programs *Firing Line* and *Crossfire*. In the following viewpoint, Kinsley argues that American workers are anything but lazy; more Americans are working longer per year than ever before. But Kinsley maintains that despite their hard work, Americans are reaping little benefit. He points out that income gains for many Americans are due to working longer hours, not better pay per hour—an indicator of a declining standard of living. Kinsley also warns that Americans' desire for consumer gratification is harmful because it leads to low rates of savings and investment.

As you read, consider the following questions:

1. What has happened to leisure time in America, according to Kinsley?
2. What does Juliet B. Schor, as quoted by Kinsley, mean by "capitalism's 'squirrel cage'"?
3. How do working hours in America compare to those in Japan, according to the author?

Michael Kinsley, "Lazy He Calls Us," *The New Republic*, February 17, 1992. Reprinted by permission of *The New Republic*, ©1992, The New Republic, Inc.

Lazy? Hey buster, are you calling American workers *lazy*??

That's what he said, all right. Japanese officials wanted to portray this 1992 remark by Yoshio Sakurauchi, speaker of the Japanese parliament, as the maundering of a senile nonentity. But it apparently reflects the views of the Japanese public. According to a *New York Times*/CBS poll, 66 percent of Japanese think Americans are "lazy" and only 13 percent think we're "hardworking." (Polling—now there's a great American export.)

The view that Americans are lazy is widespread in America, too. In [the *New Republic*, editor in chief Martin Peretz] was brooding on the subject, and praising Asian Americans for showing "that hard work is still rewarded here, in a country that needs more hard work."

Americans Work Hard

Whatever ails the American economy, though, it cannot be blamed on laziness. Americans work astonishingly hard, compared with both our own recent past and most of our trade competitors. Juliet B. Schor, an associate professor of economics at Harvard, dishes the grim figures in her intriguing 1991 book, *The Overworked American*. The average working American puts in 163 more hours a year than twenty years ago. That's the equivalent of an extra month of work. Men are working on average two-and-a-half weeks longer, women seven-and-a-half weeks longer. The pattern is consistent across various occupations and income levels. More women are working. More teenagers are working (53.7 percent). Average American work time is way up even if you include those whose work time is zero (retirees, students, the unemployed, etc.).

Commuting time is up, too—by an average of twenty-three hours (almost three working days) a year. Paid vacation time is down by 3.5 days a year. Despite the huge increase in the number of working wives, time spent on household chores has not declined. Women do a bit less, men do a bit more, the total is constant. Decades of technological advances from indoor plumbing [to] vacuum cleaners to food processors have simply illustrated Parkinson's Law: "With all these labor-saving innovations, no labor has been saved. Instead, housework expanded to fill the available time." (The one exception: microwave ovens.) Schor blames excessive American standards of cleanliness.

From their peak in the pits of the Industrial Revolution, working hours declined steadily until the 1940s. Everyone assumed this would continue. During the Depression, the Senate actually passed a bill mandating a thirty-hour work week to relieve unemployment. As late as the 1950s sociologists heartached over what Americans would do with all their leisure time. But the "leisure crisis" has turned out to be the exact opposite: people and society are frazzling from the stress of overwork.

Schor's take on all this is a bit odd. She sees the essential villain as consumerism, spurred by the capitalist system's ever receding mirage of material bliss. Convinced that the next purchase will satisfy us, we work harder to buy it, only to want something else. We are on a treadmill, "imprisoned in capitalism's 'squirrel cage,'" caught in an "insidious cycle of 'work and spend.'" Noting primly that "there are numerous examples of societies in which *things* have played a highly circumscribed role," Schor also observes that money can't buy happiness: the percentage of Americans reporting to pollsters that they were "very happy" peaked in 1957.

The Fallacy of Fallen Productivity

From the end of the 1960s to the present, Americans have increased the time they spend at work by about 160 hours—or nearly one month—per year. This is equally true for people in glamour jobs and line workers at McDonald's. And it's true for women as well as men.

It's a fallacy that the productivity of American workers has fallen. The level of productivity of the U.S. worker has more than doubled since 1948. In other words, we could now produce our 1948 standard of living in less than half the time it took in that year. That's largely because of technological change, greater investment and increased skills on the part of the work force.

Juliet B. Schor, *Newsweek*, February 17, 1992.

Schor's solution? A conscious social decision—implemented in a variety of government policies—to accept a lower standard of living in exchange for more leisure time. I wonder how many Americans would actually be interested in such a deal. Although Schor seems quite left-wing, her best allies here might be social-issue conservatives, eager for more women to stay home and tend to their families. How many of them will admit, though, as Schor frankly does, that their social engineering project implies a lower gross national product?

Make of Schor's vision what you will (and I don't dismiss it out of hand), you needn't agree about the evils of materialism in order to explain the increase in American working hours. As a study by the congressional joint Economic Committee ("Families on a Treadmill") points out, even in strictly material terms Americans are running ever faster just to stay in the same place.

The study compares two-parent families with children in 1979 and 1989. For most, the wife's real hourly pay rose only slightly and the husband's actually declined. Except for the top fifth, any increase in total family income came from working longer hours, not from better pay for hours worked. If you're working harder to afford the same lifestyle, your standard of living has declined, even if the official standard of living statistics don't reflect that.

Working Harder, Getting Nowhere

Working harder is not the answer for the American economy. We are already working harder, and it's getting us nowhere. Yes, the Japanese still put in more hours a year than we do, on average. Schor figures they outwork us by six weeks a year. She paints a convincingly gruesome picture of a society where "thousands of workers have become victims of karoshi, or 'death by overwork.' Otherwise perfectly healthy, they keel over at their desks. . . ." (West Germans, on the other hand, work an average of eight weeks a year less than we do.) But longer hours cannot explain Japan's economic performance. That's because Japan's work hours have been decreasing, America's have been increasing, and even so their economy has been growing far faster than ours.

Since 1975 Japan's output per person has increased by almost half while America's has increased by a mere 12 percent. This Japanese achievement is not the result of working longer hours— Japanese work fewer hours than they did in 1975. It is mainly the result of Japan's high rates of savings and investment—including the social investment in education.

Thus Juliet Schor may be right for the wrong reason. America's desire for immediate and unending consumer gratification may or may not be leading us to work too hard, but it's definitely leading us to save and invest too little. Unless we curb our present appetites, we won't see the gains in productivity that could allow us to have more things and more time as well in the future.

But meanwhile, just don't call us lazy.

"It would be highly beneficial to [baby boomers]— and ultimately to the future of our nation—to rediscover and embrace the traditional morals and values they discarded as hopelessly obsolete."

Baby Boomers' Values May Be Detrimental

Warren P. Mass

Baby boomers are often criticized for lacking the traditional values related to economic security and hard work held by previous generations. Absent these values, many baby boomers are interested only in themselves and the pursuit of pleasure, Warren P. Mass maintains in the following viewpoint. Mass cites a study by Harvard professor D. Quinn Mills, who finds that baby boomers are largely cynical and insecure about American institutions such as business and government. Mills identifies common traits among baby boomers: valuing experiences over possessions, fun over duty, and opportunity over security. Despite these faults, Mass credits baby boomers for their honesty and their intolerance of bureaucracy. He concludes, however, that baby boomers need to be educated about morality, personal responsibility, and their national heritage of constitutional government.

As you read, consider the following questions:
1. How did economic conditions differ as baby boomers and their parents were growing up, according to the author?
2. What are the different categories of boomers, according to the work of D. Quinn Mills, as cited by Mass?
3. In Mass's opinion, how could baby boomers' values be useful?

Warren P. Mass, "Changing of the Guard," *The New American*, October 4, 1993. Reprinted with permission.

The ascent of Bill Clinton to the Presidency was trumpeted as more than just a routine changing of the guard. Just as John Kennedy was noted for being the first President born in the 20th century, Mr. Clinton is the first chief executive born after World War II—a "baby boomer"—and symbolizes for many the ultimate replacement, by attrition, of the "older generation." Such is apt to provoke a sense of alarm, even distress, among those on the senior side of the "generation gap." They may be concerned as to what this abrupt generational change portends for America.

Articles about the baby boomer phenomenon have saturated the features sections of newspapers for years, surveying the influence of boomers in American society on everything from politics, to business, to arts and entertainment, to tastes in food and fashion. But although most such features are interesting, they rely more on casual observation than scientific study. They tend to be, therefore, more entertaining than educational.

This writer did, however, come across a controlled study of the boomer phenomenon, conducted in 1987, by D. Quinn Mills, a professor at the Harvard Business School. Mills' results have been published in the book *Not Like Our Parents: How the Baby Boom Generation Is Changing America.* Bearing in mind that all studies are fallible, and that much has happened in our country even in the few years since 1987, Professor Mills' work is nonetheless enlightening.

Historical Discontinuity

According to Mills, differences between generations are caused by "major historical discontinuities, such as wars, depressions, or major technological advances." Undoubtedly, the two most significant events influencing the *parents* of baby boomers were the Great Depression and World War II. Mills found from his studies that the Depression made the generation growing up in the '30s economically insecure and preoccupied with material needs. However, the great mobilization and common patriotic effort of World War II gave this same generation a sense of security concerning their government. The federal government had led the nation to victory and provided its returning veterans with educational and housing benefits.

The post-War generation, in contrast, grew up in the prosperous '50s and '60s and felt secure about economic conditions. However, the unpopularity and blatant mismanagement of the Vietnam War made this generation cynical and insecure about government, a cynicism which unfortunately has extended to their attitudes about religion and business. Mills found that boomers are somewhat prone to a low-grade rebellion toward established cultural institutions, the result of lack of education about their American heritage. As Mills observed, baby boomers "know who they are as individuals, but they don't know America. They are only dimly aware of our nation's history; they are rarely reflective; and though they know themselves as a group, they are not good at articulating what makes them special."

Common Traits

Of course, when analyzing the post-War generation, one is tempted to overgeneralize. But like all large groups in a society, individual differences abound with baby boomers. Mills established several broad categories to describe different types of boomers: the "pleasure seekers" (or subscribers to a hedonistic lifestyle); the "competitors" (typified by the 1980s "yuppie" phenomenon); the "trapped" (those finding it difficult to change their state in life due to economic or other considerations); the "contented" (a majority of boomers, consisting of those who are satisfied with their roles in society); and the "get highs" (escapists, who have never quite outgrown the 1960s).

Among these broad groups, Mills was nonetheless able to identify certain common traits distinguishing baby boomers from the World War II generation. For example:

- Boomers value experiences over possessions (e.g., they are more apt to spend discretionary income on travel rather than on kitchen appliances).
- Boomers value fun more than duty. Mills noted:

  People of the older generation looked upon work as an obligation. . . . A person did not expect to enjoy work. . . .

  Baby boomers have a different attitude. They will not accept work solely as drudgery. Whether they are professionals or blue-collar workers, they want work to be enjoyable.

  "Our employees want us to provide eight hours a day and forty hours a week of interesting, enjoyable, personally satisfying work," the president of a large industrial corporation told [Mills]. "Because we can't provide what they want, our people turn off and productivity and quality are awful."

  In place of duties, obligations, and chores, young people want activities that help them grow, gain new experiences, and feel good about themselves.

  This is the first generation in American history to insist that work be fun.

Economics: The Good and Bad

- Boomers value opportunity over security. Mills found that while the generation growing up during the Depression and experiencing World War II developed a deep concern for security, the baby boom generation has had very little sense of economic insecurity. (This was the case in 1987, when the study was conducted. One expects that the state of our economy in the mid-1990s may evaporate some of this sense of security.)

While World War II veterans often sought secure employment in large corporations, baby boomers often see large corporations as too bureaucratic. "What is valued by baby boomers, and increasingly by society as a whole, is initiative and independence and entrepreneurship," Mills observed. Small wonder, then, that the sort of companies thriving in today's economic climate are energetic, entrepreneurial, high-tech firms such as (to give one example) Microsoft Corporation.

Happiness—Expected but Not Found

Somewhere in the Seventies, or the Sixties, we [baby boomers] started expecting to be happy, and changed our lives (left town, left families, switched jobs) if we were not. And society strained and cracked in the storm.

I think we have lost the old knowledge that happiness is over-rated—that, in a way, life is overrated. We have lost, somehow, a sense of mystery—about us, our purpose, our meaning, our role. Our ancestors believed in two worlds, and understood this to be the solitary, poor, nasty, brutish and short one. We are the first generations of man that actually expected to find happiness here on earth, and our search for it has caused such—unhappiness.

Peggy Noonan, *Forbes*, September 14, 1992.

With regards to economic matters, the generation gap has had both positive and negative ramifications. On the one hand, the boomers' abandonment of the traditional work ethic might be viewed as making American industrial concerns less competitive vis-à-vis the Japanese, who supposedly value such traits to a high degree. On the other hand, the rejection of large corporations by boomers in favor of small firms may help break the talent monopoly of the large, multi-national corporations and help smaller, more entrepreneurial ventures. Because of the close association between many of the so-called "Fortune 500" companies and the Eastern political establishment, positive socio-political benefits may result from the independent, anti-establishment streak of many boomers (even if they are not quite sure exactly what "the Establishment" is).

Conflicting Signals

As to what to expect from boomers in the political world, they have sent conflicting messages. During the '60s, at the height of the anti–Vietnam War protests, the conventional wisdom held that the baby boom generation was both "liberal" and "anti-establishment." (Of course, this represented a contradiction for those who realized that the Establishment *was* "liberal"—i.e., that America's most powerful and influential institutions were making their resources available to those causes that would tend to increase the size and influence of government.)

Boomers Gone Astray

Then, during the Reagan years, we were told that the baby boomers had matured and settled into a comfortable conservatism. However, according to Mills:

> Voting for Reagan and against Carter made baby boomers seem conservative. But the liberal and conservative labels don't fit well. Boomers generally don't fit the traditional political categories.

Mills identified the prevailing political attitude of baby boomers as individualistic: "The representative boomer is socially liberal and economically conservative, and when the two conflict, he or she makes a choice or a compromise on the spot."

It is this tendency toward instant compromise, made without the benefit of sound education in American history and the principles of constitutional government, that leads the baby boomer generation astray. True individualism—tempered by a strong moral and historical foundation—is the ideal political system for a people committed to governing themselves through self-restraint. Unfortunately, we do not presently live in such a society; more personal responsibility and morality is needed to enable people to govern themselves.

Some Hope

The baby boomers' skepticism of government, born during the tumultuous 1960s and the Vietnam War protests, may indeed be a healthy characteristic if channeled properly. Boomers tend to be intolerant of bureaucracy, which may be useful in encouraging the dismantling of the federal leviathan. But this generation must also be made to realize that, in order to reduce the size of government, government handouts and unconstitutional programs must go.

According to Mills, baby boomers are altruistic by nature and maintain some strong guiding principles. They especially regard the virtue of honesty and abhor hypocrisy in any form. Political leaders would do well to keep this in mind, and strive to maintain honest and straightforward ethics rather than follow the path of least resistance.

It would be highly beneficial to the members of this generation—and ultimately to the future of our nation—to rediscover and embrace the traditional morals and values they discarded as hopelessly obsolete. Baby boomers as a whole are a curious lot, and are receptive to learning, but tend to take little on faith. (If Missouri is the "Show Me" state, the boomers are the "Show Me" generation.) They are indeed the future of our nation, and must be educated in morality and freedom if they are to become tomorrow's patriots. One thing is certain: They cannot be ignored.

> *"We sense that [boomers] are reaching out to commit themselves to something of importance, yearning for relationships and connections, longing for more stable anchors for their lives."*

Baby Boomers Have Rewarding Values

Wade Clark Roof

The values of baby boomers, the generation of Americans born between 1946 and 1964, have played an important role in shaping American culture, Wade Clark Roof argues in the following viewpoint. Roof asserts that maturing baby boomers should not be thought of as the "Me Generation" because they value meaningful commitments to their spouses and children. Roof also contends that boomers are intent on strengthening their inner and outer lives; they are open to spirituality and concerned about their communities. Roof is a professor of religion and society at the University of California at Santa Barbara.

As you read, consider the following questions:

1. How strongly do baby boomers value a belief in one's self, according to Roof?
2. What influence will baby boomers and their children have on religion, in Roof's opinion?
3. According to the author, what effect will baby boomers have on community?

Excerpts from *A Generation of Seekers: The Spiritual Journeys of the Baby Boom Generation* by Wade Clark Roof. Copyright ©1993 by Wade Clark Roof. Reprinted by permission of HarperSanFrancisco, a division of HarperCollins Publishers, Inc.

Virtually all aspects of the lives of baby boomers—their family styles, moral values, work habits, political views—defy simple generalizations. There are many white, upscale boomers, but there are also millions of blue-collar, minority, single-parent, and poor boomers. Polls show they are tolerant in matters of lifestyle and committed to women's issues, yet many call for a return to traditional family values. They cherish the freedom of individual expression, yet agree there should be greater respect for authority. Aside from whatever unites them as a generation, they are divided along lines of age, education, economic class, gender, and lifestyle, making them anything but a monolith.

Partly for this reason, the boomers are an easy target for caricature. At various times they have been called the Pepsi Generation, the Rock Generation, the Love Generation, the Now Generation, the Me Generation. Labels come and go, but some kind of label always seems to pop up. As Paul C. Light has observed, "The baby boomers have always been known by a handful of stereotypes—hippies in the 1960s, yuppies in the 1980s. Ask the average American to define the baby boomer of today, and he or she will likely think of yuppies or grumpies on Wall Street, or Dinks [Dual incomes, no kids] in the suburbs, long before remembering the real people just down the street."

We [the author and several University of Massachusetts graduate students] have tried to get beyond stereotypes to the real people. We have interviewed hundreds of boomers on the telephone. We have gone out and met scores of them, asking about their experiences and life histories. We have visited churches and synagogues, conducted group interviews, and talked to them in more casual settings—at folk festivals and retreat centers, in seminaries, on airplanes, at bars. Everywhere we have gone—primarily in California, Massachusetts, North Carolina, and Ohio—we have listened to their stories. While our aim was to learn as much as possible about their religious and spiritual biographies, we have found out a great deal as well about their work and careers, their marriages and families, their visions of the country and its future, their hopes and dreams. . . .

Midlife Boomers

Many boomers are now approaching middle age, or that stage of life often talked about as midlife. "Forty is the old age of youth and the youth of old age," so the adage goes. However one cares to view it, reaching forty marks a significant passage in life's journey. Midlife is popularly thought of as a time of crisis, but it is more appropriately viewed as a time of transition. Developmental psychologists describe it as a transition from early adulthood into later adulthood, a juncture when people often reexamine their lives, their past and anticipated future, their most cherished values and commitments. This can be a period of uncertainty and emotional strain, but it can also be highly challenging and self-enriching. It is a time when adults experience a capacity for growth and maturity, which potentially can occur at any life stage but is especially likely at midlife.

Boomers are now experiencing, as is common in life's passages, a sense of aliveness and freshness, an openness to new spiritual sensitivities. They are at a critical juncture of affirming life's meanings and fundamental values and of dealing with spiritual voids, of looking back upon their lives as a means of preparing to move forward. Psychologist John Roschen speaks of a "second journey into self." He points out that many young Americans are inwardly appraising self but are also moving outward toward others. In this second journey of self, they are revising their notions of who they are as their lives spiral outward to spouses, to families, to the wider communities. Boomers are no longer, if ever most of them were, to be thought of as the "Me Generation" caught up in their own selfish pursuits; instead, this is a maturing generation of individuals concerned not just with their inner lives, but with their outer lives. We sense that they are reaching out to commit themselves to something of importance, yearning for relationships and connections, longing for more stable anchors for their lives. To quote Roschen:

> This balanced care for self and others brings out the virtues of connectedness, intimacy, love, fairness, a sense of justice, and commitment to duty which yearn to be reclaimed in the lives of many in the baby-boom generation. Fulfillment versus responsibility, and individual ambition versus the needs of others are at the crux of the baby-boomers' midlife dilemma.

How the boomers deal with their lives at midlife is important, not just for themselves, but for the country. American culture as a whole could be profoundly affected in the years ahead. . . .

A Sense of Commitment

[A] trend toward commitment is apparent in the boomers we interviewed. Mollie Stone, a single mother in Massachusetts who told us about her days as a "flower child" in Central Park, is the most obvious case of someone deeply immersed in her own self, but who is now trying to revise the giving-receiving compact. Today she would like to be married and to have a more stable family life. Partly a reflection of demographics, many boomers—like Mollie—are now in their mid- to late thirties and early forties and are concerned with marriages, families, and parenting. But there appears to be something more—a profound search for ways to reach out and connect with others, and to find a more satisfying balance of concerns for self and for others. Commitment amounts to what pollster Daniel Yankelovich describes as a "giving/receiving social compact," and many today are recognizing that such a compact is open to revision as people's lives and circumstances change.

Exploring New Ways

[Baby boomers] are still exploring, as they did in their years growing up; but now they are exploring in new, and, we think, more profound ways. Religious and spiritual themes are surfacing in a rich variety of ways—in Eastern religions, in evangelical and fundamentalist teachings, in mysticism and New Age movements, in Goddess worship and other ancient religious rituals, in the mainline churches and synagogues, in Twelve-Step recovery groups, in concern about the environment, in holistic health, and in personal and social transformation.

Wade Clark Roof, *A Generation of Seekers*, 1993.

Though much energy is now directed at working out a meaningful and balanced sense of commitment, this does not mean that boomers, by and large, have abandoned their expectations for fulfilling lives. To the contrary, whatever revisions of the giving-receiving compact are occurring, it is in the context of some deeply held values that crystallized during their years growing up and continue to be of great importance to them. One is tolerance. Eighty-seven percent in our survey said there should be more acceptance of different lifestyles. Social background, level of education, and region of country do not matter: Boomers generally hold to the view that lifestyles should be a matter of personal choice. Tolerance was extended in their generation to those not just different racially or socioeconomically, but with differing sexual orientations and lifestyles. Options in virtually all realms of life are taken for granted.

Self-Reliance

Another value they hold dear is belief in themselves. Eighty-six percent of our respondents say that if you believe in yourself, there is almost no limit to what you can do. Seventy-one percent say a person who is strong and determined can pretty much control what happens in life. Even failure is seen as something to be blamed on the individual, not society. Sixty-six percent agree that if someone does not succeed in life, usually it's his or her own fault. The better educated and those most deeply influenced by the counterculture are somewhat less inclined to agree, and more likely to see society as playing a part affecting people's life chances, but self-reliance is a tenet of faith among boomers. "Brought up in an environment of change," writes Michael Maccoby, "they have learned to adapt to new people and situations, and to trust their own abilities rather than parents or institutions. They value independence, and they accept responsibility for themselves."

Victims of their own great expectations, many in this generation have experienced a disheartening gap between their perceived potential and realized achievements. Economic opportunities failed to keep pace with their aspirations. Many with college degrees were forced to settle for jobs and incomes lower than what they had assumed was befitting of college status. The optimism of the 1960s faded in the 1970s—a decade remembered for gas lines, inflation, and a rising cost of living. The tightening of the economy came at just the time when many of the older boomers were forming families, trying to buy their first homes, and discovering the difficulties of maintaining marriages, raising children, and having satisfying careers, and optimism gave way to the "big chill." One-third of our respondents report having to "scale down their expectations"—true for both the older and younger waves. Expecting so much in life, they have discovered that nothing—homes, family, love, friendship, wealth—comes easily.

A Focus on Self

A third value is the belief that strength comes from within. When boomers are asked to describe themselves, they focus on personal, individual qualities. Both their successes and failures may contribute to a greater introspectiveness. A focus on self helps to explain, for example, the high priority given to family, friends, and interpersonal relationships. Having been estranged from more organized formal institutions, many still prefer a more personal means of relating to the social world. Much energy is spent in personal relationships, obviously a source of immense satisfaction. It likely accounts for why so many boomers turn to therapy and counseling as a solution to problems and why they like a high degree of personal service in the marketplace. Introspection also bears on openness and sharing of feelings. Asked to evaluate a list of changes from the time of their parents' generation, respondents in [a 1986] *Rolling Stone* survey chose one change above all others: 83% felt that greater openness and willingness to share personal feelings was a change for the better.

These are hardly new values. The quest for psychological well-being itself has roots reaching deep into the American past. As early as the mid-1800s, Ralph Waldo Emerson, in his essay on "Self-Reliance," had written of his opposition to tradition and conformity and looked to individuals relying on their own inner resources as a means to truth and wisdom. He called upon people to recognize the power within them and to use that power for their own fulfillment. In his writing on "Nature" and "Wealth," he further elaborated on the expansive qualities of the human spirit: "Who can set bounds to the possibilities of man?" he asks, and then implicitly answers his question by reminding his readers that "the world exists for you." Optimism, personal transformation, and the union of mind and matter were all Emersonian themes that later generations of "positive thinkers"—from Mary Baker Eddy to Norman Vincent Peale—would draw on. Members of the boomer generation have felt a special affinity with such thinkers and have been inspired by their teachings. . . .

Greater Wisdom

In their innermost beings, the "children of the sixties" know that religion, for all its institutional limitations, holds a vision of life's unity and meaningfulness, and for that reason will continue to have a place in their narrative. In a very basic sense, religion itself was never the problem, only social forms of religion that stifle the human spirit. The sacred lives on and is real to those who can access it.

Far from having been in vain, their explorations have served to bring them to a greater wisdom. Life takes on richer meaning for those who are wise enough to know that in exploring, life begins to look more like an ever-evolving spiral than a vicious circle.

Wade Clark Roof, *A Generation of Seekers*, 1993.

Looking into the future, we find reasons to expect that boomer trends will have a long-lasting influence. The changing patterns of family and religion for boomers and their children are crucial. High rates of interfaith marriage and continuing large numbers of blended families will result in new generations of children with weak institutional religious ties. Denominational boundaries within Protestantism will likely erode further, as increasing numbers of Americans grow up knowing very little about their religious heritages. Better known will be the general faith traditions—Roman Catholicism, Judaism, Islam, and Protestantism clustered into its liberal and conservative camps. A highly privatized and relativistic approach to religion, already practiced by large numbers of boomers, will probably become even more widespread in a society that has no strong religious center. Both privatism and relativism in matters of faith and practice will be sustained in a culture where the importance attached to choice is so deeply rooted. Spirituality will naturally be subject to fads and fashions, quick-fix techniques that promise easy solutions. The self-help movement itself risks loss of credibility with its endless proliferation of Twelve-Step groups and perpetuation of the notion that ours is a society of victims. Even so, it seems unlikely that there will be any great turning away from concerns with the self and its spiritual quests.

Changing values will have a continuing impact as well. The value shifts of the 1960s and 1970s—that is, the countercultural values, later described as post-material values—create the context for understanding the religious and spiritual transformations. . . . In our view the value shifts were not a temporary aberration—a sudden outburst of hippies and flower children—to be followed by a return to the normalcy of the past. The counterculture came and went, but many of the values associated with it, such as libertarian aspirations, greater egalitarianism, ecological consciousness, and an enhanced concern with the self, are all now deeply entrenched in American life. The evidence points to an enduring pattern of changing American values. A major study of the children born to countercultural parents shows, for example, that even though they behave fairly conventionally, they are more aware than other children of such issues as women's rights and ecology. The parents taught strong values to their children, values that continue to set the children apart from others. Even the children from families that became more conventional in appearance and lifestyle as time passed believed more in gender equality and environmental causes than did their friends from families that had always been conventional. The point is that the 1960s ushered in cultural changes that have lasted and are now being transmitted to the next generation. What was once on the cultural margins now permeates the cultural mainstream. Much of what the parents' generation struggled for is taken by their heirs as the accepted values by which we live. . . .

Concern for Community

As boomers age we can expect increased attention to *creating* new forms of community. A more settled life, the end of childbearing, and greater concerns about health and well-being should all create conditions for more community. Boomers will likely invest their energies in those institutions where there is freedom to create—be they religious or otherwise. They may actually reach out to one another in ways we have yet to imagine. "Networking" may become a deeper, more encompassing concept than it is now. Already there are signs of a rediscovery of village forms of life, of a co-housing movement, and of cooperatives. Out in the future will come an elderculture with a concern to preserve values and traditions—including, no doubt, community as a cherished value. One expectation already advanced is that the creation of community inspired in their youth may blossom again in their old age. They may have unfinished business to return to once they are no longer absorbed in careers and rearing families.

This speculation aside, we can say that, despite the language of individualism, a concern for community is already very real to them. The sense of group identity known from the time of their youth has not been lost on them in their more individualistic, more competitive middle years. In fact, many may yearn nostalgically for its return. Many whose consciousness had been formed by the sixties told [Louise Bernikow,] the author of a study on loneliness in America, that at one time they "had a feeling of belonging to something larger than themselves, whether the antiwar, women's or civil rights movement or the youth culture." The feeling was gone but not forgotten.

"Public schools are delivering precisely the product of humanistic education that they have been asked to deliver."

Public Schools Have Subverted Religious Values

Robert W. Lee

Many conservative and other Americans deplore the absence of religious values in public schools. In the following viewpoint, Robert W. Lee argues that public schools have abandoned religious values in favor of secular humanism, inculcating children with dangerous messages that promote promiscuity, drug use, and a lack of respect for life. Lee contends that students are being enticed to discard the values and religious beliefs of their families and create their own sets of values. Lee is a contributing writer to the *New American*, a biweekly conservative magazine.

As you read, consider the following questions:

1. What are some of the components of the "death education curriculum," according to Samuel Blumenfeld, quoted by the author?
2. In Lee's opinion, how are school-based or school-linked health clinics undermining parental rights?
3. On what basis does the author criticize school drug-education programs?

Robert W. Lee, "Mind Pollution," *The New American*, August 8, 1994. Reprinted with permission.

Dr. Thomas Sowell, a senior fellow at Stanford University's Hoover Institution, claims that government schools in America today are carrying on "unrelenting guerrilla warfare against the traditional values of society and against the very role of families in making decisions about their own children." Sowell is not exaggerating. More than a decade ago, the *Humanist* magazine (January/February 1983) ran an article in which John J. Dunphy, *summa cum laude* graduate of the University of Illinois-Edwardsville, bluntly declared that "the battle for humankind's future must be waged and won in the public school classroom by teachers who correctly perceive their role as the proselytizers of a new faith." Such teachers, Dunphy stated, will be "utilizing a classroom instead of a pulpit to convey humanist values in whatever subject they teach, regardless of the educational level—preschool day care or large state university." Classrooms, Dunphy maintained, "must and will become an arena of conflict between the old and the new—the rotting corpse of Christianity . . . and the new faith of humanism. . . ."

Humanism in Action

Education analyst Samuel Blumenfeld contends that school programs supposedly intended to assist students in "clarifying" their values are instead enticing students "to discard the values and religious beliefs of their families and create new sets of values reflecting their own personal desires and leanings, particularly those regarding sex." Many youngsters, for example, have "been encouraged by values clarification to reject the traditional Judeo-Christian prohibitions against sexual perversion and adopt an open and assertive homosexual lifestyle."

Values clarification, Blumenfeld asserts, "is humanism in action." One of its exercises, the lifeboat survival game, has students decide who must die on an overcrowded lifeboat so that the others might live. In his book *The Leaning Tower of Babel*, Richard Mitchell explains that "the verdict must be 'relevant,' conducive to 'the greatest good for the greatest number,'" and focus on "accepted notions of 'social usefulness.'" Which means that the "children who 'play' the game usually decide to dump an old clergyman, a man who is supposed to be prepared for that sort of thing," whereas a "young country-western singer will be preserved. She has many long years ahead of her in which to maximize her potential and serve the greatest good by entertaining the greatest number."

Another scenario, described by Blumenfeld, has fifteen persons alone in a bomb shelter after a nuclear holocaust. They have food and other supplies sufficient to keep only seven alive until it is safe to emerge from the shelter. Each is delineated by age, race, religion, education, profession, and lifestyle, after which students are required to determine which seven deserve to live.

A process that pressures impressionable youngsters to make such decisions based solely on the social utility of those involved is truly Hitlerian in its implications. It tends to bolster support for such lethal real-world policies as abortion and euthanasia, two of the stated objectives (along with the "right" to suicide) of major humanist declarations and manifestos.

Ramirez/Copley News Service. Used with permission.

Menninger Foundation senior psychiatrist Dr. Harold M. Voth has noted the abundance of evidence suggesting that "children are being scarred" by values clarification exercises "that spread pessimism, depression, and a hatred of life." Likewise, many are being harmed by instruction in "death education." As explained by Samuel Blumenfeld in *The Blumenfeld Education Letter* for June 1990, "the purpose of death education is to 'desensitize' children to death—to remove or reduce that reasonable, rational, and useful antipathy to death that helps us preserve our lives. It is when children begin to see death as 'friendly' and unthreatening that they begin to be drawn into death's orbit and lured to self-destruction."

Virtually every school subject is vulnerable to such death conditioning, from reading and math to shop and art (where children draw death-related pictures). Blumenfeld notes that typically, components of the death education curriculum entail

> questionnaires delving into the child's view of death and dying;
> the writing of obituaries, eulogies, epitaphs, and wills; planning
> funerals; visits to cemeteries and mortuaries; reading stories
> and books about death; and discussing abortion, euthanasia,
> and suicide. The whys and hows of suicide are discussed, and
> suicide notes are written. In some visits to funeral homes, chil-
> dren try out coffins; in math they measure each other for
> coffins, and in shop they build model coffins. Children also
> study the death customs of other cultures and develop a death
> vocabulary. In one second grade class in Lowell, Massachusetts,
> the children used the information in an obituary to work out
> arithmetic problems. Some death education exercises include
> fantasizing about dying.

On June 15, 1994, the Gallup Organization released a poll in-
dicating that 5 percent of American teenagers say they have attempted suicide and 12 percent say they have come close to trying it. The reported suicide rate for adolescents has tripled since
1950. In December 1991, the *Journal of the American Medical
Association* reported that school suicide prevention programs,
supposedly intended to help teens, were instead increasing depression in teens who had tried to commit suicide, some of
whom told researchers that "talking about suicide makes some
kids more likely to try to kill themselves."

Rabid environmentalism may also be contributing to the problem. Beginning in the earliest grades, schoolchildren in many
schools are being indoctrinated about the supposed dangers of
asbestos (unsafe classrooms), radon (unsafe basements at home),
cancer-causing chemicals (unsafe food), lead (unsafe water),
ground-level ozone and carbon monoxide (unsafe air), etc. Many
scientific studies have confirmed that stress resulting from con-
tinuous, gnawing fear not only generates the sort of emotional
problems often associated with suicide, but also erodes the immune system in a way that opens the door to serious physical
health problems as well. Environmental fearmongering may be
doing more long-term damage to the physical and emotional
well-being of our schoolchildren than any alleged environmental
threats could do.

"Safe Sex"

In their 1968 book *The Lessons of History*, historians Will and
Ariel Durant warned,

> No man, however brilliant or well-informed, can come in one
> lifetime to such fullness of understanding as to safely judge
> and dismiss the customs or institutions of his society, for these
> are the wisdom of generations after centuries of experiment in
> the laboratory of history. A youth boiling with hormones will
> wonder why he should not give full freedom to his sexual de-

sires; and if he is unchecked by custom, morals or laws, he may ruin his life before he matures sufficiently to understand that sex is a river of fire that must be banked and cooled by a hundred restraints if it is not to consume in chaos both the individual and the group.

Concerns about teen pregnancy and AIDS have served as the catalyst for an explosion of "safe sex" courses that are ignoring that crucial lesson of history and loosening the few restraints that still exist. They are predicated on the ethically obtuse proposition that, while it is best not to rob banks, those who just can't resist should pull ski masks over their heads to reduce the chance of getting caught. Such courses not only condone, but in many instances serve to encourage, premarital sex, homosexuality, and other sexual experimentation and aberration.

A Higher Authority

The time has come to renew our public commitment to our Judeo-Christian values—in our churches and synagogues, our civic organizations and our schools. We are, as our children recite each morning, "one nation under God." That's a useful framework for acknowledging a duty and an authority higher than our own pleasures and personal ambitions.

Dan Quayle, *Human Events*, May 30, 1992.

The award-winning video *Sex, Drugs, and AIDS*, narrated by actress Rae Dawn Chong, has been used in many junior and senior high schools. Its central message is that premarital sex is "cool," even expected of adolescents, but that "hip" teens will "play it safe" by using condoms. An emotional interview with a young man whose homosexual younger brother is dying of AIDS underscores the point that homosexuality should be viewed as an acceptable alternative lifestyle.

So devoted are some public school systems to promoting homosexuality that "National Coming-Out Day" is celebrated with as much enthusiasm as graduation day. In February 1993, the Massachusetts "Governor's Commission on Gay and Lesbian Youth" produced a report recommending, "Learning about gay and lesbian people, including their experiences and contributions to society, should be integrated into all subject areas" including "literature, history, the arts, and family life."

In New York and Massachusetts, public school programs supposedly intended to promote "tolerance" for homosexuality are actually designed to re-educate children and wrest them away from the values taught by their parents. Typical of such efforts was the controversial "Children of the Rainbow" curriculum, which (like the Massachusetts program) sought to indoctrinate children in the "gay rights" ideology by saturating classroom subjects with pro-homosexuality messages. New York Assembly-woman Deborah Glick, an open lesbian who supported the Rainbow curriculum, explained, "I think that the reality is that most of the parents themselves have tremendous prejudice and bigotry that have been passed on for generations. . . . And the reality is that we as a society . . . must provide a counterbalance to what kids are obviously learning at home."

Reaping the Harvest

In 1970, prior to the sex education and condom craze insti-gated by the AIDS scare, two-thirds of all births to teens be-tween 15 and 19 were within the confines of marriage. By 1988, the ratio was reversed, with two-thirds born outside wedlock. According to one study, girls using birth control devices under the guidance of a Los Angeles clinic increased the number of their sexual encounters by 50 percent. Similarly, psychologist Dr. William R. Coulson, director of the Research Council on Ethnopsychology, reported that students exposed to public school sex education programs are 50 percent more sexually in-volved than students who are not. According to Coulson, the "experienced kids started teaching the inexperienced. It never flows from the virgin to the non-virgin."

Public schools in the District of Columbia were first in the na-tion to implement kindergarten-through-12th-grade sex educa-tion programs beginning in the late 1950s. They were so "suc-cessful" that by 1975 DC became the first major city in the country to have more abortions than live births and more births outside wedlock than within. And when Dr. Joseph Zanga, chairman of the Division of General Pediatrics and Emergency Care at the Medical College of Virginia, surveyed the results of "safe sex" programs around the country, he too concluded that they encourage, rather than prevent, teenage sexual activity. California, for example, introduced a "safe sex" curriculum in the 1970s, after which the state's teen pregnancy rate soared from close to the national average to 30 percent above, and teen abortions tripled. In contrast, teen pregnancy rates fell in such states as South Dakota and Utah after "modern" sex education classes were replaced with more traditional tutelage.

In 1986, then–Surgeon General Dr. C. Everett Koop issued his enormously influential (and error-laden) report on AIDS in which, after assuring readers that "value judgements are absent," he urged that sex education begin in "the lowest grade possible" and include information on "homosexual relationships." He also favored advertising condoms on network television. It has all come to pass, and [former] Surgeon General Joycelyn Elders carried the message to American youth that sex is a "healthy part of our being, whether it is homosexual or heterosexual," and has suggested that condoms be given to children as young as eight. Indeed, the *New York Times Magazine* for January 30, 1994, reported that Dr. Elders has a "safe sex" bouquet (condoms in floral arrangement) proudly displayed on her desk, and claims, in response to critics who have labeled her the "Condom Queen," that if she could "get every young person who is engaged in sex to use a condom in the United States," she "would wear a crown with a condom on it!" Yet, as noted by a 1992 minority report of the House Select Committee on Children, Youth and Families, condoms not only "do not change the behavior which puts teens at risk," but "the evidence shows that when condoms are used by teenagers the failure rate is higher than in the general population—as high as 30%."

Condom Conduits

School-based and school-linked health clinics have also generated their share of controversy and opposition throughout the country, primarily because they serve as conduits for the distribution of condoms and other birth control devices, abortion referral information, lessons in "safe" sex, and other aspects of the humanistic agenda favored by such groups as Planned Parenthood, the most aggressive advocate of such clinics.

Many such clinics also undermine parental rights and responsibility by refusing to let parents know when services are requested by, and rendered to, their minor charges. In 1992, for instance, District of Columbia Public Health Commissioner Mohammed Akhter announced that all public high school students would be eligible to receive condoms from school nurses, even should parents object by sending a note from home, and that parents would not be notified should one of their children request a condom. School Superintendent Franklin Smith had initially ruled that parental wishes would be honored, but he was overruled by Commissioner Akhter, who asserted: "Dr. Smith has the responsibility for the administration of the school system, and the principals and teachers are responsible for the education of the children. But we are the ones responsible for the health care needs of the children. These are my clinics. When a child crosses the door and enters into the nurse's suite, any communication between the child and the nurse is confidential." Which led syndicated columnist Don Feder to observe that it apparently means that "when a child enters a school clinic, he sheds parental authority at the door."

As solutions for the many problems associated with teen promiscuity and sexually transmitted diseases, school sex education, school-based clinics, and school-sanctioned condom crusades are equivalent to fighting fires with blasts of oxygen.

"Responsible" Drug Abuse

Many school drug programs also appear to be aggravating, rather than ameliorating, the problem they are supposed to solve. As far back as 1979, education writer Barbara Morris documented the case against school anti-drug programs which refuse to take a firm moral stance, but instead serve mainly to stimulate curiosity while advertising the pleasures associated with "getting high." One National Institute of Mental Health publication cited by Morris in her best-selling book, *Change Agents in the Schools*, was entitled *How to Plan a Drug Abuse Workshop for Teachers*. Used as a model for training teachers, it asserted that at all grades "a nonmoralizing presentation is essential" and urged that only "open minded individuals, as opposed to those known to have fixed or hostile positions [against drugs], would preferably be selected [as drug education teachers] except where inservice training might change an attitude or where an individual is included as a foil demonstrating the disadvantage of inflexibility."

In the November 1987 *Reader's Digest*, Peggy Mann, author of *Marijuana Alert*, reported that the "drug-education courses offered in our nation's schools too often carry this incredible message: If you do drugs 'responsibly,' it's okay." Note that it is the same siren song sung by the sex educators. One "educational" filmstrip cited by Mann extolled the medical qualities of marijuana and the "euphoric feeling of relaxation, contentment, inner satisfaction; the sensations of floating beyond reality" induced by the weed. And one of the three books on drug abuse most commonly found in school libraries, *Licit and Illicit Drugs*, by Edward M. Brecher, asserts that those who use mescaline (a hallucinatory drug) have found that its "most spectacular phase comprises the kaleidoscopic play of visual hallucinations in indescribably rich colors . . . the 'seeing' of music in colors or the 'hearing' of a painting in music." Which led Mann to ask rhetorically, "What adventurous youngster would not want to try mescaline or LSD" after reading *that*?

A quarter-century ago, writing in the August 1969 issue of *Chalcedon Report*, noted theologian and scholar Dr. Rousas J. Rushdoony observed, in words as pertinent now as then, "We are getting today what we have paid for: our public schools are delivering precisely the product of humanistic education that they have been asked to deliver. To deny Christian faith a place in education, to convert schools into statist agencies, and then to expect anything other than what we have, is the mark of a fool."

"Parochial or church schools . . . have their own reason for being and should not be defended by indicting the public schools for being secular."

Public Schools Are Not Hostile to Religion

James E. Wood Jr.

By U.S. Supreme Court decree, public schools are forbidden from teaching religious values. In the following viewpoint, James E. Wood Jr. agrees with the Court and argues that public schools should be free from religious influence to maintain academic freedom and integrity. Nevertheless, Wood asserts, public education is not hostile to religion; study about religion should be included in schools. Wood contends that religious conservatives attack what they call "secular humanism" in public education in an attempt to Christianize the schools. Wood is director of the J.M. Dawson Institute of Church-State Studies at Baylor University in Waco, Texas.

As you read, consider the following questions:

1. According to Wood, what is the "twofold significance" of the present censorship campaign aimed at the public schools?
2. Why does Wood believe students should learn about religion?
3. What has been the effect of pressure by religious groups on textbook publishers, according to the author?

Excerpted from "The Battle over 'Secular Humanism' in the Public Schools" by James E. Wood Jr., in *Why We Still Need Public Schools: Church/State Relations and Visions of Democracy*, Art Must Jr., editor (Buffalo: Prometheus Books). Copyright 1992 by Art Must Jr. Used by permission of the publisher.

For more than two decades, the public schools of America have largely come to be perceived by the New Religious Right as dominated by "secular humanism." Writing in 1979, United States Senator Jesse Helms of North Carolina expressed a view that is still widely shared: "When the U.S Supreme Court prohibited children from participating in voluntary prayers in public schools, the conclusion is inescapable that the Supreme Court not only violated the right of free exercise of religion of all America; it also established a national religion in the United States—the religion of secular humanism."

In the seventies and eighties, "secular humanism" gradually became a code word for all the evils in American society, largely replacing "communism" as the greatest threat facing America and its democratic institutions in the fifties and sixties. "Godless communists" and "their fellow travelers" of only a few decades ago were now labeled "secular humanists." In the words of Tim LaHaye, one of the founders in 1979 of the now-defunct Moral Majority, "secular humanism" is "the world's greatest evil."

In a series of widely distributed books on "secular humanism," LaHaye charged that most of the evils in the world today can be traced to "secular humanism," which he saw as having taken over the government, the media, and education in America. Similarly, Pat Robertson contended that "secular humanists" have stolen the government, the courts, and the public schools from America's God-fearing majority, and it is up to Christians to win back these institutions. The allegedly pervasive influence of "secular humanism" was seen by its foes as constituting a new form of religious establishment.

Attacking Public Schools

Without defining "secular humanism," the New Religious Right perceives it as being widespread throughout American society. The focus of the movement's crusade against "secularism humanism" is directed at the public schools. That is where, it is charged, the "immoral indoctrination" of impressionable minds is occurring. The charge is twofold: contrary to the United States Supreme Court decisions on religion and the public schools, the public schools are teaching a religion to children that is antithetical to "Judeo-Christian values"; and the religion being taught is "secular humanism." To its adversaries, "secular humanism" embodies anti-moral and anti-Christian ideas that undergird the liberal educational and political philosophy that has come to control America in recent decades. Opposition to "secular humanism" in the public schools has expressed itself in censorship of public school textbooks; objection to the teaching of evolution; and widespread disapproval of various courses in the public school curriculum, particularly in social studies.

"Secular humanism" is blamed for progressive education, the exclusion of religion from the public schools, the decline of ethical and moral values, sexual promiscuity, the rise of drug abuse, and the waning of respect for authority.

Special blame for the triumph of "secular humanism" is placed on the United States Supreme Court. In the words of Pat Robertson, the Court's decisions on religion and the public schools made "atheism the only acceptable religion for America's schoolchildren." Charging that the public schools have suffered "an inculturation of values totally contrary to the Judeo-Christian tradition," Robertson singled out the public schools as being "so fallen that they have become jungles." In 1984, he predicted that in the next twenty years all schools in America would be private. In his book *The Battle for the Public Schools*, LaHaye charged that "public schools have become conduits to the minds of our youth, training them to be anti-God, anti-moral, anti-family, anti-free enterprise, and anti-American." "Public education," he wrote, "is controlled by elitists with an atheistic, humanistic viewpoint." In a similar vein, Jimmy Swaggart declared, "The public school system, gutted by secular humanism, is literally attacking the home, the family, the structure of this country." "I don't have any good words about the public school system. If it weren't for the Christian school system, this country would have gone to Hell in a handbasket." The charge is repeatedly made that the Supreme Court's decisions outlawing public school-sponsored religious education classes, prayer, and devotional Bible reading officially established "secular humanism" in the public schools. Thereby, it is said, the Supreme Court joined atheists and agnostics in considering traditional religion irrelevant. "Secular humanism" is perceived to be the established religion of the public schools, which some have called "government seminaries of secular humanism."

Censorship Campaigns

In recent years, most of the battles over public school textbooks, often resulting in the adoption of strict guidelines of censorship, have centered on the broad charge of the incorporation in these books of the teachings of "secular humanism." By and large the courts have not been willing to uphold parental grievances against the public school curriculum and public school textbooks. In 1975, in one of the most widely publicized censorship cases, a West Virginia federal district court rejected the charges of some parents that a series of English textbooks undermined their religious beliefs and established the religion of "secular humanism" in the public schools. The district court ruled that it would take "a complete loosening of the imagination" to conclude that the inclusion of allegedly godless and profane books in the public schools constitutes an establishment of the religion of "secular humanism." The West Virginia decision was consistent with a New York case some years earlier, in which that court denied the appeal of parents to ban certain classics in English literature (e.g., *Oliver Twist* by Charles Dickens and the *Merchant of Venice* by William Shakespeare) that were found to be offensive on religious grounds. Similarly, the Michigan Appellate Court ruled against curriculum grievances based upon the religious views of the plaintiffs.

In the 1980s, legislation was introduced in several states to disallow those subjects in the public school curriculum that were viewed to be incompatible with basic Christian teachings. On the local level, book banning and book censorship took place in public schools throughout the country. . . .

Serious, Non-Indoctrinative Study

There are some on the Religious Right who would have only their brand of Christianity taught in the schools, and there are some on the Secular Left who would have no mention of religion at all—except in safely historical contexts. I have argued for serious, non-indoctrinative study of various religions (along with serious, non-indoctrinative study of secular ways of thinking), not just for their historical significance, but as living traditions that help orient us in a complex and confusing world. This is, after all, the overriding purpose of education: to orient us in the world.

Warren A. Nord, *Social Education*, September 1990.

There is nothing new about censorship. It has a long history and has frequently cropped up in the United States, aimed particularly at books in public libraries and public schools. The present censorship movement, however, which is primarily aimed at the public schools, holds a twofold significance that warrants special concern. First, there is the phenomenal rise in the incidents of attempted censorship of public school, and second, there has been a shift away from a focus on a particular book or literary work to a broad assault on the public school curriculum.

Today, few would question that censorship of public school textbooks is on the rise, and has, indeed, become a national problem. Recently, Arthur Kropp, president of People for the American Way, reported that there is an explosion of censorship created by religious bigotry, specifically aimed at removing certain textbooks from the public school curriculum. One study of the 1986–1987 academic year reported 156 censorship incidents, constituting a 22 percent increase over the previous year. Reports of organized efforts by parents and organizations to censor public school textbooks have become commonplace throughout the country. Another recent study has documented a 160 percent increase in incidents of censorship during the mid-1980s. At least half of these incidents are reported to be aimed not at single books or specific library materials, but at a broader agenda involving not only individual courses but also virtually the entire curriculum of the public schools. In the 1989–1990 school year, some 244 incidents took place, while in the preceding year only 172 efforts were made to withdraw public school texts from classroom use.

Targeting School Boards

Many local groups of parents, encouraged and supported by outside organizations such as Pat Robertson's National Legal Foundation, Mel and Norma Gabler's Educational Research Analysts, Phyllis Schlafly's Eagle Forum, Beverly LaHaye's Concerned Women for America, the California-based Traditional Values Coalition, the Christian Educators Association International (CEAI), the National Christian Education Association (NCEA), and Citizens for Excellence in Education (CEE), are pressuring school boards and state legislatures to adopt restrictive measures for the selection of public school textbooks and the development of the public school curriculum. Failure to accomplish censorship through these measures is met with threats of legal suits against public school administrators, teachers, and school boards. All of these groups seek, in effect, to introduce sectarian religion into the public school classroom.

Robert L. Simonds, who founded both the NCEA and the CEE in 1983, has asserted in written statements that his goal was to encourage fundamentalist teachers and school administrators to "take dominion" over the public schools. The former (NCEA) encourages teachers to "model what they believe" and to "emphasize moral and spiritual values" in their instruction, while the latter (CEE) encourages the formation of groups to promote fundamentalist Christians as school board candidates.

The recent wave of censorship of public school textbooks is primarily directed at imposing a sectarian Christian viewpoint on the public schools and wresting them from the concept of the secular public school. In the words of Mel and Norma Gabler, who have waged campaigns on censorship of public school textbooks throughout the country as well as in their home state of Texas, "acceptable textbooks should be passed on high morality, fixed values, Christian concepts, and a proper portrayal of our nation's great heritage." Similarly, CEE's stated goals are "to bring public education back under the control of Christians" and "to change the atheist-dominated ideology of secular humanism in our schools' texts, curriculum, and teachers' unions."

Government neutrality toward religion in the public schools

has come to be viewed by many as government hostility toward religion. In a series of decisions bearing on religion and the public schools, the United States Supreme Court has frequently addressed this issue, but for many the assurances of the Court have been of no avail. In 1948, in the *McCollum v. Board of Education* case, the Court went out of its way to make the point as follows: "To hold that a state cannot consistently with the First and Fourteenth Amendments utilize its public school system to aid any or all religious faiths or sects in the dissemination of their doctrines and ideas does not . . . manifest a government hostility to religion or religious teachings. A manifestation of such hostility would be at war with our national tradition as embodied in the First Amendment's guaranty of the free exercise of religion."

The assault on the public schools not only continues, but also has greatly accelerated since the early 1980s. So great is the assault that in the thinking of some observers, the American public school may well be on the way to becoming "an endangered species." While the public schools are subjected to a wholesale indictment for their neutrality toward religion, nonpublic schools, the vast majority of which are religious, have come to be described, according to one study of the movement, as "the most rapidly expanding segment of formal education in the United States."

The battle over "secular humanism" in the public schools is dangerous because, while "secular humanism" remains largely undefined by fundamentalists, it is assumed that the term is somehow to be equated with secular*ism*, and, therefore, must be destructive of all religious and moral values. The truth is that nonreligious or secular humanism does not mean, let alone require, the rejection of Judeo-Christian religious and moral values. To be sure, whenever and wherever Judeo-Christian or other traditional religious values are denigrated in the public schools, it should be condemned as incompatible with the secular character of American public education and the guarantees of the First Amendment.

Separating Humanism and Religion

Unfortunately, the attack on "secular humanism" in the public schools is all too often but a thinly veiled attack on the public schools themselves—both on their academic freedom and their academic integrity. Much of the myth of "secular humanism" has been perpetrated by those who seek to Christianize the public schools, to make them more responsive to their own particular or sectarian religious views, rather than let them remain schools in which a secular or nonreligious approach to the study of history, science, government, and literature prevails. The study of humankind, human experience, and human values is quite properly the focus of the public schools, while inculcation of religious beliefs, religious experiences, and religious values is the focus of religious education that is rooted in the home and the church or synagogue.

Parochial or church schools and programs of religious education have their own reason for being and should not be defended by indicting the public schools for being secular in their teaching. America's public schools are necessarily committed to *human* values, *human* achievements, and *human* capabilities, in which the activities, interests, and historical development of humankind are made central in education. It is for this reason that public schools enjoy the support of public funds while parochial or church schools which are committed to a particular religious worldview are denied public funds. While public schools are not to be committed to any religious worldview as such, the secular public school cannot fulfill its role without giving serious consideration to the place of religion in the life of humankind and society. As the United States Supreme Court declared in 1963, "It might well be said that one's education is not complete without a study of comparative religion or the history of religion and its relationship to the advancement of civilization."

Greater Study of Religion

[There] has been a growing, now very broad, consensus for incorporating a much greater study of religion into public education. Although there continues to be considerable concern about whether this can be done well in practice, there is widespread—and growing—agreement in principle that religion must be taken much more seriously.

Warren A. Nord, *Social Education*, September 1990.

Admittedly, religion continues to receive short shrift in the public school curriculum. Several recent studies of American history textbooks, for example, reveal that very little attention is given to the role of religion. This phenomenon cannot be ignored and cannot be justified, but this fact alone does not warrant the charge that the public schools are hostile toward religion or that "secular humanism" has become the established religion in the public schools. In spite of the earnest efforts of a variety of educators to establish institutes and to provide curriculum resources aimed at giving greater attention to the teaching *about* religion in the public school curriculum and the categorical assertion by the U.S. Supreme Court that "one's education is not complete without a study of . . . religion," it must be acknowledged that far too little attention is given to the study about religion in the public school curriculum.

Again, an explanation of this neglect of religion studies in the public school is not to be found in the unwarranted claim of a hostility toward religion on the part of the public schools or the courts. Rather, the reasons for this lack of attention to religion are to be found in the very problems associated with teaching about religion in the public school curriculum, among which are fears of controversy on the part of public school officials and public school administrators, widespread disagreement as to what should be taught concerning religion, an already crowded curriculum, and the lack of trained teachers and teacher education programs to carry out lesson plans of religion studies within the existing curriculum requirements of the public schools. The fact remains, however, that teaching about religion is integral to education, and that to omit the role of religion in history, society, and the world at large is not a complete education.

Religious Studies Programs

The place of study about religion in public education has come to be recognized by a wide range of educational and religious groups. Various national organizations have analyzed and observed the neglect of study about religion in the public school classroom. Several years ago, the eight thousand–member Association for Supervision and Curriculum Development published a report on religion studies in the public school curriculum in which it deplored the fact that public school textbooks "virtually ignore religion." Paul Vitz of New York University, in his study, sponsored by the National Institute of Education, of sixty representative social studies textbooks, found that none of them "contain one word referring to any religious activity in contemporary life." A wide range of religious denominations—Catholic, Protestant, and Jewish—have urged the implementation of religion studies in the public schools and participate, along with many professional educational organizations, in the National Council on Religion and Public Education. Recently, a broad coalition of sixteen religious and educational groups published a pamphlet titled "Religious Holidays in the Public Schools" with the purpose of helping teachers to deal with basic issues surrounding the celebration and appreciation of religious holidays. The sponsoring organizations included, among others, the American Association of School Administrators, the American Academy of Religion, the American Federation of Teachers, the American Jewish Committee, the National Association of Evangelicals, the National Council of Churches, the National Council for Social Studies, and the National Education Association.

It should also be noted that a variety of programs aimed at the inclusion of religion in the public school curriculum have been initiated in such states as Florida, Indiana, Kansas, Minnesota, North Carolina, and Pennsylvania. The National Endowment for the Humanities issued a grant to North Dakota State University and the North Dakota Department of Public Instruction to develop and implement a training program for the inclusion of teaching about religion in the public school curriculum. In November 1990, the Georgia State Board of Education approved a program to encourage and to train public school teachers to teach about religion in the public schools. Sponsored by the First Liberty Institute of George Mason University in Virginia, the program selected Georgia as the national pilot for the implementation of the program. The Institute hopes to serve as a national teacher-training and resource center for public school curriculum development in this area.

Pressure on Publishers

In spite of these hopeful signs, publishers of public school textbooks continue to feel pressure to avoid controversial subjects and to bow to the will of organized groups whose aim is to censor public school textbooks. Thereby, out of economic considerations, publishers are inclined to surrender their freedom to cover significant educational issues simply because they are controversial. Well-organized and repeated efforts toward religious censorship of public school textbooks inevitably have had, and continue to have, a chilling and inhibiting effect on public school administrators and classroom teachers in dealing with the phenomenon of religion. Fortunately, because of recent court decisions including those of the United States Supreme Court and lower courts, and at the urging of various educational and religious groups, publishers are becoming more willing to review their textbooks with regard to the place given to the role of religion. For those educators who are easily intimidated, the result can be one of accommodation to the pressures of religious censorship to the point that the academic integrity of the public school and the public school educator is eroded and substantially weakened. While the battle over "secular humanism" in the public schools is far from over, the pejorative use of "secular humanism" as the established religion of the public schools needs to be seen as unfounded and unjustified, largely made by persons who seek to make the public schools more responsive to their own sectarian religious views.

Periodical Bibliography

The following articles have been selected to supplement the diverse views presented in this chapter.

Deborah Baldwin	"As Busy as We Wanna Be," *Utne Reader*, January/February 1994.
Daniel Benjamin and Tony Horwitz	"German View: 'You Americans Work Too Hard—and for What?'" *The Wall Street Journal*, July 14, 1994.
William J. Bennett	*The Index of Leading Cultural Indicators*, vol. 1, 1993. Available from the Heritage Foundation, 214 Massachusetts Ave. NE, Washington, DC 20002-4999.
Charles W. Colson	"Where Did Our Conscience Go?" *Focus on the Family*, January 1994. Available from PO Box 35500, Colorado Springs, CO 80935-3550.
Thomas B. Edsall	"An Up-Close Look at the 'Values' Battle," *The Washington Post National Weekly Edition*, October 17–23, 1994.
Amitai Etzioni	"U.S. Schools Rediscover the Virtue of Virtues," *Insight on the News*, December 26, 1994. Available from 3600 New York Ave. NE, Washington, DC 20002.
Albert R. Hunt	"A Domestic Peace Corps with a '90s Twist," *The Wall Street Journal*, August 18, 1994.
Michael Kinsley	"Back from the Future," *The New Republic*, March 21, 1994.
John Lukacs	"To Hell with Culture," *Chronicles*, September 1994. Available from PO Box 800, Mount Morris, IL 61054.
Dan Quayle	"Coming to Grips with the Poverty of Values," *Conservative Chronicle*, September 28, 1994. Available from PO Box 11297, Des Moines, IA 50340-1297.
Joseph Raz	"Multiculturalism: A Liberal Perspective," *Dissent*, Winter 1994.
Lillian B. Rubin	"'People Don't Know Right from Wrong Anymore,'" *Tikkun*, January/February 1994.
Woody West	"Schools Are Crucial Battlefield in the War of American Ideals," *Insight on the News*, November 28, 1994.

Is America in Decline?

Chapter Preface

Coping with a sluggish economy in the 1990s, many Americans began taking a harder look at their jobs, future prospects, and personal financial security. As economist and author Edward N. Luttwak put it in December 1994: "The problem in question is the unprecedented sense of personal economic insecurity that has suddenly become the central phenomenon of life in America . . . for virtually all working Americans."

Faced with the economic constraints of the early 1990s, many companies have "downsized"—sharply reducing their numbers of permanent, full-time employees and permanently eliminating many positions that formerly offered secure, lifelong careers. This corporate restructuring has left many Americans, particularly younger workers and workers with young children, feeling pessimistic about their jobs and futures.

Consider the Millers, a Missouri couple with four young children interviewed by the *New York Times*. "Sure, we've got four [part-time jobs]," said Craig Miller, a laid-off sheetmetal worker who had previously earned more than $15 an hour and who had planned to purchase a home. "So what? So you can work like a dog for $5 an hour. For people like us, I'm afraid the good times are gone for good." Many younger workers face similar prospects. According to U.S. Bureau of Labor Statistics economist Dan Hecker, "We're getting more college graduates than we are college-level jobs. About 20 percent of the college graduates end up in non-college jobs."

According to many more Americans, however, prospects are not so bleak. In a February 1994 *New York Times* poll of nearly seven hundred non-self-employed workers, 31 percent responded that they saw a "big future" and 49 percent "some future" in their line of work in the next five to ten years. Two-thirds expressed satisfaction with their choice of occupations.

Whether they are optimistic or pessimistic about better jobs and incomes, Luttwak writes, "what most working Americans now seem to want is . . . security for the jobs and income they already have." Jobs—their availability and quality and people's satisfaction with them and their incomes—are just one measure of the success and strength of America. The authors in the following chapter debate this and other indicators of whether America is in decline.

"There is a coarseness, a callousness, a cynicism, a banality, and a vulgarity to our time."

Moral Conduct Is in Decline

William J. Bennett

William J. Bennett served as America's first "drug czar" in the 1980s and is now a popular voice of the conservative right. In the following viewpoint, Bennett asserts that America suffers from a moral and spiritual deficiency. He argues that *acedia*, an aversion to spiritual things, is on the rise and is the basis for social pathologies such as crime, illegitimacy, and divorce. Bennett is the editor of the best-selling *The Book of Virtues* and a fellow at the Heritage Foundation, a Washington, D.C., think tank.

As you read, consider the following questions:

1. On what basis does Bennett caution against blaming liberals for social disorders?
2. Why does Bennett disagree that religious faith has no place in the public arena?
3. Why can politics not solve America's moral afflictions, according to the author?

From William J. Bennett, "Getting Used to Decadence: The Spirit of Democracy in Modern America," *The Heritage Lectures*, no. 477, 1993. Reprinted by permission of The Heritage Foundation, ©1993.

A few months ago I had lunch with a friend of mine, a man who has written for a number of political journals and who now lives in Asia. During our conversation the topic turned to America—specifically, America as seen through the eyes of foreigners.

During our conversation, he told me what he had observed during his travels: that while the world still regards the United States as the leading economic and military power on earth, this same world no longer beholds us with the moral respect it once did. When the rest of the world looks at America, he said, they see no longer a "shining city on a hill." Instead, they see a society in decline, with exploding rates of crime and social pathologies. We all know that foreigners often come here in fear—and once they are here, they travel in fear. It is our shame to realize that they have good reason to fear; a record number of them get killed here.

Today, many who come to America believe they are visiting a degraded society. Yes, America still offers plenty of jobs, enormous opportunity, and unmatched material and physical comforts. But there is a growing sense among many foreigners that when they come here, they are slumming. I have, like many of us, an instinctive aversion to foreigners' harshly judging my nation; yet I must concede that much of what they think is true.

I recently had a conversation with a Washington, D.C., cab driver who is doing graduate work at American University. He told me that once he receives his master's degree he is going back to Africa. His reason? His children. He doesn't think they are safe in Washington. He told me that he didn't want them to grow up in a country where young men will paw his daughter and expect her to be an "easy target," and where his son might be a different kind of target—the target of violence from the hands of other young males. "It is more civilized where I come from," said this man from Africa. I urged him to move outside of Washington; things should improve.

Something Has Gone Wrong

But it is not only violence and urban terror that signal decay. We see it in many forms. *Newsweek* columnist Joe Klein recently wrote about Berenice Belizaire, a young Haitian girl who arrived in New York in 1987. When she arrived in America she spoke no English and her family lived in a cramped Brooklyn apartment. Eventually Berenice enrolled at James Madison High School, where she excelled. According to Judith Khan, a math teacher at James Madison, "[The immigrants are] why I love teaching in Brooklyn. They have a drive in them that we no longer seem to have." And far from New York City, in the beautiful Berkshire mountains where I went to school, Philip Kasinitz, an assistant professor of sociology at Williams College, has observed that

Americans have become the object of ridicule among immigrant students on campus. "There's an interesting phenomenon. When immigrant kids criticize each other for getting lazy or loose, they say, 'You're becoming American,'" Kasinitz says. "Those who work hardest to keep American culture at bay have the best chance of becoming American success stories."

Symptoms of Decline

According to a recent poll, 73 percent of Americans worry that the nation is experiencing a moral decline. They are right to be concerned.

The symptoms of America's social decay hardly bear repeating. The explosive rise of illegitimacy since 1960 has plunged millions into material poverty and moral dependence. An epidemic of crime has created a climate of fear in many neighborhoods and schools. Much of our popular culture is dominated by promiscuity, violence—or both. Worse yet, our judicial and educational systems often seem helpless to stem the rising tide of social decay.

James A. Baker III, *The Washington Times*, July 11, 1994.

In 1992 an article was published in the *Washington Post* which pointed out how students from other countries adapt to the lifestyle of most American teens. Paulina, a Polish high school student studying in the United States, said that when she first came here she was amazed by the way teens spent their time. According to Paulina:

In Warsaw, we would talk to friends after school, go home and eat with our parents and then do four or five hours of homework. When I first came here, it was like going into a crazy world, but now I am getting used to it. I'm going to Pizza Hut and watching TV and doing less work in school. I can tell it is not a good thing to get used to.

Think long and hard about these words, spoken by a young Polish girl about America: "When I first came here it was like going into a crazy world, but now I am getting used to it." And, *"I can tell it is not a good thing to get used to."*

Something has gone wrong with us.

This is a conclusion which I come to with great reluctance. During the late 1960s and 1970s, I was one of those who reacted strongly to criticisms of America that swept across university campuses. I believe that many of those criticisms—"Amerika" as an inherently repressive, imperialist, and racist society—were wrong then, and they are wrong now. But intellectual honesty demands that we accept facts that we would sometimes like to wish away. Hard truths are truths nonetheless. And the hard truth is that something *has* gone wrong with us.

America is not in danger of becoming a Third World country; we are too rich, too proud, and too strong to allow that to happen. It is not that we live in a society completely devoid of virtue. Many people live well, decently, even honorably. There are families, schools, churches, and neighborhoods that work. There are places where virtue is taught and learned. But there is a lot less of this than there ought to be. And we know it. John Updike put it this way: "The fact that . . . we still live well cannot ease the pain of feeling that we no longer live nobly."

Empirical Evidence of Social Regression

Let me briefly outline some of the empirical evidence that points to cultural decline, evidence that while we live well materially, we don't live nobly. In 1993 I released, through the auspices of the Heritage Foundation, *The Index of Leading Cultural Indicators*, the most comprehensive statistical portrait available of behavioral trends over the last thirty years. Among the findings: since 1960, the population has increased 41 percent; the gross domestic product has nearly tripled; and total social spending by all levels of government (measured in constant 1990 dollars) has risen from $142.73 billion to $787.00 billion—more than a five-fold increase.

But during the same thirty-year period, there has been a 560 percent increase in violent crime; more than a 400 percent increase in illegitimate births; a quadrupling in divorces; a tripling of the percentage of children living in single-parent homes; more than a 200 percent increase in the teenage suicide rate; and a drop of 75 points in the average S.A.T. scores of high-school students.

These are not good things to get used to.

Today 30 percent of all births and 68 percent of black births are illegitimate. By the end of the 1990s, according to the most reliable projections, *40 percent* of all American births and *80 percent* of minority births will occur out of wedlock.

These are not good things to get used to.

And then there are the results of an on-going teacher survey. Over the years teachers have been asked to identify the top problems in America's schools. In 1940 teachers identified them as talking out of turn; chewing gum; making noise; running in the hall; cutting in line; dress code infractions; and littering. When asked the same question in 1990, teachers identified drug use; alcohol abuse; pregnancy; suicide; rape; robbery; and assault.

These are not good things to get used to, either.

Consider, too, where the United States ranks in comparison with the rest of the industrialized world. We are at or near the top in rates of abortions, divorces, and unwed births. We lead the industrialized world in murder, rape, and violent crime. And in elementary and secondary education, we are at or near the bottom in achievement scores.

The American Ethos

These facts alone are evidence of substantial social regression. But there are other signs of decay, ones that do not so easily lend themselves to quantitative analyses (some of which I have already suggested in my opening anecdotes). What I am talking about is the moral, spiritual, and aesthetic character and habits of a society—what the ancient Greeks referred to as its *ethos*. And here, too, we are facing serious problems. For there is a coarseness, a callousness, a cynicism, a banality, and a vulgarity to our time. There are just too many signs of de-civilization— that is, civilization gone rotten. And the worst of it has to do with our children. Apart from the numbers and the specific facts, there is the ongoing, chronic crime against children: the crime of making them old before their time. We live in a culture which at times seems almost dedicated to the corruption of the young, to assuring the loss of their innocence before their time.

This may sound overly pessimistic or even alarmist, but I think this is the way it is. And my worry is that people are not unsettled enough; I don't think we are angry enough. We have become inured to the cultural rot that is setting in. Like Paulina, we are getting used to it, even though it is not a good thing to get used to. People are experiencing atrocity overload, losing their capacity for shock, disgust, and outrage. . . .

Sick Television

There is a lot of criticism directed at television these days—the casual cruelty, the rampant promiscuity, the mindlessness of sit-coms and soap operas. Most of the criticisms are justified. But this is not the worst of it. The worst of television is the daytime television talk shows, where indecent exposure is celebrated as a virtue. It is hard to remember now, but there was once a time when personal failures, subliminal desires, and perverse taste were accompanied by guilt or embarrassment, at least by silence. Today these are a ticket to appear as a guest on the Sally Jessy Raphael show, or one of the dozen or so shows like it. I asked my staff to provide me with a list of some of the daytime talk-show topics from one two-week period. They include cross-dressing couples; a three-way love affair; a man whose chief aim in life is to sleep with women and fool them into thinking that he is using a condom during sex; women who can't say no to cheating; prostitutes who love their jobs; a former drug dealer; and an interview with a young girl caught in the middle of a bitter custody battle. These shows present a two-edged problem to society: the first edge is that some people want to appear on these shows in order to expose themselves. The second edge is that lots of people are tuning in to watch them expose themselves.

This is not a good thing to get used to.

Who's to blame? Here I would caution conservatives against the tendency to blame liberals for our social disorders. Contemporary liberalism does have a lot for which to answer; many of its doctrines have wrought a lot of damage. Universities, intellectuals, think tanks, and government departments have put a lot of poison into the reservoirs of national discourse. But to simply point the finger of blame at liberals and elites is wrong. The hard fact of the matter is that this was not something done to us; it is also something we have done to ourselves. Liberals may have been peddling from an empty wagon, but we were buying.

Much of what I have said is familiar to many of you. But why is this happening? What is behind all this? Well, again, intelligent arguments have been advanced as to why these things have come to pass. Thoughtful people have pointed to materialism and consumerism; an overly permissive society; the writings of Rousseau, Marx, Freud, Nietzsche; the legacy of the 1960s; and so on. There is truth in almost all of these accounts. Let me give you mine.

Spiritual *Acedia*

I submit to you that the real crisis of our time is spiritual. Specifically, our problem is what the ancients called *acedia*. *Acedia* is the sin of sloth. But *acedia*, as understood by the saints of old, is not laziness about life's affairs (which is what we normally think sloth to be). *Acedia* is something else; properly understood, *acedia* is an aversion to and a negation of *spiritual* things. *Acedia* reveals itself as an undue concern for external affairs and worldly things. *Acedia* is spiritual torpor; an absence of zeal for divine things. And it brings with it, according to the ancients, "a sadness, a sorrow of the world." *Acedia* manifests itself in man's "joyless, ill-tempered, and self-seeking rejection of the nobility of the children of God." The slothful man hates the spiritual, and he wants to be free of its demands. The old theologians taught that *acedia* arises from a heart steeped in the worldly and carnal, and from a low esteem of divine things. It eventually leads to a hatred of the good altogether. And with hatred comes more rejection, more ill-temper, sadness, and sorrow.

Spiritual *acedia* is not a new condition, of course. It is the seventh capital sin. But today it is in ascendance. In coming to this conclusion, I have relied on two literary giants—men born on vastly different continents, the product of two completely different worlds, and shaped by wholly different experiences—yet writers who possess strikingly similar views, and who have had a profound impact on my own thinking. It was an unusual and surprising moment to find their views coincident.

When the late novelist Walker Percy was asked what concerned him most about the future of America, he answered:

> Probably the fear of seeing America, with all its great strength and beauty and freedom . . . gradually subside into decay through default and be defeated, not by the Communist movement . . . but from within by weariness, boredom, cynicism, greed and in the end helplessness before its great problems.

And here are the words of the prophetic Aleksandr Solzhenitsyn (echoing his 1978 Harvard commencement address in which he warned of the West's "spiritual exhaustion"):

> In the United States the difficulties are not a Minotaur or a dragon—not imprisonment, hard labor, death, government harassment and censorship—but cupidity, boredom, sloppiness, indifference. Not the acts of a mighty all-pervading repressive government but the failure of a listless public to make use of the freedom that is its birthright.

What afflicts us, then, is a corruption of the heart, a turning away in the soul. Our aspirations, our affections, and our desires are turned toward the wrong things. And only when we turn them toward the right things—toward enduring, noble, spiritual things—will things get better. . . .

Actions Depend on Philosophy

Our actions depend, in the end, on our basic philosophy toward life. It makes an enormous amount of difference, for example, if a person is guided by the two great commandments ("Thou shalt love the Lord thy God with thy whole heart, soul, mind and strength, and thou shalt love thy neighbor as thyself"), or if he is guided by a more modern outlook: "If it feels good, do it." One of the reasons that we have seen a breakdown of moral order during the last quarter-century is that many people's underlying beliefs have changed.

William J. Bennett, *The San Diego Union-Tribune*, August 7, 1994.

In identifying spiritual exhaustion as the central problem, I part company with many. There is a disturbing reluctance in our time to talk seriously about matters spiritual and religious. Why? Perhaps it has to do with the modern sensibility's profound discomfort with the language and the commandments of God. Along with other bad habits, we have gotten used to not talking about the things which matter most—and so, we don't.

One will often hear that religious faith is a private matter that does not belong in the public arena. But this analysis does not hold—at least on some important points. Whatever your faith—or even if you have none at all—it is a fact that when millions of people stop believing in God, or when their belief is so attenuated as to be belief in name only, enormous public consequences follow. And when this is accompanied by an aversion to spiritual language by the political and intellectual class, the public consequences are even greater. How could it be otherwise? In modernity, *nothing* has been more consequential, or more public in its consequences, than large segments of American society privately turning away from God, or considering Him irrelevant, or declaring Him dead. Fyodor Dostoyevsky reminded us in *The Brothers Karamazov* that "if God does not exist, everything is permissible." We are now seeing "everything." And much of it is not good to get used to.

Social Regeneration

What can be done? First, here are the short answers: do not surrender; get mad; and get in the fight. Now, let me offer a few, somewhat longer, prescriptions.

1. Let me suggest that our first task is to recognize that, in general, we place too much hope in politics. I am certainly not denying the impact (for good and for ill) of public policies. I would not have devoted the past decade of my life to public service—and I could not work at the Heritage Foundation—if I believed that the work with which I was engaged amounted to nothing more than striving after wind and ashes. But it is foolish, and futile, to rely *primarily* on politics to solve moral, cultural, and spiritual afflictions.

The last quarter-century has taught politicians a hard and humbling lesson: there are intrinsic limits to what the state can do, particularly when it comes to imparting virtue, and forming and forging character, and providing peace to souls. . . .

2. We must have public policies that once again make the connection between our deepest beliefs and our legislative agenda. Do we Americans, for example, believe that man is a spiritual being with a potential for individual nobility and moral responsibility? Or do we believe that his ultimate fate is to be merely a soulless cog in the machine of state? When we teach sex-education courses to teen-agers, do we treat them as if they are young animals in heat? Or do we treat them as children of God?

In terms of public policy, the failure is not so much intellectual; it is a failure of will and courage. Right now we are playing a rhetorical game: we say one thing and we do another. Consider the following:

- We say that we desire from our children more civility and

responsibility, but in many of our schools we steadfastly refuse to teach right and wrong.
- We say that we want law and order in the streets, but we allow criminals, including violent criminals, to return to those same streets.
- We say that we want to stop illegitimacy, but we continue to subsidize the kind of behavior that virtually guarantees high rates of illegitimacy.
- We say that we want to discourage teenage sexual activity, but in classrooms all across America educators are more eager to dispense condoms than moral guidance.
- We say that we want more families to stay together, but we liberalize divorce laws and make divorce easier to attain.
- We say that we want to achieve a color-blind society and judge people by the content of their character, but we continue to count by race, skin, and pigment.
- We say that we want to encourage virtue and honor among the young, but it has become a mark of sophistication to shun the language of morality.

Education and Religion

3. We desperately need to recover a sense of the fundamental purpose of education, which is to provide for the intellectual *and* moral education of the young. From the ancient Greeks to the founding fathers, moral instruction was the central task of education. "If you ask what is the good of education," Plato said, "the answer is easy—that education makes good men, and that good men act nobly." Thomas Jefferson believed that education should aim at improving one's "morals" and "faculties.". . .

4. As individuals and as a society, we need to return religion to its proper place. Religion, after all, provides us with moral bearings. And if I am right and the chief problem we face is spiritual impoverishment, then the solution depends, finally, on spiritual renewal. I am not speaking here about coerced spiritual renewal—in fact, there is no such thing—but about renewal freely taken.

The enervation of strong religious beliefs—in our private lives as well as our public conversations—has de-moralized society. We ignore religion and its lessons at our peril. . . .

In his 1950 Nobel Prize acceptance speech, William Faulkner declared, "I decline to accept the end of man." Man will not merely endure but prevail because, as Faulkner said, he alone among creatures "has a soul, a spirit capable of compassion and sacrifice and endurance."

Today we must in the same way decline to accept the end of moral man. We must carry on the struggle, for our children.

"We have examined the evidence employed to prove that America is experiencing a moral crisis and found it unconvincing."

Moral Conduct Is Not in Decline

Jeffrey W. Hayes and Seymour Martin Lipset

In the following viewpoint, Jeffrey W. Hayes and Seymour Martin Lipset reject the charge that individualism has fostered systematic moral decline in America. Studying trends related to crime, drug abuse, sexual behavior, and the family, Hayes and Lipset conclude that America's moral conduct remains strong, evidenced by such factors as a reported decrease in drug use among youths and the resilience of the two-parent nuclear family. Hayes is a graduate student in the University of Chicago's political science department. Lipset, a sociology professor at George Mason University in Fairfax, Virginia, is a senior scholar at the Progressive Policy Institute, a Washington, D.C., think tank.

As you read, consider the following questions:

1. What is the relationship between crime and economic success, according to Robert Merton, cited by the authors?
2. What moral comparisons do Hayes and Lipset make between America and other industrialized nations?
3. How can moral decay be avoided, in the authors' opinion?

From Jeffrey W. Hayes and Seymour Martin Lipset, "Individualism: A Double-Edged Sword." Reprinted with permission from vol. 4, no. 1, Winter 1993/94 *The Responsive Community*, 2020 Pennsylvania Ave. NW, Suite 282, Washington, DC 20006.

The decline of contemporary morality in the United States has been heralded by no less of an authority than Pope John Paul II who, during his 1993 visit to Denver, warned of "a serious moral crisis . . . already affecting the lives of many young people, leaving them adrift, often without hope, and conditioned to look only for instant gratification." The Pope is certainly not alone in his admonitions. The contention that America's problem is fundamentally moral seems to capture a national mood, which historian Daniel Boorstin has recently called a "startling renaissance of the New England conscience." Those who argue that today's America is in the throes of moral decline cite a combination of rising crime rates, the dissolution of the traditional family, increased drug use, excessive litigiousness, and the spread of relativism to bolster their case. And their argument seems to be winning the day, for whether or not America's moral fabric is actually coming apart at the seams, there is no denying that the impression of moral decline is pervasive.

The most forceful attempts to explain America's moral decline have held excessive individualism responsible for the rending of the nation's social and political fabric and the corresponding decline of moral norms. And to be sure, individualism is a significant force in American culture, one with widespread impact on Americans' views of their social obligations. It seems intuitive, therefore, that if morality is actually decaying, this elemental aspect of American ideology must somehow be playing a role.

It would be a mistake, however, to accept the argument of moral decline without taking a second look. While these social trends are disturbing and some of them recent, others have surprisingly long-standing roots in our society. Still others have been granted exaggerated importance in the quest to demonstrate our decay. Moreover, even if the case for such a decline were as strong as sometimes supposed, the connection between that decline and American individualism is far from evident.

A Double-Edged Sword

In reality, American morality is quite complex, particularly because of paradoxes within our culture that permit pernicious and beneficial social phenomena to arise simultaneously from the same basic value. That is, American individualism is something of a double-edged sword: it fosters a high sense of personal responsibility, independent initiative and voluntarism, even as it encourages self-serving behavior, atomism, and a disregard for communal goods. More specifically, American individualism threatens traditional forms of community morality, and thus has historically promoted particularly virulent strains of social problems. At the same time, it represents a tremendous moral asset, encouraging the self-reflection necessary for responsible judgment and fostering the strength of voluntary communal and civic bonds. To argue, therefore, that individualism has caused systematic moral decline ignores the extent to which American morality itself is beholden to the strength of individualism.

Emphasizing moral individualism, however, should not imply that the individual is the historical starting point for either society or morality. Humans are not solitary creatures with no need for companionship or support, and their cooperation requires trust between actors that is only possible if everyone exercises a minimum of self-restraint and goodwill; morality is both the cause and effect of this trust. Still, the exercise of morality in the context of modern American society requires an account of the role of individualism as a moral force.

Moral Decline or More of the Same?

To some extent, perceptions of American moral decline result from a persistent moralism within our culture that leads Americans to evaluate our nation and society according to pure ideals. No country could ever measure up to our standards. Flooded with reports of rapid social, economic, and political changes, we look for an overarching explanation in the failure to live up to our moral ideals.

Though historically moralistic, America's egalitarian and meritocratic foundations tend to undercut just those institutions that sustain the values that so concern us. The United States was born out of a revolution that sharply weakened the hierarchically rooted community values of the European Old World, and enormously strengthened individualistic, egalitarian, and antistatist ones. In the Old World, an aristocratic upper class dictated to the lower classes most social and economic norms. America, however, had no stable ruling class to promote such standards of moral conduct and fair play. Social problems have, therefore, always been ascribed to the lack of stable ethical standards. If the Pope stresses American social developments as evidence of an emerging crisis of ethics, he is not alone in American history.

Partisans of the so-called decline of morality [argument] cite rising crime rates as elemental to their argument. Between 1960 and 1989, homicides in America rose from 5.1 to 8.7 per 100,000 per year, while larcenies increased from 1,726 to 5,077. Sociologist Charles Derber posits the cyclical recurrence of periods of what he terms "wilding," in which lawlessness, disorder, and immorality threaten the stability of society. According to Derber, "Wilding is American individualism running amok." In recent years, Americans' perceptions of increasing lawlessness have fed fears that civil society is collapsing.

Crime is a problem to which distinctive American cultural

traits (individualism among them) have certainly contributed. Before concluding simply that individualism causes crime, however, it is important to understand the relationship between crime, morality, and individualism in American life. In explaining lawlessness in American history, historian Robert Merton stresses that American society places a premium on economic success and upward mobility. "The *moral mandate* to achieve success," he argues, "thus exerts pressure to succeed, by fair means if possible and by foul means if necessary."

The Importance of Religion in America

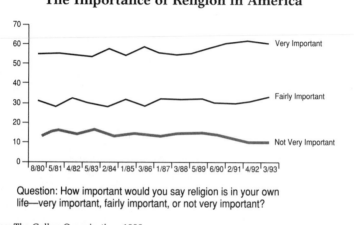

Question: How important would you say religion is in your own life—very important, fairly important, or not very important?

Source: The Gallup Organization, 1993.

Describing the tendency to commit illegal acts for socioeconomic advancement as a "moral mandate" is seemingly oxymoronic. But work and economic success in America are, as Max Weber emphasized, enshrined in the country's Protestant sectarian traditions. Higher crime rates may represent the underside of this work ethic: those without ready access to capital, education, and good jobs turn to "foul means" to make it.

Drugs: Not a New Problem

Drug use is another societal problem many attribute to moral failure. Yet it too is nothing new. From widespread alcohol consumption in early America to, as J. Hector St. John Crèvecoeur comments in his 1782 *Letters from an American Farmer*, the adoption by the women of Nantucket of "the Asiatic custom of taking a dose of opium every morning," Americans have not historically been morally above the use of drugs. As technology gives modern society more sophisticated and different narcotics—from morphine during the Civil War to cocaine in the late nineteenth century to "free-base" cocaine in the 1980s—some Americans have always used them.

Of particular concern have been media reports of growing drug abuse in the nation's schools. But the proportion of youth who report using illicit drugs appears to be on a long-term decline. National survey data compiled by the Institute for Social Research at the University of Michigan reveal that marijuana use has fallen since 1978, and the percentage of twelfth graders who claimed to have used any illicit drug steadily dropped from a peak of 66 percent in 1981 to 41 percent, the lowest level since the survey began. Alcohol consumption by minors has also dropped, daily drinking falling by one-half from its 1979 peak of 7 percent of respondents.

The common stereotype of our morally directionless youth is contradicted not only by the lower percentages trying drugs but also by the increased disapproval high-schoolers express toward virtually all types of drug use. These trends are even more striking because they shatter common misconceptions about race and drugs: by almost every measure (use of marijuana, cocaine, LSD, stimulants, barbiturates, crack, alcohol, and cigarettes), African-Americans are consistently less prone to use illicit substances than either whites or Hispanics.

Lawsuits Abound

Paradoxically, though various forms of illegality thrive in this country, America is a society profoundly rooted in law. A potent orientation toward individual rights continues to shape the attitudes of the population. The complaint that Americans go to court at the drop of a hat has become commonplace, and the American eagerness for legal settlements to our disputes has led many to question the morality of litigation as "our basic form of government." We have more lawyers per capita, more malpractice, and more environmental and occupational safety suits than anywhere else in the world. Is this excessive litigiousness indicative of our inability to deliberate and form amicable agreements amongst ourselves?

Again, however, if American legal habits represent a crisis of morality, it is one we have been experiencing for over 200 years. Alexis de Tocqueville noted the contractual and litigious character of Americans in the 1830s, as have countless other observers throughout our history.

Sex, Adultery, and Family Values

The family has been regarded as a vital source of morality in traditional and modern societies alike. The United States, however, is exceptional in that its rates of divorce and single-parent families rank by far the highest among the advanced societies. This lead in family fragmentation, however, is not a recent development. Heightened divorce rates in the United States go back to the nineteenth century. "At the turn of the twentieth century," writes sociologist David Popenoe, "the United States' divorce rate was already more than twice that of France and England (and about six times the rate of Sweden)."

Not surprisingly, warnings of the extinction of the traditional family have been widespread. Yet the cherished, 1950s-style nuclear family is not as fragile as many believe. Reviewing the current literature on the American family in *The New Republic*, Ann Hulbert argues that alternatives to the traditional family have always existed but "have never beckoned for long as a competing ideal." Hulbert goes on to argue: "The two-parent nuclear family norm, alternately revered and distrusted as a homogeneous standard, is not ready for replacement. . . . [T]he two-parent family continues to prevail, though neither widely nor simply."

Moral Conduct and Individualism

Has there been a deterioration of moral conduct? Probably not. But we have been given ample proof that extending commitment to our national idea, which centers around a profound individualism, is by no means an unmixed blessing. As the U.S. has progressed in recognizing the worth and the claims of people previously excluded from the Declaration's promise, it has also encouraged tendencies which have destructive possibilities, liable to see the individual as too radically autonomous and leave him too narrowly self-serving. In seeking to improve the moral conduct of the nation, earlier generations of Americans have had to build on the positive elements of the country's individualist ethic, so as to curb its dark side. Ours is surely no exception.

Everett C. Ladd, *The Responsive Community*, Winter 1993-94.

Though voluminous and often confusing, the data support this assessment: 83 percent of white families and almost half of all African-American families are headed by married couples. Statistics on the state of the African-American family have been especially misleading. For instance, sociologist Christopher Jencks notes that while the growth of illegitimate births as a percentage of all African-American births has increased from one-fifth in the early 1960s to over three-fifths in the 1990s, this is not so much a function of a growth in births among the unmarried as a great decline among the married.

For both African-American and white America, the family

structure remains relatively traditional. Compared to citizens of other developed countries, Americans are considerably more likely to marry at some point in their lives, tend to wed at earlier ages, have larger families, and are less likely to engage in non-marital cohabitation. Recent changes to the modern American family have not so much threatened its dissolution as shaped its internal dynamics, which are now defined by the fact that both parents now work outside the home. The nuclear family remains intact even as it undergoes fundamental and complex internal change.

Related to worries over the failure of the family as society's moral anchor are concerns regarding the loosening of sexual mores. Those who believe in the current moral decline view the sexual revolution of the 1960s and 1970s as a nightmare of teen pregnancies and lascivious sexual practices. But this perception is exaggerated. In reviewing new research by the Kinsey Institute, sociologist Andrew Greeley cites surveys that argue against notions of waning American sexual morality. Three-quarters of respondents to a national poll believe that most Americans engage in extra-marital affairs, but nine out of ten say that they personally have been faithful. Greeley concludes that "Americans think that sexual behavior has in general turned permissive, even though they . . . generally engage in behavior which is in most respects not incompatible with traditional morality."

"Everything's Relative"

Perhaps the most bludgeoned symbol of the decline of morality in America is not a tangible social ill at all, but rather a philosophical trend. Relativism, which posits the ultimate indefensibility of any moral position and the inherent equality of all cultural forms, is widely blamed for the disintegration of societal standards of judgment and behavior. All of the social and economic problems discussed above have been attributed, at one point or another, to America's acceptance of relativism. But, as theorist Jacques Barzun points out, "No idea working alone has ever demoralized society, and there have been plenty of ideas simpler and more exciting than relativism."

Moreover, the evidence does not suggest that Americans view morality as somehow indeterminate or incommensurate. After examining survey results, polling authority Everett Carll Ladd maintains that "more often than not, the data indicate there is in fact considerable agreement on the norm. If we are going to hell in a handbasket, it is not because the preponderance of Americans have abandoned their attachment to some older verities." To the contrary, they are much more likely than Europeans or Canadians to believe in absolute morality. When asked in the 1990 World Values Survey whether absolute or circumstantial standards apply to moral dilemmas, the great majority of Europeans and Canadians replied that morality is circumstantial. Americans, in harmony with their sectarian traditions, are more likely to view morality as absolute. And, as can be documented, religious literalism, inerrantism, and belief in Biblical truths are stronger in America than in the rest of the industrialized world.

Individual vs. Communal Moralities

We have examined the evidence employed to prove that America is experiencing a moral crisis and found it unconvincing. This is not to say that the country does not face contemporary moral challenges. Clearly it does. The communitarian perspective—represented by the writings of Robert Bellah, Philip Selznick, and Amitai Etzioni—views the reinvigoration of community as the most promising means of confronting America's moral challenges. . . . Communitarians argue that norms of responsibility to the collective whole should somehow be "emphasized" in order to "counterbalance" the destructive tide of individualism and selfishness in modern America. But the scale is not out of whack. Social developments in America have always been wrought with complicated contradictions, successes and failures. The way to ensure that we avoid moral decay is not to alter the culture, but rather to illuminate the ways in which we can use the moral tools with which our individualistic culture provides us so that we can fix the social problems generated by the underside of individualism.

"It is not too much to say that America has been
experiencing the rise of internal barbarism."

America Faces a
Civilizational Crisis

Dwight D. Murphey

A number of social crises—from violent crime to poverty to dis-
honesty—plague America, Dwight D. Murphey argues in the
following viewpoint. Murphey asserts that these crises taken as
a whole constitute an internal barbarism that tears at the fabric
of American society. However, Murphey contends, much of the
public does not recognize the threat of these crises to the nation.
Murphey is an associate editor of the bimonthly *Conservative
Review* and a business law professor at Wichita State University
in Kansas.

As you read, consider the following questions:

1. Why do many Americans misperceive the severity of social
   crises, in Murphey's opinion?
2. According to Murphey, how have blacks contributed to and
   been affected by social problems?
3. What is the economic impact of fraud, according to the
   author?

From Dwight D. Murphey, "America's Civilizational Crisis: The Rise of Internal Barbarism,"
Conservative Review, vol. 4, no. 5, September/October 1993. Reprinted with permission.

This past Fourth of July, my wife and I and some friends drove to a spot two miles north of the giant fireworks display that is put on annually at Wichita's Cessna Stadium. From there, we saw all of the dazzling color at a distance. We lost out on much of the awe-inspiring effect, but preferred that to becoming entangled in parking and traffic problems.

As it turned out, there was an additional reason to avoid a large crowd. When the show was over and thousands of people streamed out of the stadium to find their cars, a member of one of Wichita's many gangs started shooting at another. A reputed gang member was killed—and so, too, was a 53-year-old woman, a person totally separate from the gangs, whose last conscious act was that of helping a disabled friend walk back toward the parking lot.

This killing has had a searing effect in Wichita. Many such deaths have a remote quality about them, amounting in our consciousness to nothing more than another stranger's being struck down by the great anonymous wash of violence that is "out there." But not this one. It told hundreds of thousands of people just how close the horror has come. It means that the flood of barbarism is lapping at all our doors. The bullet that killed Barbara Gragg could just as well have killed any of us.

It would be comforting to think of Barbara Gragg's death as an isolated phenomenon, or even to think of "gang shootings" more generally as a generic sort of problem in itself. In many ways, that is precisely what we do: The criminal justice system will treat her death as an individual case, prosecuting her killer if it can identify him; and much discussion is going on about how to combat gangs.

Internal Barbarism

But these things are more than specific incidents or even classes of incidents. They are part of a general disintegration of the cement of our civilization. Put together with a great many other facts about contemporary life, they take on a vastly broader dimension: *it is not too much to say that America has been experiencing the rise of internal barbarism. . . .*

Many people still don't understand that the widely varying details of the barbarism relate to a whole. They see each separately, and just don't perceive them as comprising a seamless web of civilizational decay.

Most people refuse to think in terms of long-term cause and effect. It is more comfortable simply to accept what is, and to consider the "worrier" as a mere ideologue or some sort of neurotic. Most of the professionals around whom I've worked, in law and in academia, have been oblivious to the things that have concerned conservatives.

There are other reasons, too, that the decadence isn't generally perceived as such. The fact that it is a human phenomenon has as an unavoidable corollary the further fact that many of our contemporaries either embody or embrace some aspects of it. In order fully to understand the problem, they must come to grips with their own lives. In part, for example, the rise in barbarism is a result of the disintegration of the family, itself the result of still other factors. But do young couples who live together without benefit of marriage, or who give birth to a child out of wedlock, or who place themselves in welfare dependency through their self-destructive conduct, see themselves as part of a civilizational problem? No, they just don't think of their own behavior in those terms.

Before citing specifics, it is worth noting that some of the particulars relate to concentrated centers of barbarism and others to our national life in general. It is easy to spot the barbarism as it exists within the major pockets that have come into being; but it is manifested, too, in an overall decline.

Examples of Barbarism

Here is a representative sample of conditions and events, taken from recent press clippings, that illustrate the problem:

1. Violent crime. The annual FBI study entitled "Crime in the United States, 1991" reported that in that year violent crime continued to grow rapidly. The 1.9 million violent crimes that were reported constituted a five percent increase over the prior year—and a 45 percent increase over 1982. A growing number of young people between 10 and 17 were arrested for crimes ranging from murder to rape, robbery, drug abuse and weapons violations.

In part, this occurred among whites, but to a very large extent it was a black phenomenon, with a 145 percent increase. For white juveniles, there was a 251 percent increase in heroin and cocaine arrests; for blacks, a 2,373 percent increase.

A study by a University of Pennsylvania professor, based on arrest records of men born in Philadelphia between 1945 and 1958, found that two-thirds of violent crime is committed by a mere seven percent of those arrested. This seven percent produces three-fourths of the rape and robbery—and virtually all of the murder. The Rand Corp. has called these the "superfelons." If all of them were incarcerated between 16 and 30, a massive reduction in crime would occur—but it would require another 1,000,000 prison beds.

2. Carjacking deaths. A news report in September 1992 tells of killings in Los Angeles, New York City and Maryland in which "carjackers" have shot and killed drivers to steal their cars right out from under them. Car theft rose 23 percent in the five years from 1987 through 1991, and "carjacking"—unheard of until recently—has come to amount to two percent of the total.

3. Drugs. The use of cocaine started to drop in 1986, but in early 1993 a federally funded survey conducted by the University of Michigan found that eighth-graders are increasingly getting into drugs of all kinds, including marijuana, cocaine, LSD and inhalants. 11.2 percent of these 13- and 14-year-olds said they had tried marijuana.

4. Crack babies. The figure is a little dated now, but in late 1989 the United States Attorney for Kansas wrote a letter to Wichita's leading newspaper telling of "200,000 babies born in the United States who are affected by cocaine and crack cocaine."

Civilization at Stake

As a people, we have many national life-threatening problems of a mundane character. One thinks of the almost terminal disorder of our country's fiscal affairs, our citizens' inability to save and plan for the future, homelessness, the deterioration of our educational system, the existence of urban violence and drug-related crime. I believe, however, given a restoration of values, that disorders can be overcome. But one should be deeply worried by the ills in our society that point to a fatal fragmentation of the society created in America since the early 1600s. What's at stake is our branch of Western civilization. Many thoughtful Americans are concerned about survival of the inner values of our civilization, the weakened standards of our civilization, under the conditions which exist today and which are likely to exist in the opening decades of the 21st century.

Anthony Harrigan, *The St. Croix Review*, June 1992.

5. Shoplifting rampage. It is worthwhile to leave statistics occasionally to see the stark reality of individual cases. One of the most ludicrous episodes occurred when the Texas Southern University "Ocean of Soul Marching Band" went to Tokyo to participate in the halftime ceremonies at the December 6, 1992, football game between Kansas State University and the University of Nebraska. Just before the band was to fly back to the United States, its members were taken shopping at an electronics mall. Approximately $22,000 worth of electronics products were shoplifted. Japanese police didn't allow the group to leave until the goods were handed out of the buses. "One by one," a police official said, "about 100 products were passed to the back doors of the buses." Back in the States, the University wound up abolishing its band program.

6. *The Magic Johnson example.* Before we move on to the statistics about sexually transmitted diseases, AIDS, and the number of children born out of wedlock, it's worth noting excerpts cited in the press from Magic Johnson's book *My Life:* "As long as nobody gets hurt, what's wrong with sex between unmarried adults? . . . Just about every time the bus brought us back to our hotel," he wrote, "there would be 40 or 50 women waiting in the lobby. . . . Some were secretaries. Some were lawyers. Quite a few were actresses and models. Others were teachers, editors, accountants or entrepreneurs. . . . Most of these women were college-educated professionals. . . . Every day, hundreds of perfumed letters arrived. . . . Some of the mail got pretty explicit."

Our now non-judgmental vocabulary has dropped the word "whore." It is easy to see why. Such a moral epithet made sense when the word applied to a limited class of women. If Magic Johnson's narrative is to be believed, however, that behavior has become so common that there is no longer a limited class of people to whom it applies. What are we to think of the lawyers, teachers, editors and models he describes? What are we to think of him?

7. *Sexually transmitted diseases.* Reports are that three million American teenagers contract venereal diseases—now called "sexually transmitted diseases"—every year. Syphilis is at its highest level in 40 years, with 134,000 new cases annually. There are now 500,000 new genital herpes [cases] annually, cumulatively infecting an estimated 25 million Americans. Add to this a total of 24 million cases of human papilloma virus (HPV) and 1.3 million new cases of gonorrhea every twelve months.

8. *AIDS deaths.* The estimate in early 1993 was that, by 1995, 330,000 Americans will have died of AIDS, and about one million carry the HIV virus. A hopeful report is that AIDS seems to be remaining centered in "socially marginalized groups" and isn't spreading as quickly into the heterosexual, non-drug-using population as once anticipated.

In July 1993, the Clinton administration proposed spending $2.7 billion in the following fiscal year on all aspects of AIDS. This represents a 28 percent increase over the prior year.

Crises Facing Blacks and Families

9. *Children out of wedlock.* In excess of one million babies are born out of wedlock in the United States every year. This is an enormous problem within the black community, where 65 percent of the babies are illegitimate (as much as 80 percent in certain cities). It is worth noting, however, that more than half of the million babies are born to white mothers.

There is a strong connection between out-of-wedlock births, low birthweight, high infant mortality, and poverty. A January

1992 article by Nicholas Eberstadt in the *Wall Street Journal* reported that "infant mortality in 1988 was two-fifths higher for blacks than for babies born in Puerto Rico. . . . Among blacks, the incidence of low birthweight is not only higher than that of virtually any other Western population but also twice as high as that of U.S. whites. Yet the incidence among U.S. whites is high as well—nearly twice that of Norway."

10. Black disintegration. Although there has been a growing black professional class, much of the rest of the black community is a "disaster area" so far as the disintegration of civilized values is concerned.

William Bennett observed in 1992 in the *Wall Street Journal* that the "Great Society effort [is] now well into its third decade—at the cost of more than $2.5 trillion." Despite (or arguably because of) this historically unprecedented effort, "blacks comprise almost half of the prison population. The homicide rate for black males aged 15 to 24 has increased by 40 percent since the mid-1980s. . . . Forty percent of those murdered in the U.S. are black men killed by other black men."

Charles Murray pointed out in 1990 that even during the economic boom of the 1980s, 37 percent of young blacks stayed out of the labor market. "What are they doing?" he asked. "While they are out of the labor force, they survive off relatives, girlfriends, hustles, maybe drugs or crime. What they aren't doing is saving for the future, marrying the women they get pregnant, supporting the children they father. Neither are they acquiring the job skills. . . ."

This is a matter of grave concern to the excellent circle of black conservatives whose writings appear in, say, the *Issues & Views* journal. They ascribe that deterioration to the disincentives of the welfare state itself and to the "blame white society" attitudes inculcated by the sort of "leadership" that has prevailed, in league with the American Left, among blacks.

Single Parents and Poverty

11. Crumbling families. The disintegration of family structure has by no means been limited to the black minority. A representative of the Wichita School District reported in 1986 that "the largest number of women in U.S. history—67 percent of women between the ages of 18 and 34—are in the labor force." He said that "marching along with these couples are young single-parent families maintained chiefly by women" and that "the number of divorced mothers more than doubled between 1970 and 1982."

There is a direct correlation between unmarried parentage and poverty. An article by Robert Rector in the *Washington Times* in September 1992 told how "the poverty rate for married-couple families was just 5.6 percent [in 1990]. For married couples with a full-time worker it was just two percent. By contrast, the poverty rate of female-headed families was a staggering 32.2 percent." He pointed out that "in 1959, 28 percent of poor families with children were headed by women. In 1992, 60 percent . . . were headed by single mothers."

12. *Astronomical increase in spending on "the poor."* A recent chart prepared by John Cogan of the Hoover Institution shows that, *in constant 1989 dollars*, governmental expenditures for the poor increased from approximately $18 billion in 1962 to $140 billion in 1991.

13. *Declining academic achievement.* Michael Novak, in a 1990 *Forbes* magazine article, tells us that "hardly a day goes by without some test showing how incompetent our youngsters are in math, geography, history, politics—or almost anything worthwhile. . . . This dumbing down is not for want of opportunity, years in school, money for books, travel and massive exposure to the media."

Dishonesty and Fraud

14. *Loss of integrity.* Honesty and personal integrity have little appeal to a major portion of American society. A February 2, 1992, report in the *Wichita Eagle* observed that "critics say fraud has been an important force in pushing up the premiums Americans have to pay for auto insurance, from $40 billion to $100 billion since 1980." The article points to "fraudulent claims—everything from reporting accidents that never happened, to exaggerated car damage to faked injuries." "In Massachusetts, the insurance commissioner estimates that fraud and abuse account for as much as 40 percent of auto insurance claims. The insurance industry has long estimated fraud at 10 percent of auto claims filed. On Long Island, N.Y., Nassau County police have concluded that 50 percent to 60 percent of the hundreds of people who report their cars stolen from the Green Acres shopping mall . . . have actually abandoned or destroyed them for the insurance money."

The manifestations of barbarism are all around us. They reflect a spiritual condition in which millions of people see nothing beyond their own immediate urges, and feel themselves a part of no common morality.

It is a problem of the "underclass," black and otherwise; but it goes much further, too. I am reminded of a case told about on television a few nights ago: An agricultural employer hired illegal immigrants to do farm labor, but without health insurance; when one of the workers developed a health problem, he ran up a $50,000 unpaid medical bill at a local hospital. No doubt all of us who *do* pay our medical bills and *do* have medical insurance are picking up the tab for that $50,000. But do you suppose that farm employer cares?

The honest American stands, in effect, like a giant oak covered by parasitical, life-sucking vines. Add up the fraud, the passed-along costs such as the medical bill, the enormous volume of shoplifting and the equally voluminous employee theft, and what do we have?—a vast incubus on the backs of productive people.

15. Why our civilization endures. This recital of barbarism is not intended to suggest that there are not millions of people who *are* honest, responsible, hard-working and productive. Indeed, it is due to them that we are able to go on as a civilization at all. . . .

It is imperative that we reaffirm our commitment to a free society and to civilization. The barbarism must not be allowed to define our existence, even as we combat it. For example, our recourse must be to law, not to the vigilantism that will inevitably grow if lawful measures aren't taken; to an increased demand for what is truly valuable in art and music, films and literature, not to censorship. Otherwise, the barbarism will have struck its worst blow within our own souls.

"There is no question but that the media play a central part in defining the crisis of the moment."

America's Crises Are Often Exaggerated

Barbara Ehrenreich and Todd Gitlin

Many media critics argue that what are considered crises are not as serious as they appear or are exaggerated by the media. In the following viewpoint, Barbara Ehrenreich and Todd Gitlin maintain that the media are responsible for transforming many issues into so-called crises. Ehrenreich and Gitlin contend that the media largely define current issues, report the seriousness surrounding them, and then rely on polls to elevate the issues into "crises." The authors argue that public concern toward these crises, such as terrorism and drug abuse, grows and wanes as the media play up or disregard various issues, in cycle fashion. Ehrenreich is an author and a columnist for *Z Magazine*. Gitlin, a sociology professor at the University of California at Berkeley, is a contributing writer to numerous publications.

As you read, consider the following questions:

1. What are some examples of mass panic in modern America, according to the authors?
2. Why do Ehrenreich and Gitlin believe the public is receptive to media-boosted crises?
3. Why are more crises gaining public attention more rapidly, in the authors' opinion?

Barbara Ehrenreich and Todd Gitlin, "Panic Gluttons," *The Washington Post*, March 7, 1993. Reprinted with permission.

America is afflicted by a peculiar volatility. One threat after another seems to arise out of nowhere and seize our attention for weeks at a time. A bomb goes off in the World Trade Center and the next day terrorism has become the threat to end all threats. Then the spotlight moves to cults. In 1993, the threat was the supposedly still-born presidency of Bill Clinton. (After the ravages of Nanny-gate and gays in the military, many were surprised to find that we still had a president.) In 1992, the imminent peril was the resurgence of racism and racial violence. In the summer of 1990 it was Saddam Hussein. In 1985, it was missing children.

The issues are usually real enough, but the sudden public fixations, coming in synchronized waves of alarm, reflect a dangerous dynamic linking the media, the polls, politicians and the public. Instead of approaching public problems systematically, soberly, consistently, we seem to lurch, fearfully from spasm to spasm, like a paranoid in search of fresh enemies.

Amplifying the Public Mood

Mass panics and moralistic fixations are nothing new, of course. Twentieth-century Americans have repeatedly enthused over wars or cringed from such threats as "white slavery," "reefer madness" and domestic communism. But in the last 15 years or so, a new dynamic has come into play, causing alarms and enthusiasms, once launched, to intensify, obliterating alternative views. Briefly put, the media not only highlight the new issue, they also tend to amplify the public mood they have themselves helped set in motion. Stories about how grave the problem is soon share space with stories telling us how worked up people are becoming—and citing the polls to prove it. The issue can be as serious as police brutality or as chimerical as Satanic child abuse cults. Once it "resonates," it tends to mushroom.

This is what is called, in cybernetics, a positive feedback system. Instead of a self-correcting process (the classic example is a thermostat, which turns down the furnace when the temperature rises far enough), we get a self-accelerating loop. The new dynamic joining the media and the public generates mounting concern, even frenzy—until ultimately, boredom sets in and the hunt is on for a fresh fixation.

Follow the Leader

The first step, in the launching of a media-fed frenzy, is the identification of the issue. There is no question but that the media play a central part in defining the crisis of the moment. On this, social scientists have reached as firm a consensus as social scientists ever do. The media don't necessarily tell people what to think, but they do—if only through sheer repetition—tell people what to think *about*.

There wouldn't be an issue, though, if media heads didn't tend to swivel in the same direction. Since it often isn't obvious just what "the news" is, editors and producers tend to follow the leader. Collective insecurity combines with competitive frenzy. If the flagship media have done the story, so must everyone. "Your boss will yell at you or refuse to believe you if you're too far afield," says Tom Goldstein, dean of the journalism school at the University of California, Berkeley. "It's safer to follow."

That is, until the boredom begins.

Less Reality than Fiction

On television and in newspapers, reality and truth have long since fallen by the wayside, replaced by what can be called a culture of lying.

Hard facts and figures in the news are generally accurate—that much is necessary to maintain the credibility of the entire exercise. But the presentation of the facts frequently degenerates into a hodgepodge of artificial crises and falsely heightened plot lines. The media are less a window on reality than a stage on which officials and journalists perform self-scripted, self-serving fictions.

Paul H. Weaver, *The New York Times*, July 29, 1994.

Let's take . . . terrorism. While you might not know it from the network news, terrorism's panic appeal existed long before the World Trade Center blast. Recall, if you will, the media-driven alarm about terrorism in 1986 when Americans canceled overseas vacations in record numbers in the wake of a spate of overseas bombings and hijackings. By April 1986, a CBS/*New York Times* poll rated terrorism "the most important problem facing this country today." Then as now, an American's chances of dying in a terrorist attack were minuscule. As *Newsweek* reported, we were 124 times as likely to choke to death.

By the fall of 1986, terrorism had been all but forgotten as public anxiety swung to America's new "number-one problem"—drugs. In this case, there was legitimate basis for concern. But the alarm over drugs, crack in particular, tended to sweep aside the facts that illegal drug use in general had been declining since 1979 and that crack accounted for only a tiny share of the declining total. Suddenly it became big news that, according to *New York Times*/CBS News polls, more Americans chose drugs as "the most important problem facing this country today" than any other issue. Drug frenzy subsided in 1987, but surged again in the fall of 1989, after President George Bush's speech announcing, to great fanfare, an escalation of the "drug war." Drugs were ranked "the most important problem" by a staggering 64 percent of Americans—only to slide dramatically again when the spotlight moved away.

Then, in December 1990, a *Newsweek* cover story on the ostensible surge in campus "thought police" inspired a flock of copy-cat cover stories. These in turn generated network pieces and seemingly inexhaustible grist for the Sunday talk shows. One consequence, of course, is that as journalists dwell on "political correctness," there's less time for, say, the fiscal crisis of the universities. Attention is a scarce resource, whether for journalists or the public.

Potential Crises

Not every issue has the makings of a great fixation. Some issues, like unemployment, may be news, but we don't rely on the media alone to tell us how important they are. We can see for ourselves. The issues that best suit the media-panic cycle are those of which few of us have first-hand experience. When the issue is child-molesting cults or Saddam Hussein or missing children or Lyme disease or killer bees, hardly any of us have reality checks.

The selection of potential crises also tends to have a definite ideological tilt, though hardly for conspiratorial reasons. Journalists have long had a habit of deferring to news-making elites, who are also, of course, journalistically essential "sources." That affects the way many stories are covered. Media analyst Jeff Cohen of Fairness and Accuracy in Reporting points out that the nuclear freeze movement, which had majority support in the mid-1980s, never attracted media attention on the scale, say, of the pro-war mood of early 1991. Similarly, the wave of racist incidents reported on campuses in 1989 never coalesced into a cover story or a major "threat to civil liberties"—unlike "political correctness," an issue more congenial to the then-regnant conservatives.

The Influence of Polls

Once an issue is launched, the polls come into play. If polls show that the issue is attracting significant levels of public concern, it is likely to get more coverage—as well as more attention from political figures—and hence, of course, to elicit still more public concern. Many issues fall flat at this stage for sheer lack of response. Despite heavy media coverage, "political correctness" never quite achieved the status of a serious problem.

But when an issue does begin to take off, the media managers are poised to monitor the slightest ripple it stirs in the public psyche. The networks and major newspapers started their own polling services in the mid-1970s, deciding that public opinion is itself a form of news. By 1988, the extent of media reliance on polls was, according to I.A. "Bud" Lewis, who directed polling for both NBC News and the *Los Angeles Times*, "wild, and the curve is escalating."

Now, there are not only vastly more polls, but reporters have more access to them. As Richard Morin, director of polling for *The Washington Post*, points out, once poll results find their way into data bases, the wire services and other journalists circulate the findings still further, often oversimplifying them in the process. This flurry of poll data helps high-level gatekeepers, especially in television, decide which issues are "hot" and deserve coverage. At best, the polls can help correct the media themselves as when polls showing Clinton's popularity after the 1993 State of the Union [speech] signaled a shift in the mood of presidential coverage.

The catch is that many polls ask about topics which have already been defined, in the media, as "issues" or "news." Thus, for example, ABC News's first poll on drug use came in the summer of 1986, after wide coverage of [professional basketball prospect] Len Bias's death from a cocaine overdose. So polls often end up simply confirming the media gatekeepers' notions of which stories are important and which events have moved on to become "crises." Treating the polls as "news" means of course that public sentiment—often simplified to cartoonish extremes—gets fed right back to the public along with other reports on the "crisis." The cycle continues.

Once an issue has risen to the top, there is, for a while, no incentive to buck the trend. Journalists are loath to wonder aloud whether a "war" is really the best approach to drug abuse, or whether the rights and wrongs of the Gulf War should be debated or whether Clinton's budget plan is really as advertised when the polls have united behind the president. Thus, during the Gulf War, television virtually eliminated antiwar views, although the public and prominent influentials were deeply divided right up to the eve of hostilities. Within days after the war began, support for the war was itself a big story, with local news channels encouraging towns to compete for the highest number of flags and yellow ribbons displayed. One television commentator who criticized the war was dropped with the explanation: "We don't want to contradict the national mood." The polls had spoken.

Part of the Loop

In fact, the public is not just an object of manipulation, but a key component of the loop. We may not pick the issues that become our occasional fixations. We may never see our deepest concerns—for economic security or individual dignity—fed back to us as "crisis." Yet we accede, more or less readily, to each fresh alarm as it comes along. We go for the adrenaline boost, and then, when the threat vanishes from our field of vision, withdraw back into lethargy and irritation. Our spasms and fixations rarely solve problems, yet after each cycle, somehow, we find ourselves available for the next—only to succumb to eventual boredom and withdrawal.

One reason why we acquiesce is that there are fewer and fewer settings in which people can meet to define and evaluate issues on their own, through the slow and time-honored process of discussion. Union halls and political clubs, for example, were once centers of vibrant grassroots debate. Today, unions are in sharp decline, and political managers are more comfortable organizing focus groups than community forums. Politics belongs to the pros—the handlers, pollsters and consultants who orchestrate "themes" largely out of media ephemera.

While talk shows, televised town meetings and push-button "interactive" polling a la Ross Perot may have advisory value and give some people a platform for testifying, they are no substitute for forums where people deliberate and have the chance to change each other's minds.

It may be too that we have become accustomed to these spasms and alarms. They provide a short-lived sense of community, a high of collective identity. We are, as a people, growing more different from one another—less white, more polyglot, more tribal. Marketers target Zip Codes. Cable TV expedites fragmentation. In the metropolises where American style is made, culture circulates in the plural. In times of social disruption and transition, amid economic distress, the market for panic improves.

One reason the panic cycles are becoming shorter, the media-boosted spasms more intense, is that we lack a fixed enemy to give us unity and purpose. For decades, the Cold War solved our identity problems on the cheap. Communism overshadowed all other menaces and helped define us by showing what we were not. As soon as glasnost dawned, the search for new enemies was on—drugs, Japanese industrialists, Manuel Noriega, Saddam Hussein, maniacal captains of cults.

What Could Be Done

It's long past time to break the cycle. Instead of surveying the horizon for the next sensation, political leaders should lead, the media should inform and so on as the civics books prescribe. Rather than invite individuals to deliver themselves of on-the-spot opinions about hitherto unheard-of situations, polls could give respondents a chance to learn and debate. But there is no technical fix for the public withdrawal from ongoing political life. The mass addiction to fixations and panics reaches deep. The public, by this time, has come to expect news that either entertains, frightens or flatters preconceived notions. And neither newsmakers nor media managers dare risk popularity by letting the public down.

But great spasms of collective feeling mobilized from above are, after all, more the stuff of Nuremberg [site of Nazi war-crime trials] than of democracy. Real democracy, in a day-to-day sense, is messier, more fractious and infinitely more demanding. It is an open-ended process, not a loop. A revived and toughened democratic process could itself be a fine source of collective identity for the post–Cold War era. We should not need an enemy, or the frisson of an overnight panic, to show us how much we have in common.

"Lauren is a member of the first generation since the Great Depression that can expect to have a lower standard of living than its parents."

The American Dream Is Dying

Katherine S. Newman

Following World War II, Americans' standard of living reached new heights. What came to be known as the American dream— new homes and cars, college educations, vacations, and other amenities—was realized by more Americans than ever before. In the following viewpoint, Katherine S. Newman contends that the American dream is now out of reach for millions of Americans—the baby boomers. Despite hard work and "playing by the rules," and anticipating lifestyles equal to or greater than those their parents enjoyed, many baby boomers have found themselves shut out of the American dream, Newman argues. Indeed, she maintains, many of them despair of ever living "the good life." Newman is an anthropology professor at Columbia University in New York City. She is the author of *Falling from Grace: The Experience of Downward Mobility in the American Middle Class* and *Declining Fortunes: The Withering of the American Dream*, from which this viewpoint is excerpted.

As you read, consider the following questions:

1. What was the driving force behind the America dream, according to the author?
2. How can government help America recover from its economic malaise, in Newman's opinion?

Lauren Caulder was born in the halcyon days of the 1950s, when prosperity was a given and the formula for achieving it was clear. You drove yourself in school, got into a respectable college, picked a practical career, and pushed ahead with your nose to the grindstone. At the end of this long march lay the accoutrements of the good life: homeownership, family, and the security of a middle-class standard of living. Even as the currents of the American cultural revolution of the late 1960s swirled around her, Lauren doggedly followed the prescription for entry into the middle class and landed the kind of job that should have made it all possible, as a midlevel administrator of a federal lending program.

A Shriveling Dream

Something went awry in Lauren's life in the 1980s. Just when the fruits of her labor should have begun to pay off, the carrot at the end of the stick began to shrivel. Homeownership, that essential piece of the American dream, became an impossibility. Prices escalated to ridiculous levels and closed Lauren out. Unable to afford her own home, Lauren thought she could at least enjoy the benefits of her hard work through an occasional shopping spree or a winter holiday on a sunny island. Instead she discovered that even without the burden of a mortgage, she was still boxed in by a budget that never seemed to stretch far enough for the odd, spontaneous purchase. These days, every dime in her bankbook is committed: she is reasonably solvent, but there is no room for indulgence. This would not be such a problem if Lauren were just starting out; she could afford to wait her turn. But she is nearly forty years old now. All that lies ahead is endless penny-pinching, without much equity to show for it:

> Every time I think I've made a financial breakthrough, something comes along that knocks me right out of the water. You think, okay, finally everything is paid off. Great, now we can start saving for such and such. Car breaks down. No use fixing it anymore. You've got to buy a new one or worse yet pay for a $750 transmission job. There you go. Now you're back in the hole, charged up on your credit card. . . . Something always comes along to wipe out everything that you might think is a winning achievement. You never seem to get over the hump and put it behind you.

Why has Lauren's standard of living fallen so far short of what she thought it would be? Her father, a quiet man of working-class origins and modest means, worked all his life in the advertising industry as a copywriter. Together with his wife, who stayed home to raise the Caulder clan, he was able to buy into a comfortable suburban community and give Lauren and her siblings a solid high school education at the local public school, swimming lessons at "the club," a chance to learn a musical instrument, and occasional travel to interesting vacation spots. Mr. Caulder's life is testimony to the great American dream: his hard work paid off in a better life for himself and his kids. His upward mobility ensured that serious want never intruded into Lauren's childhood.

A Fading Dream

Do you feel the American dream will be easier or harder to attain in the future? (Asked of one thousand Americans)

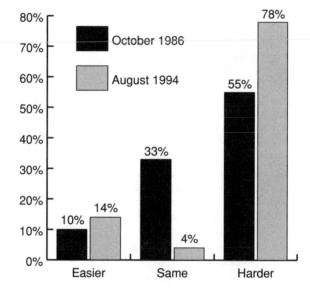

Source: Luntz Research Cos. for the Hudson Institute; 1986 data from the Roper Organization.

The Caulder children were raised to respect traditional virtues of family and frugality, but they were also provided the emblems of affluence that were, after all, part of the reason their parents labored so hard. What was an achievement to be proud of for Mr. Caulder's generation became an expectation, a norm, an entitlement in his daughter's generation. If you became a certain kind of person—educated, cultivated, serious, motivated, hardworking—you were entitled to expect the same benefits in your life. Remaining a card-carrying member of the middle class was the most natural state of existence imaginable for baby boomers like Lauren who were raised amid its splendors.

But as Lauren left the 1980s behind—the decade dubbed by the media, the president, and a passel of economists as the longest period of expansion in the economy's postwar history—all she could see was the life-style she had taken for granted receding farther and farther from her grasp. She is better educated than her father; her job pays more than his ever did; she has a professional identity that her mother never even dreamed of—she should be sitting on top of the world. At the very least, Lauren tells herself, she and her husband are entitled to do as well as her parents did on one modest salary. Yet the gap between what should be and what is feels as large as the Grand Canyon:

> I'll never have what my parents had. I can't even dream of that. I'm living a lifestyle that's way lower than it was when I was growing up and it's depressing. You know it's a rude awakening when you're out in the world on your own. . . . I took what was given to me and tried to use it the best way I could. Even if you are a hard worker and you never skipped a beat, you followed all the rules, did everything they told you you were supposed to do, it's still horrendous. *They lied to me.* You don't get where you were supposed to wind up. At the end of the road it isn't there. I worked all those years and then I didn't get to candy land. The prize wasn't there, damn it.

Lauren is a member of the first generation since the Great Depression that can expect to have a *lower* standard of living than its parents. Children of the post–World War II economic boom, they entered adulthood in an era of economic uncertainty, where news of shuttered factories, bankruptcies, junk-bond nightmares, and white-collar unemployment is the stuff of daily headlines. Gone is the notion that each generation improves on the lot of its parents. In its stead comes the dread Lauren feels: she is on a treadmill that will never support a lifestyle even remotely like the one she knew as a child. Where Lauren's parents could expect to live in a nice house at low cost, have a family when they felt like it, and support their expenses on a single income, Lauren knows that she cannot afford a house, that she and her husband both have to work, and that children are a luxury that will be hard to afford.

No Way Out

Lauren's father, Andrew, a widower for some eight years now, recently sold the house he had owned for thirty years. This lovely New England–style home—too big for a man alone, with its four bedrooms and a large yard—had cost him $15,000 in the late 1950s, nearly twice his yearly income. While that was no small amount of money for Andrew, the 4 percent veteran's mortgage he received as thanks for his military service brought the cost within reach. The Caulder homestead fetched an astounding $400,000 in 1990, a sum so vast it makes Lauren laugh and weep at the same time. There is simply no way she can imagine ever earning enough money to buy her natal home now, or anything even remotely similar.

If Lauren could scale back her expectations, change her ambitions with every fluctuation of the consumer price index, she would have lower blood pressure. Instead, she boils over at being so tightly constrained, so unable to see past this month's paycheck:

> I'm not able to go anywhere. The lack of upward mobility and foreseeing no way out of my current situation is very frustrating. I couldn't take a more expensive apartment, couldn't buy a new car, can't take a vacation I want to take. It's just being frustrated everywhere I turn. Not being able to do the things you want to do with the money you are earning to enjoy your life. Being constantly browbeaten by the economy.

Most perplexing of all from Lauren's perspective is the fact that she always resisted the temptation to deviate and instead stuck to the straight and narrow path that was supposed to ensure that this would not happen. She followed the rules: she didn't party too much or get involved in drugs. She finished a respectable college degree, and she has steadily worked her way up the public-sector hierarchy to a responsible, even important, job. In her youth, the rewards for this good behavior were forthcoming, and she was lulled into the expectation that goodies come to those who work and wait. It seems a cruel hoax:

> I've always killed myself for a reason. I killed myself in school to get the good grades, and that was the reward, thank you very much. I got my A's. All the way along, I was rewarded in just the way I was supposed to be. . . . That was what the book said. And then you get out here to the real world and suddenly the last chapter is a sad joke. You're told you work hard for a living and you can buy a house in [your hometown], or the next town down the line that's a little cheaper. But it's not true and it's really very perturbing.

Lauren sees the real world as a rude awakening from a perfect childhood. Her upbringing made her naïve and gullible. Unseen forces have taken advantage of her faith in the work ethic, leaving her feeling duped.

Accepting Their Lot

Americans are an optimistic lot. It is part of our cultural heritage, if not our daily experience, to assume that even when times are tough, the situation is bound to improve. Even in the depths of the Great Depression, the government tried to capitalize on the average Joe's belief that prosperity was just around the corner. Unfortunately, the members of Lauren's generation do not see the economy in this light. They are beginning to believe that the slump they have experienced is permanent, something they will have to get used to, even though they find this "fact" difficult to accept. Although they have lost their optimism, they have yet to come to terms with the new reality of downward mobility.

Baby boomers find it hard to accept their lot because more than their own lot is at stake. The fall they have experienced relative to their parents may well have serious consequences for their own children. Wendy Norman, a high school classmate of Lauren's, spends a lot of time thinking about the advantages her parents conferred upon her: comfort and enrichment without extravagance—ballet lessons, the occasional theater trip, and lazy summer days down at the pool. While Wendy was lucky to have all these things, her parents were fortunate too. The economic history of the 1950s made it possible for them to do far more for Wendy than their own parents had been able to do for them in the dreary days of the Great Depression. The Normans took pride and pleasure in being able to provide Wendy with so many advantages. Wendy is fairly certain, however, that she will *not* experience the satisfaction that comes from knowing that she has "done right" by her own kids:

> I guess our grandparents and our parents, what kept them moving and motivated was that they were trying to do for their children. Improve their children's lot. I think they achieved that and for the most part were probably happy in it. That gave them the happiness, the self-fulfillment. I don't think we have that in our generation.

Wendy and her baby-boom counterparts across the nation are worried that those critical advantages, those aspects of personal biography social scientists call "cultural capital," may be lost to their own children in the 1980s and 1990s. Their kids may have to settle for less: for mediocre schools, libraries that are closing down due to lack of revenue, and residence in less affluent communities with fewer amenities. . . .

Baby Boomers' Concerns

[Baby boomers] may well want to know why so little attention has been paid to their concerns, particularly in light of how much attention is given to the problems of other groups: the elderly, the poor, the cities. Boomers are likely to open a generational conversation on the subject of equity and it will not be a pleasant one, for their complaints already evoke countercharges that they are a spoiled generation with inflated expectations, a critique they sometimes level at themselves. If the economic prospects of the boomers continue to sag, the country may hear the sound and fury of promises unfulfilled and hard work gone unrewarded. And this will be just the beginning of the generational debate: in time, the "baby-bust" generation will surely ask why they should have to bear the burden of supporting the boomer generation in retirement. . . .

This does not augur well for the soul of the country in the twenty-first century. Every great nation draws its strength from a social contract, an unspoken agreement to provide for one another, to reach across the narrow self-interests of generations, ethnic groups, races, classes, and genders toward some vision of the common good. Taxes and budgets—the mundane preoccupations of city hall—express this commitment, or lack of it, in the bluntest fashion. Through these mechanistic devices, we are forced to confront some of the most searching philosophical questions that face any country: what do we owe one another as members of a society? Can we sustain a collective sense of purpose in the face of the declining fortunes that are tearing us apart, leaving those who are able to scramble for advantage and those who are not to suffer out of sight?

The American Dream—Economically and Spiritually

Many of those who define the American Dream in economic terms blame government for its demise. According to this view, wasteful federal spending, excessive taxation, and a mounting federal deficit and national debt have left a yoke around the necks of future generations, impeding their ability to achieve their dream. Those who see the American Dream in spiritual terms see the moral decay of a nation besieged by crime and violence. To them, the American Dream is dying along with our nation's spirit. Values such as support for community and personal responsibility, once so cherished, seem abandoned. Institutions such as the family, church and school that had nurtured the American Dream for two centuries have been weakened.

Frank Luntz and Ron Dermer, *The Public Perspective*, September/October 1994.

There will be little left of the nation if we withdraw into our own little corners and refuse to "pay" for anyone else's needs. If the fortunes of the generations diverge to the point where they cannot see each other's legitimate claims and heartfelt dilemmas, we may well see the development of warring interest groups competing for politically sacred identities: the inviolable elderly, the deserving children, the baby boomers holding IOUs because they have yet to claim their fair share, the burdened baby-bust generation that did not get to "come to the party" in the 1980s. This is a nightmare vision of American politics that we cannot afford to entertain. We cannot allow public policy debates to descend to the level of squabbles over who is spoiled, about which ethnic groups deserve the good life and which

144

should be excluded, about who is really deserving of a decent retirement or adequate medical care. The social contract upon which we all depend requires some recognition of the common rights and legitimate aspirations of all Americans for a share of the good life.

Help from the Economy

In explaining our fate, American culture tends to subtract large forces from our lives—economic trends, historical moments, and even government policies that privilege one group over another—and looks instead to the individual's character traits or values for answers. Ask members of the postwar generation about their extraordinary experience of upward mobility and you are likely to hear a sermon on the importance of hard work and "your own bootstraps." The GI Bill, low-interest mortgages, and the booming economy of the 1950s and 1960s will barely rate a mention in this tale of upward mobility. But the truth is that the hard work paid off only because economic conditions over which no individual had control made it possible and because government policies provided a helping hand.

In the legacy of the GI Bill, the WPA [Works Progress Administration, 1935–1943], and a host of other government initiatives lies the kind of active program for recovery we sorely need today. These programs created confidence that we lack at present that there are measures we can take, investments in the well-being of all Americans that will actually make a difference. The Great Depression was a far worse economic calamity than anything we have seen since, and we found our way out of it. It is true that part of that trajectory of success came about because the United States was arming itself for World War II, a catalyst for government spending that few would want to see repeated. But the lesson we might take from the experience of the nation's recovery from the blight of the 1930s is that we need not assume that nothing can be done to move the economy and the generations that depend upon it out of the current malaise. We can ask and should ask what government can do as well as what private industry can do. And when we have finished that agenda, we must ask as well what we must do for one another if the present generations and those that follow are to claim their own share of the American dream.

=====

"What we're doing is doubling our real standard of living in a single generation."

=====

The American Dream Is Alive

Kenneth Silber

Despite gloomy predictions from some commentators, there is much evidence that people can still live the American dream, Kenneth Silber argues in the following viewpoint. According to Silber, one statistic—real, per capita, disposable income—shows that income nearly doubled from 1960 to 1992. Silber also cites a poll that shows almost two-thirds of Americans reporting a better standard of living than their parents. Silber maintains that positive developments that the media ignore—such as the rise in women's earnings, declining interest rates, and increased availability of homes for future homebuyers—prove that the American dream can be achieved. Silber is a contributing writer for *Insight*, a weekly magazine published by the *Washington Times*.

As you read, consider the following questions:

1. According to Cheryl Russell, quoted by Silber, what are the expectations of "baby busters"?
2. What changes in America's population during the past two decades does the author note?
3. How do people's assessments of their own economic condition differ from their view of the state of the country in general, according to Russell, as cited by Silber?

Journalists and social scientists have long asserted that the standard of living in the United States is declining—a piece of conventional wisdom that has become a staple of Bill Clinton's rhetoric. The historical pattern of each generation prospering more than its predecessor has been broken, claim these cultural observers, who say that today's younger Americans cannot expect to match, let alone exceed, the living standards of their parents.

The pundits have focused on the baby boom generation, the roughly 77 million Americans born between 1946 and 1964, a group that has grown larger in recent years as as a result of immigration.

In the 1960s, the first boomers to hit college campuses sparked both praise and condemnation for their political activism. Throughout the 1970s and 1980s, their entry into adulthood provoked a marketing frenzy as corporations tried to judge the generation's tastes, giving rise to one of the most infamous stereotypes of recent history—the affluent, self-involved yuppie.

A Victimized Generation

Lately, that image has given way to a new characterization of the boomers as victims of economic decline. Katherine S. Newman, a Columbia University anthropologist, is a prominent advocate of the latter point of view. In *Declining Fortunes: The Withering of the American Dream*, published in 1993, she writes that the boomers comprise "the first generation since the Great Depression that can expect to have a *lower* standard of living than its parents."

Newman draws a sharp contrast between the boomers and their parents' generation (called the "postwar generation" because its members entered adulthood in the years following World War II). There is, she writes, a striking difference between their economic fates: "the postwar generation, beneficiaries of an expanding private sector and generous government benefits, and the baby-boom generation, heirs to the vagaries of deindustrialization, deregulation, speculative gains in the housing market, and unprecedented competition driven by their own numbers."

Newman, along with others who have sounded the alarm about falling living standards, argues that those born after the baby boom face even bleaker prospects.

"The fury of the twentysomething generation may be directed at the wrong people, but there can be no question that they have a lot to complain about," she wrote in a *New York Times* op-ed article. "America's youth have been even more savagely affected by the declining state of the economy than the boomers." This younger generation, variously known as "baby busters" and "Generation X," was born during a period of relatively low fertility. (Although there is disagreement about precisely when the baby bust occurred, many demographers place it from 1965 to 1977.)

Numbering some 47 million, the busters "are expecting to live like middle-aged people, when in fact they're entry-level workers," says Cheryl Russell, a demographer and author of *The Master Trend: How the Baby-Boom Generation Is Remaking America.* "I think they have overly high expectations for themselves at too early an age." Younger Americans often regard as necessities products that their parents would have considered luxuries. "Our concept of what the basics are is much more elaborate today," she says, "so that even though we are near a peak of affluence in this country, we don't feel that we are rich."

As a result, busters have adopted a kind of self-protective cynicism. "Sometimes I wonder why we haven't all committed mass suicide, because we don't have a hell of a lot to look forward to," a 23-year-old woman told the *Wall Street Journal.* . . .

Measuring Income

But do we live in a period of declining fortunes? Are younger Americans experiencing—or in danger of experiencing—a lower standard of living than their parents? The answer is complicated by the fact that there is no universally accepted way to define and measure standards of living.

Many economists seek to resolve this ambiguity by focusing on something quantifiable: income. In particular, economists often measure the standard of living by using a little-publicized Commerce Department statistic: personal income, on a per-capita basis, after taxes and adjusted for inflation. This statistic—technically known as "real, per-capita, disposable income"—provides a picture very different from that presented in the litanies of decline. Income, by this measure, rose more than 93 percent from 1960 to 1992. (It declined between 1990 and 1991, as it has during previous recessions, but regained much of this ground the following year and in late 1993 is near an all-time high.)

"What we're doing is doubling our real standard of living in a single generation" says Fabian Linden, executive director of the consumer research center at the Conference Board, a research organization in New York. "This is not a unique experience. In the comparable prior period, it doubled as well." Indeed, says Linden, such dramatic improvements repeatedly have occurred in American history, with incomes doubling every 35 to 40 years. It is a pattern, he asserts, that shows no sign of ending.

In fact, income statistics tend to understate the extent to which the buying power of consumers has increased over the decades, since they do not take into account improvements in the quality and range of available products. They do not reflect the difference in sound quality between today's compact-disc players and the phonographs of a previous era, for example, nor the power of modern personal computers beyond that of the most sophisticated machines decades ago.

Moreover, according to Richard A. Easterlin, an economist at the University of Southern California, pessimism about living standards often is based on excessively narrow measures of income. "A lot of the assertions about the deterioration in living standards [are] based upon the movement in the earnings of males, particularly males of particular educational groups," he says.

Alive and Well

The American Dream is alive and well. More precisely, the American ideology is fundamentally strong, and continues to show in the present era the resilience it has over the past two centuries. Americans worry about deficiencies in their performance, as they should, but the great majority of them show no fundamental loss of confidence in either the moral worth of their society's fundamental organization or its capacity to help them achieve—as much as any can—the best possible earthly life.

Everett Carll Ladd, *The Public Perspective*, September/October 1994.

As Easterlin sees it, research that focuses on men's incomes understates improvements in living standards by ignoring the rise in women's earnings in recent decades; likewise, focusing on high school graduates overlooks the increase in college attendance (and the resulting higher incomes) of recent generations. He also notes that researchers sometimes confuse cyclical patterns with long-term trends and thus make misleading comparisons of one generation in a year of economic downturn with another in a year of economic growth.

Wrong Comparisons

Another misleading comparison, Easterlin says, is one that appears not in academic literature but rather in people's own assessments of their well-being. "When the boomers are comparing themselves with their parents, they're not comparing themselves with their parents 25 years ago," he says. "In fact, most of them don't know how well their parents were doing 25 years ago. What they're doing is comparing themselves with their parents as of the present time."

Easterlin points out that such assessments ignore the fact that most people's incomes rise over the course of their working lives; people at relatively early stages in their careers tend to earn less than those nearing retirement age. Income generally peaks between ages 45 and 55. The important question is how different generations are doing at comparable ages—and in this regard, Easterlin notes, the boomers' average incomes are outpacing those of the previous generation. "Short of something like the Great Depression of the 1930s, it is almost inconceivable that they would end up worse off than their parents, on average."

The tendency of incomes to rise over the course of people's careers helps explain recent changes in the distribution of income in the United States. Often, the contention that living standards are falling is combined with an argument that inequality is on the rise. Newman, for example, writes that "we saw a marked increase in the divide between haves and have nots over the course of the 1980s: record numbers of American families were pushed into poverty, while those fortunate few who were already at the top of the income scale added enormous sums to their coffers."

During the past two decades, however, the portions of the population consisting of young adults and the elderly—groups that tend to earn relatively low incomes—grew quickly, while the relatively high-earning middle-aged group shrank to a smaller percentage of the population. Linden expects these trends to start reversing over the course of the 1990s as the boomers move into middle age.

One item that any generation would regard as part of "the basics" is housing, and the availability of housing is a topic often raised by those who see living standards in decline. "For the baby-boom generation—and even worse for those coming behind them, the so-called Generation X—there was a significant delay in getting into the housing markets," says Newman. "And for many it was just impossible and still is impossible.". . .

Home Ownership

While recent decades have seen a rise in the amount of labor required to purchase housing, this has been more than offset by a decline in the amount of labor needed to buy other goods. The Conference Board's Linden calculates that 22.7 hours of labor were required to provide the average household with a week's supply of food, clothing and shelter in 1960—compared with 21 labor-hours in 1990. The price of shelter went up—from 6.3 labor-hours per week in 1960 to 9.7 in 1990—but the corresponding figures for food and clothing declined by an even larger amount.

The coming years, moreover, may see home ownership rates resume their historical rise. One reason for this is that interest rates have declined sharply from the elevated levels seen in the 1970s and 1980s, a development that should make mortgages easier to obtain. (Newman, however, is not optimistic about this prospect, arguing that even as interest rates fall, other economic obstacles will block access to the housing market. "The trouble is that those interest rates are coming down, but unemployment is not coming down," she says.)

Demographics should also help make housing more attainable. The large number of baby boomers brought a commensurate increase in the demand for housing, which helped push prices up. The smaller size of the baby-bust generation should translate into less upward pressure on real-estate values.

"When the buster generation comes along, to some degree they will have an advantage," says William H. Frey, a demographer at the Population Studies Center of the University of Michigan. Frey notes that homeowners have a tendency to "trade up," buying progressively more expensive houses; the aging of the boomers, he says, will help increase the availability of lower-priced homes.

Meanwhile, the aging—and death—of the postwar generation will result in houses and other assets being passed along to the boomers. "If you make the pessimistic assumption that people don't live forever, somebody's going to inherit all that," says Linden.

Edward N. Wolff, an economist at New York University, estimates that the boomers will receive an average inheritance of about $50,000. Inheritance, in any generation, is unequally distributed, with some individuals receiving a lot and others receiving little or nothing. But Wolff notes that the boomers, as a group, will receive far more than what was inherited by any previous generation. "This transfer of wealth, as far as I can tell, is really unprecedented in its magnitude," he says.

Changes Among Women

Other trends cited in Newman's book as evidence of economic decline could be given alternative interpretations. In discussing the changing role of women in recent decades, for example, Newman writes, "It is clear that the wholesale entry of women into the labor market is practically the only thing that kept the average middle-class family afloat. With men's wages stagnating and the cost of living rising, it was women to the rescue."

Linden, on the other hand, notes that in recent years women have received slightly more than half of all college degrees awarded, up from about one-third in 1960, a sign that they are working not out of economic necessity but rather because they prefer to have careers. "During the 1980s, which was an extraordinarily prosperous decade, you got a surge, a tidal wave, of women into the labor force," he says. "It becomes palpably absurd to say all of this is the result of the desperate need to make ends meet.". . .

Newman's book is hardly alone in focusing on negative developments while ignoring positive ones. Rarely are headlines devoted to rising incomes or increased life expectancy. Says Linden, "The press finds it far more attractive to peddle bad news than good news, for the simple reason that good news is a bore."

One result, argues Russell, is that many people develop an unduly negative view of the state of the country—even while maintaining a positive assessment of their own condition. "There's a big difference between the personal and the general," says Russell. As she sees it, "people are much more optimistic about the prospects for their children than they are about American children [in general]. They are much more optimistic about their personal finances than they are about the national economy."

Indeed, a poll taken by the Conference Board in 1992 indicates that most people, when asked about their own family's living standards, do not subscribe to the theory of decline. Asked how they would compare their present standard of living with that of their parents during the last years in which they were living at home, 63 percent responded that they were better off than their parents, 23 percent said their living standards were the same and 14 percent reported a decline. Among respondents under age 35, nearly three-quarters said their conditions were better than or the same as those of their parents—despite the fact that the respondents were in early stages of their careers, whereas, during their last years at home, the parents had been in or near their peak earning years.

The poll, based on a national sample of 5,000 households, also found that a large majority in every age group believed they had greater opportunities than their parents did at the same age. And fewer than 16 percent expected their children's living standard to be lower than their own.

Problems and Improvements

Such numbers, of course, do not mean that poverty and hardship have vanished from the United States. Linden notes that some segments of the population—such as single parents and high school dropouts—face relatively bleak economic prospects. "We have some very real social problems," he says, but these should not be confused with the "mainstream of the economy."

Linden also argues that economic trends should not be confused with cultural ones. "You might feel that music is deteriorating, movies are deteriorating and television is deteriorating," he says. "Art galleries are not open as many hours as they used to be. [But if] you take something a little bit more vulgar—like how many bucks do we spend, in real terms, as compared to what we had 10 years ago—we're doing very well indeed."

These economic improvements, however, may receive little notice from commentators. Notes Linden, "If you say all's well, you're a fool and an optimist, naive and a bore. But if you say things are terrible, the American dream is tarnished—you're a caring, concerned philosopher."

So what will happen to the baby busters? According to some analysts, they will face favorable conditions in the labor market, precisely because of the relatively small size of their generation. "As we move further into this decade, we're going to encounter a very slow growth in the number of people of working age," says Linden. "It's going to have a positive effect on wages and job opportunities."

"At its most destructive, American culture's mean streak holds out the potential to promote even more violence in . . . society."

The Dark Side of Popular Culture

Nina J. Easton

American society and popular ("pop") culture exhibit increasingly cruel—and violent—characteristics, Nina J. Easton argues in the following viewpoint. Easton maintains that from radio and television to the attitudes of children and adults, insults, mean-spiritedness, and violence permeate our culture. Pop culture not only reflects the nastiness in society, Easton contends, but intensifies those feelings and encourages the malicious and violent tendencies many people harbor. Easton is a staff writer for the *Los Angeles Times Magazine*, a weekly publication.

As you read, consider the following questions:

1. According to Easton, who are the targets of personal attacks in mainstream entertainment?
2. How does barbed humor differ between older and newer television shows, according to Easton?
3. Why does the author believe there is much concern with television's effect on children?

In the 1990s, "dissin'" is fast becoming a national pastime. Cutting insults, crude put-downs and vulgar and vicious personal lampoons are dominating mainstream entertainment—even while political leaders urge us to put people first. More than ever, comedy draws the most laughs when it's at the expense of someone else. "Humor has devolved to allow more extreme forms of brutality and insults that are normally perceived of as abhorrent," says Jennings Bryant, director of the University of Alabama's Institute for Communication Research. "It is pushing the bounds of propriety."

Today's personal attacks often are aimed close to home—at family members, girlfriends, co-workers, teachers. In an age of political correctness, these are safe targets, not likely to generate a rash of protest from hypersensitive organized interests. So are celebrities, who are fast slipping from their privileged positions with fawning fans and press. Fat jokes are popular; fat people aren't a protected lobby. Sexual put-downs are in; who other than religious zealots would challenge them in the post-sexual-revolution age?

Invective in the Media

Barbed humor is the staple of relationship game shows. If the couples connect on the popular dating games *Love Connection* and *Studs*, sexual innuendoes bubble forth. But if they don't, the insults fly: She was fat, he was cheap, she was cold, he was a bore. "Kiss him? I'd rather make out with a sidewalk," quips one *Studs* contestant. . . .

Fictional characters on contemporary TV shows have a staff of writers to script them, so their insults are wittier, but equally vicious. On Fox's popular *Married . . . With Children*, a running gag of intrafamily ridicule, Al Bundy wonders why his wife Peg didn't marry a man more like her father: "Or weren't there any chronically unemployed social parasites the month you were in your prime?" The satirical variety show *In Living Color* is more reckless, taking aim at black women, gays and even, in an off-color skit about a spastic handyman, the handicapped. . . .

The 1992 Emmy telecast turned especially unpleasant: In the midst of Hollywood's counterattack on the Republicans' own mean-spirited family-values campaign, Diane English—creator of *Murphy Brown*, one of TV's saltier put-down artists—burst out: "I couldn't possibly do a worse job raising my kid alone than the Reagans did with theirs."

In children's entertainment, the superhero has evolved into a superbrat. Cartoons feature 6-year-old child-animals who slam doors in the faces of innocent characters and maniacally kick villains in the shins. The star of the hit movie *Home Alone 2* is a 10-year-old snot who delights in setting up vicious pranks for the villains, any one of which would, in real life, maim or kill a person. (When was the last time anyone survived a brick to the head from three stories up?) The fantasy alter ego of a sweet young woman in *Drop Dead Fred*, a video cult favorite with the 8-year-old set, greets her mother with such salutations as, "It's megabitch! Get me the ax! No, get me a chain saw!"

©1994, *Boston Globe*. Distributed by Los Angeles Times Syndicate. Reprinted with permission.

Radio shockjock Howard Stern's obscenities are what draw the ire of the Federal Communications Commission and the press, but biting cruelty is also his stock in trade. When Dick Cavett, who disclosed his shock-therapy treatment for depression, called Stern's show to lend support in his battles against the FCC, Stern offered this in return: "So how many volts did you take to the head?" One of his ugliest comments was made while his partner read the celebrity news one morning: "Big, fat Kirstie Alley. It's a good thing she had a miscarriage. If she got pregnant, her breasts would be sagging to the floor."

Stern's popularity is skyrocketing: He airs in 10 cities [as of February 1993], including Los Angeles, where he has the top-rated morning show, and he has launched a TV talk show. Radio-industry officials note that other radio talk-show hosts around the country now are borrowing Stern's style.

Even while some commentators complain that PC-ism is choking free expression, American popular culture is rich with examples of misogyny, racism and homophobia. In rap and heavy metal music, especially, women are routinely referred to as bitches and "ho's" (short for whores); gays are faggots. Need some anti-Semitism? The syndicated TV series *Uptown Comedy Club* featured a skit about the law firm of "Judacy," where Hasidic lawyers sing, "I really want to sue you. I really want to overcharge you." Rush Limbaugh has sunk to disturbing lows on his radio show, such as this tirade against AIDS and abortion activists: "Get out of our schools. Get out of our churches. Take your deadly, sickly behavior and keep it to yourselves."

There's something equally mean about the increasingly violent voyeurism that permeates American TV news and entertainment today—from the airing of domestic squabbles on talk shows like *Geraldo* to [the] shooting of a woman by her estranged husband at a Florida cemetery, captured by a Spanish-language news crew and disseminated nationwide.

Psychological Violence

Whatever form this invective takes, media researchers call it "psychological violence," and they are concerned that just as hundreds of studies link TV to a more violent society, the decline in civility in popular culture will alter our behavior toward each other. "It's worrisome," says Alvin Poussaint, associate dean at the Harvard Medical School and former consultant to the now-defunct *Cosby Show*. "I don't think this is just reflecting reality. It's also part of *encouraging* reality. For a lot of vulnerable people, especially children, this is putting suggestions in their heads, or at least lowering their defenses against impulses they might have." Poussaint also worries that trends in popular culture contribute to an increased difficulty among many young people in discerning right from wrong.

What is the reality that America's tastemakers are helping to shape? More confrontational social relationships, for one. John Murray, head of the Human Development and Family Studies Department at Kansas State University, doesn't permit his children, age 7 and 11, to watch *Roseanne* or *The Simpsons*. The many fans of these shows point out that both TV families, despite their heavy reliance on irreverence and insult humor, demonstrate strong bonds of love. But for Murray, who studies the impact of media on children, love hidden beneath a crusty exterior isn't a satisfying rationale: "No matter what else, a steady diet of these shows conveys the sense that it's all right to be mean-spirited to each other. But if you act like that in real life, all you do is anger people. Every office, every department, every class has one person like that, and—fortunately, I guess—they're always the outsider."

At its most destructive, American culture's mean streak holds out the potential to promote even more violence in a society where cutting off someone in the fast lane can mean a bullet to the head. Social graces are not just the stuff of snobbery, notes Judith Martin, author of the syndicated "Miss Manners" column. Holding our tongues, setting internal limits on the views we express to each other, smooths the bumps in a conflict-ridden society. In our zeal to promote "open communication" at any cost—or for any laughs—we've forgotten that, Martin contends. "The total expression of every thought is not desirable," she says. "People are killing each other in the streets over insults and dissin'."

The most chilling side of this mean streak is coming straight from the mouths of soldiers and college students and children. Left to their own devices, without the benefit of network scripts or the restrictions of government censors, they create ballads rife with cruelty and brutality. Sailors at the U.S. Naval Academy march to sadomasochistic tunes that feature sex with corpses and "bitches" cut in half by chain saws. This is one current favorite: "My girl ain't got no eyes/Just two sockets full o' flies/Sometimes I even play a joke/Pull the plugs and watch her choke."

In 1992, a UCLA fraternity made headlines with songs celebrating the mutilation of women with such props as cheese graters and hot oil. The frat members apparently didn't believe they had anything to hide: They published the lyrics inside an otherwise informational orientation manual.

And on the schoolyards of Los Angeles, third-graders can be heard singing ditties like this (to the tune of "This Land Is Your Land"): "This land is my land, it isn't your land/I've got a shotgun, and you don't got one/ I'll blow your head off, if you don't get off/This land is private pro-per-ty."

Hostility and Derision

Hostility has always been an engine of humor. At the turn of the century, Sigmund Freud wrote that hostile jokes, like obscene humor, give humans an outlet for a natural emotion that civilized society otherwise forces them to repress. As Americans, we laughed when Moe pulled Larry's hair and told him to "sha-a-a-t up!" or when Abbott smacked Costello upside the head for issuing a dumb wisecrack.

Hollywood's toughest acts were packaged as working-class humor (as if, somehow, the upper classes were too refined to get angry). In Jackie Gleason's *The Honeymooners*, Ralph looks ready to slam his fist into his wife's jaw when he slugs his hand and boils, "One of these days, Alice, one of these days . . . pow!"

Archie Bunker unleashed his ridicule not only on his wife, his daughter and his "meathead" son-in-law but also on "coloreds," Jews and anyone else who wasn't a white working-class Protestant like himself.

Ralph Kramden's anger bubbled out of the frustrations of his daily life as a bus driver bored with his life and struggling to make ends meet. Gleason, who created the series, made it clear that he intended the Kramdens' bickering to take place within the context of love, and it did: "Baby, you're the greatest!" he'd say with a bearhug. Audiences saw how the extremes of Ralph's personality got him into trouble, and they laughed at him, not his targets. Similarly, Archie's insults and racism sprang from working-class frustrations, but, by surrounding him with more tolerant family members, *All in the Family*'s writers turned his views—not his victims—into objects of derision.

Today's Barbarism

The barbarism burgeoning across this country has been propagated by the culture of whites, and I do *not* mean slavery. That is long gone. What are not gone are movies, television, talk radio, books, magazines, music, art—yes, art—propagating juvenility, irresponsibility, loudness, corrupt language, sexual prowess, physical brutality, and pornography and leading to a widespread decay not only of "values" and of standards of behavior but of imagination.

John Lukacs, *Chronicles*, September 1994.

Most of today's humor and song doesn't reveal any ironic truths about the perpetrator (just as violence in film long ago ceased to comment on the nature of violence). "It's nastier and more personal. And there's very little wit in a lot of this, it's just dumbed-out and gross," complains Michael Medved, author of the 1992 book *Hollywood vs. America*.

The University of Alabama's Bryant first noticed a turning point in American humor in the mid-1970s, when, as a young faculty member at the University of Massachusetts, he saw the "Mr. Bill" skit on *Saturday Night Live*. Mr. Bill was a clay doll whose sole purpose was to be abused—his face pounded, his limbs torn—while audiences roared. "I thought, 'What in the world have we unleashed here?'" recalls Bryant. "There was no cognitive complexity. All you saw was cruelty." Fifteen years later, American audiences have become so inured to cruelty, physical or verbal, that we laugh when the Joker electrocutes his victims in *Batman*, and we actually buy the line that the "Terminator" is being compassionate when he shoots his victims in the knees instead of killing them.

When Don Rickles burst onto the national comedy scene in the '60s, lampooning Frank Sinatra and other revered celebrities, his act was new—and shocking. Two decades later, when New York's satiric *Spy* magazine first appeared, calling Donald Trump a "short-fingered vulgarian," it, too, was new and shocking, an arrival of much-needed irreverence toward the rich and powerful. But insult humor has a short shelf life; the shock wears off and audiences grow numb—*habituated* is the word researchers use. The purveyors of the satire can respond by adding more dimension to the humor, as *Spy* has done, or they can scream louder, pushing the boundaries of propriety even further, as most of Rickles' comedic heirs have.

Loving Hate

It's not hard to figure out what will push buttons in contemporary audiences. Marki Costello isn't a sociologist or marketing executive, but she probably knows this country as well as any of them: One of the game-show world's most prized talent scouts, she interviews potential contestants, thousands of them a year, for *That's Amore* and, before that, for dating-game shows such as *Love Connection*. At 26, Costello knows people. She learned the business at the knee of her late mother, who did the same job for game shows in a previous era, and she's the granddaughter of comedian Lou Costello. Costello's conclusion about contemporary culture: "I am convinced that America is dying to love to hate. We thrive off other people's gossip and misery. Humor today makes people laugh because it's shocking. When my grandpa did it, it was clever, it was thought out."

Married . . . With Children co-creator Michael Moye tackles the question from a different angle. He sees his shows as an antidote to the overweening and unreal "niceness" of sitcoms like *The Cosby Show*. "Personally," Moye says of *Cosby*, "I never lived like that or saw people who could work so hard and look so good. We thought, 'There has to be something out there for the rest of us.' So we did the dark side of the American family."

Irony and irreverence are particularly appealing to an under-40 audience weaned on *Saturday Night Live* and *Mad* magazine, as *Newsweek* media writer Jonathan Alter notes. The motto hanging in the office of one producer sums up a feeling that is widespread among younger TV writers: "No messages, no hugs."

People draw their own lines between funny and offensive. Moye, for example, calls Howard Stern's radio show "the oinking of a pig" but gives his own show longer rope because the put-downs are directed at fictional characters. Others, such as *That's Amore*'s [host] Luca Barbareschi, forgive brutal candor when it is done humorously—as it is on his show—rather than being offered up as some kind of serious social commentary on voyeuristic talk shows. That's actually a line that most of us draw without knowing it: Bryant's studies have found that audiences will even laugh at images of sexual violence when they are presented as comedy.

Rage and Separatism

That insults and cruelty are thriving in popular culture today isn't surprising. Conditions have converged to produce a climate in which this virus multiplies: There are more channels of communication today, and all the information coming through those channels is "more frank, more explicit" than ever before, says Daniel Linz, associate professor of communications at the University of California at Santa Barbara.

And popular culture is tapping a wellspring in modern society that many social observers say is brimming with rage. "During the election, reporters would write about 'voter anger' as if that was somehow separate from culture," says Mark Crispin Miller, professor of media studies at Johns Hopkins University and author of the book *Boxed In*. "But the rage is global. Everywhere you look, there is a very striking separatism going on. People are receding into their ethnic or sexual peer groups. There is an anti-cosmopolitan, antisocial movement." In Europe, neo-Nazis are on the rise, and ethnic strife is tearing the Balkans apart.

In Los Angeles County, hate crimes have tripled in the last four years. Gays, especially, are being targeted for violence throughout the country. Anti-gay ballot initiatives in three states in 1992 unleashed a torrent of gay-bashing, from threatening calls and hate mail to the firebomb killing of a gay man and lesbian in Salem, Ore.

That hatefulness seeped into the 1992 presidential campaign, when [Republican] candidate Pat Buchanan called on his audience to "take back our country" from gays and blacks and "radical feminists" like Hillary Rodham Clinton. Commentators called Buchanan's tirade the meanest prime-time political speech in American history. . . .

What the Media Reflect

To look at the relationships between society's emotional state and the way pop culture reflects it is to walk into a hall of mirrors. Even while acknowledging that pop culture reflects society, researchers also accuse image crafters and tastemakers of intensifying those raw feelings. As Miller puts it, "We are so embedded in the media spectacle that we can no longer say the media simply reflect something. They reflect a reality that they have altered." Contemporary TV and movie plots, Miller and others argue, often encourage audiences to relate to the meanness and violence rather than be frightened or repelled by it. A commonly cited example is *Silence of the Lambs:* During the film's ending—not a part of the book—audiences root for serial murderer Hannibal Lecter when he turns his lethal sights on a particularly obnoxious functionary. [A recent] crop of movies—*The Player, Glengarry Glen Ross, Unforgiven* and *Reservoir Dogs,* among them—writes *Newsday* film critic Jack Mathews, was especially rife with "loathsome male protagonists."

Increasingly, Miller argues, even advertisers—historically known for excessive sentimentality—are sneaking in appeals to rudeness and selfishness, using characters such as children who don't have to share their candy bars or women who see their beauty and thinness as life's best revenge.

Most well-documented are the links between what children see on television and what they do. It is widely accepted among those who study children and psychology that exposure to TV violence can promote aggressive behavior in young people, particularly if a child's family or neighborhood doesn't sufficiently counteract the influence. That conclusion is based on hundreds of studies, including a 1972 surgeon general's report. . . .

Experts suspect, then, that it will make some difference that in 1988, children watched a whopping 28 violent acts per hour on their cartoons. And now they can participate in the on-screen violence: In the Supernintendo video game "Final Fight," players use every means at their disposal to kill the video opponents on the screen. If a punch doesn't work, stab him with a knife. In a *Simpsons* video-arcade game, the player gets to watch the opponent crumble to the ground and die.

Outlets for Natural Emotions

All of this raises a question that researchers have yet to fully answer: Is it easier to pull the trigger or throw a fist at someone who has already been demonized, or at least dehumanized, in song or humor? Are children more likely to pick on each other or ignore their parents or tell their teachers to shove it if they see that kind of behavior on TV? Researchers can only speculate. Says Leonard Eron, professor emeritus of psychology at the University of Illinois: "The kind of humor that continually denigrates certain parts of the population can't help but build an attitude that it's OK.". . .

Before the cycle escalates further, we might do well to consider the advice of Roman statesman and orator Cicero, who wrote at the peak of the Roman empire: "If we are forced, at every hour, to watch or listen to horrible events, this constant stream of ghastly impressions will deprive even the most delicate among us of all respect for humanity."

"Is popular culture good for America? Of course it is. . . . Americans have always felt they have had something special to offer."

The Bright Side of Popular Culture

The American Enterprise

The following viewpoint is an excerpt from an *American Enterprise* special report on a March 10, 1992, conference titled "The New Global Popular Culture: Is It American? Is It Good for America? Is It Good for the World?" Sponsored by the American Enterprise Institute for Public Policy Research (AEI) in Washington, D.C., the conference featured forty panelists, including Berkeley sociologist Todd Gitlin, *Time* essayist Pico Iyer, *American Enterprise* editor Karlyn Keene, Harvard international relations professor Joseph Nye, University of Salzburg history professor Reinhold Wagnleitner, and AEI senior fellow Ben Wattenberg, who agree that American pop culture is good for America and desired by much of the world—signs that America is not in decline.

As you read, consider the following questions:

1. In Gitlin's opinion, why has American popular culture succeeded internationally?
2. What values are frequently conveyed in American films, according to Wattenberg?
3. According to Nye, what is "soft power" and American pop culture's relationship to it?

Gitlin: American popular culture is the closest approximation there is today to a global lingua franca, drawing especially the urban and urbane classes of most nations into a federated culture zone. American popular culture is the latest in a long succession of bidders for global unification. It succeeded Roman culture with its Latin language, imposed by the empire and the Catholic Church, and the so-called Marxism-Leninism of the thankfully just-ended 90 percent of the twentieth century.

Thanks to multinational corporations, Charles Bronson, Clint Eastwood, Arnold Schwarzenegger, and the multicolor chorus of Coca-Cola are the icons of the latest in one-world ideology, or better, global semiculture.

The emergence of a global semiculture coexists with local cultures and sensibilities more than it replaces them. As the Norwegian researcher Helge Rønning suggests, it's plausible to suppose that global, largely American, popular culture has become, or is in the process of becoming, everyone's second culture. It activates a certain bilingualism.

Why does American popular culture succeed? Economies of scale are a part of the explanation. The United States can simply undersell other suppliers. But no one is forcing the Danes to watch *Dallas* at gunpoint. The dominance of American popular culture is a soft dominance—in a certain sense, a collaboration.

American popular culture, as British researcher Jeremy Tunstall has argued, has been driven by a single overriding purpose: to entertain. For this reason, economies of scale aside, it is easy to see why American goods have outdone the competition—British goods were developed in large part for high-culture elevation, Soviet goods for didactic purposes.

By the time the commercial work that comes out of Hollywood, Nashville, or New York leaves our shores, American popular culture has been "pretested" by a heterogeneous public—a very large international market, in a sense, because it contains elements of foreign tastes. No competitor from the monocultures of Europe and Asia can make that claim.

A Global Success

Wagnleitner: The global success of U.S. culture is one of the important chapters in the history of the twentieth century. In Europe, from which I come, the Americanization of culture was not a byproduct of the political, military, and economic success of the United States in Cold War Europe but was actually at the center of that process. In a Europe that had been devastated, the United States became synonymous with modernity. After two bouts of European self-annihilation and self-imposed cultural ruin, it seemed that the United States had a corner on the codes of modernity.

Whatever the content and meaning of the original products of the cultural industry of the United States, for European and other youngsters American popular culture by definition always contained a strong element of protest against traditions, customs, and habits. It is the rebellious idea behind American popular culture that is so attractive. The European teenage world soon became American—but, after all, it had been an American invention. Still, the products of U.S. culture did not penetrate foreign countries automatically. The global success story has another dimension, namely, the direct and indirect support these cultural exports received from the government of the United States. This was not a secondary product of the general political, military, and economic strategy, but an important, if not the most important, means of establishing a Pax Americana.

The Appeal of American Culture

One aspect of the attractiveness of American culture to the peoples of this planet is that they can see and hear themselves in it. From Luciano Pavarotti to Wynton Marsalis, from Olympia Dukakis to Paula Abdul, our American culture is the bone and blood of the songs and sagas and dances and dramas of every people on earth. And through our paperbacks and videocassettes, we are bringing people around the world a distant but familiar echo of the music that was played at their great-grandparents' weddings and the stories that were handed down in their own homes from generation to generation.

Joseph Duffey, *The American Enterprise*, May/June 1992.

An analysis of the staggering amount of information that flows through the one-way channels of the U.S. media leads to the conclusion that we are dealing with U.S. cultural imperialism. Yet U.S. cultural imperialism acted as a welcome antidote to the imperialism of German national socialism, Austrian fascism, and Japanese militarism. The congruent anticommunist values shared between the United States occupation forces and the majorities of the liberated allows no other conclusion than that we are dealing with a classic case of self-colonization.

In 1987, 79 percent of all worldwide film and television exports originated in the United States; in 1991, European TV productions accounted for just 20,000 hours of the total 125,000 hours of airtime of all European TV stations. About three-quarters of all computer programs in the world operate by English commands.

Yet, the term Americanization represses and hides more than it explains. The development of the instant culture of the mod-

ern world has much less to do with the propagation of the supposed national characteristics of those people who live in the
United States than with the further development of the system
of capitalism. The cipher "Americanization" describes, then, the
development of a consumption-oriented social order within capitalist societies. . . .

The Best Pop Culture

Iyer: Pop culture makes the world go 'round, and America
makes the best pop culture. By now, indeed, such products represent the largest single source of America's export earnings,
even as America remains the single most popular destination for
immigrant visas. The more straitened or shut off a culture, the
more urgent its hunger for all the qualities it associates with
America: freedom and wealth and modernity.

Nowadays, though, the world that we grew up in is turning on
a carousel of dimes, and America may be coming to be seen as
increasingly redundant. Now that communism is disintegrating,
the allure of capitalism may begin to dissipate. There is a genuine sense in many parts of the world that the disciplined efficiency of a unified Europe and of the new East Asian powers
may leave America behind: the largest debtor nation in the
world, where 43 percent of all blacks are born into poverty,
seems an unlikely model for emulation. And yet, America's hold
on imaginations will remain secure.

In the cultural realm, the emphasis in the New World Order
will still fall squarely on "New World." The British make better
music, the Japanese are far ahead in technology, the Europeans
have a stronger and more self-conscious sense of their aesthetic
heritage, yet in the world of songs, movies, and images, America is still, and long will be, the Great Communicator. The capital of the world, as Gore Vidal often says, is not Washington but
Hollywood. And however much America suffers an internal loss
of faith, it will continue to enjoy some of the immunity that at-
taches to all things in the realm of myth: much as we—and everyone else—assume that the French make the best perfumes,
and the Swiss the finest watches, the suspicion will continue
that Americans make the best dreams.

The likely dominance of American culture is best borne out
by the Japanese example. As more and more of the world is being bought and taken over by the Japanese, the outlines of a
Japanese Empire are increasingly in evidence, not just in the
new Japanese colonies such as Australia's Gold Coast, Hawaii,
and [Paris's] Champs Élysées—where prices are quoted in yen
and shopgirls speak Japanese—but even in more far-reaching
fashion. Sushi and karaoke are universally understood. But the
Japanese belief that they are different from the world—or even

superior to it—tends to distance them from the outposts of their empire in a way that could never happen with the Pax Americana (for America is the world, a heterogeneous collection of all its scattered parts). . . .

American Appeal

America has become more or less a shorthand for everything that is young and contemporary. America has created so much that is regarded as promising and up-to-date that everything that's promising and up-to-date is taken to be American, even if it's Nintendo. It's less a transmission of American values than American marketing strategies, skills, and reputation. I grew up in Oxford, England, and in that great cathedral of orthodoxy and learning, we were raised on the *Beverly Hillbillies*, Jack Kerouac, and The Grateful Dead. We consumed them because U.S. television programs were better crafted than their British equivalents. Kerouac seemed much more dynamic than the British novelists in the 1950s. . . .

Nye: Market responses are a reality test, and markets show that American popular culture embodied in products and communications does have widespread appeal. Nicaraguan television played American shows even while the government fought American-backed guerrillas. Similarly, Soviet teenagers wore blue jeans and sought American recordings during the Cold War. Young Japanese who have never been to the United States wear sport jackets with the names of American colleges.

Japanese consumer products and cuisine have recently become increasingly fashionable on a global scale. They also pass the market test, but they seem less associated with an implicit appeal to a broader set of values than in the case of American domination of popular communication. In part, this may reflect the inward orientation of Japanese culture. While Japan has been extraordinarily successful at accepting foreign technology, it has been far more reluctant to accept foreigners.

Americans can be parochial and inward-oriented, too, but the ethnic openness of American culture and the political appeal of American values of democracy and human rights are a source of international influence that European nations possess to a lesser degree and communist societies have totally lost. . . .

Values as Film Themes

Wattenberg: There is indeed some violence, sex, and obscenity in American popular culture. But who says that is not part of America? More important, however, generally accepted American values are also at work: upward mobility in *Working Girl;* the fight against the establishment in *Beverly Hills Cop, Dirty Harry,* and *Thelma and Louise;* pluralism in *Driving Miss Daisy,*

Jungle Fever, and *Grand Canyon;* populism in *Rocky;* patriotism in *Top Gun;* technology in *E.T.* and *Back to the Future;* individualism in *Dances with Wolves, Home Alone,* and *Tootsie.* It would be exceptionally hard to eliminate American exceptionalism from American entertainment. And it won't happen. . . .

Influence Abroad

In 1976, South Africa introduced television. That was very late for a country as technically advanced as it is. The government had been keeping it out for a very good reason: they didn't want the country to be invaded by modern ideas. I arrived there ten years afterward. Their leading television show was *The Cosby Show,* their leading movie star was Eddie Murphy. I said to myself, "Something's got to give," and indeed, it finally did. The introduction of our popular culture, with all its vulgarity, had more influence than our trade embargo.

Richard Grenier, *The American Enterprise,* May/June 1992.

Keene: If American culture is corrupting us, I would expect some evidence of that to show up in survey data. If *Married . . . With Children* mocks the institution of marriage and family, why is it that 78 percent of high school seniors in a recent poll say that having a good marriage is extremely important to them, that 68 percent say they and their friends are working hard, and that a majority say that they regularly go to church? Only about a quarter say they or their friends have ever been sent to the principal's office.

If *Studs* glorifies premarital sex, why is it that 86 percent of young people say that premarital sex for teens is always or almost always wrong? And finally, if a movie like *The Doors* glorifies drug use, why is it that only a quarter of young people today, in contrast to a near-majority of my generation in the late 1960s, say that marijuana should be legalized?

Core values have persisted, and survey data provide us ample evidence of that. . . .

Good for America

Wattenberg: Is popular culture good for America? Of course it is, if we want to accomplish what we want to accomplish. Americans have always felt they have had something special to offer—not impose. The American missionary idea is as old as [American colonial governor] John Winthrop's City on a Hill and as recent as Ronald Reagan's [election] landslides.

During the Cold War, we spent trillions to ensure that the

world would be user-friendly to American values. That was our foreign policy. Of necessity, it had to be waged with an emphasis on defense.

With the end of the Cold War, the focus has shifted. American values are flourishing; we are on the offensive. But the frontline activity may now be in movie theaters and on television all over the world, in the pages of *Reader's Digest*, on CNN, on MTV. The influence is so pervasive that many are asking, "Is the world Americanizing?"

What is Americanization? We talk about democracy and markets. But those ideas come from something earlier, from that constellation of ideas, views, and values that travel under the flag of individualism. There are those of us who believe that American-style individualism is the most revolutionary force in the world, that it is driving both politics and economics.

I cannot tell you how long this remarkable moment will last. I can offer only my intuition—it won't last forever, it's not ending now, but the end can come quickly. So, let's make hay while the sun shines.

If popular culture is the principal instrument for the dissemination of American ideas, so be it. But it's not just popular culture. If we want to be influential, we ought to pay more attention to other ways our ideas spread: immigration, language, tourism, education, commerce, and international broadcasting, to begin a long list. . . .

Soft Power

Nye: In a post–Cold War period, we're going to find that the traditional ways of using power and military force remain important but not sufficient. There are more and more issues that you can't solve that way. In that sense, a nation's cultural and ideological appeal are going to be critical to getting others to want the things you want.

You can threaten to take away the car keys if your kids use drugs. It's much better if you have programmed them earlier not to want to use drugs. Soft power is the ability to get others to want the same kinds of things you want.

For better or worse—I think for better—the United States has done that. We have a very broad popular culture, and when I use the term popular culture, I mean everything from McDonald's to Harvard. Fifty percent of the people in this country go on to higher education. That makes it part of the popular culture.

I was in Moscow recently and went into McDonald's. What I found, in a society beset by lines, was that at McDonald's you could get what you wanted immediately. Further, in a society for which cleanliness has not been a prime value, somebody was scrubbing the floor at McDonald's constantly. . . .

The question we ought to ask ourselves is to distinguish between what you might call the formal message and the subliminal message of many of these cultural artifacts that we're sending abroad.

You can become an American very quickly. Twenty percent of the students at Harvard are Asian-American. You can come to this country and do amazing things in a very short period of time. Compare that to Japan, which everybody is so concerned about now. Japan is a very narrow, inward-oriented culture—great consumer products, but great resistance to foreigners. It's a lot harder to try to be Japanese than to try to be American.

The openness that we convey in our popular culture serves our interests. It's not just a Cold War phenomenon. Let's not be quite so elitist about the subliminal effects of popular culture. . . .

Wattenberg: Is it good for the world? I think so, but the world-niks will have to decide for themselves. More than at any time in history, people have a choice.

Many reasons are offered for American cultural dominance. Our technical virtuosity is supreme. Our industry has economies of scale that make it efficient. English is the universal language. Americans have a universal demography. European filmmakers will tell you that only Americans know how to tell a story. (That from the soil that nurtured Shakespeare and Victor Hugo!)

All true. But did those factors just happen to come together? Not likely. People everywhere want to share the American experience, to take a bite of the apple of individualism. And that is why America is not in decline. Over the centuries, great global powers have been great because they have influenced the world. America belongs to a select group of cultures that have forever transformed the world. We ought to pay more attention to the idea of a New World Order because people everywhere are interested in buying into what's happened in the new world.

Periodical Bibliography

The following articles have been selected to supplement the diverse views presented in this chapter.

Gary L. Bauer
"What Went Wrong with Our Country?" *The American Legion Magazine*, July 1994.

William J. Bennett
"Quantifying America's Decline," *The Wall Street Journal*, March 15, 1993.

Carl Bernstein
"The Idiot Culture," *The New Republic*, June 8, 1992.

The CQ Researcher
"Downward Mobility: What Happened to the American Dream?" July 23, 1993. Available from 1414 22nd St. NW, Washington, DC 20037.

George Garrett
"When Lorena Bobbitt Comes Bob-Bob-Bobbing Along: The Sorry State of Popular Culture," *Chronicles*, April 1994. Available from PO Box 800, Mount Morris, IL 61054.

Sandy Garrett
"Yes, Our Schools Can Teach Character," *Vital Speeches of the Day*, October 15, 1994.

Joseph T. Gorman
"The American Dream: From Rhetoric to Reality," *Vital Speeches of the Day*, May 1, 1993.

Jay Mathews
"Study Sees Threat to Baby Boomer Living Standards," *The Washington Post*, April 15, 1994.

Jon Meacham
"Is Little Rock Corrupting Washington? C'mon," *The Washington Monthly*, May 1994.

National Forum
Special issue on popular culture. Fall 1994. Available from PO Box 16000, Louisiana State University, Baton Rouge, LA 70893.

Robert J. Samuelson
"How Our American Dream Unraveled," *Newsweek*, March 2, 1992.

Paul Solman
"Great Expectations," *Mother Jones*, March/April 1994.

U.S. Catholic and James DiGiacomo
"Sharing the Faith: Helping Young People to Lead Moral Lives," February 1994.

The Wilson Quarterly
Special section on television and American culture. Autumn 1993.

Elizabeth Wurtzel
"Will I Ever Be Happy?" *Mademoiselle*, January 1994.

Alexandra York
"The State of the Culture," *Vital Speeches of the Day*, May 1, 1993.

How Important Are
Family Values?

AMERICAN
VALUES

Chapter Preface

Family values seem to be a daily topic of debate in the media and among politicians and others. While such discussions encompass a variety of issues and problems important to families—education, illegitimacy, morality, sexual behavior, welfare, and work, to name several—they often boil down to the advantages of two-parent families and whether single parents, stepparents, or unmarried partners can raise children adequately.

Culturally, the traditional family has been recognized as a household of husband, wife, and children. Fathers are predominantly the breadwinners, mothers may or may not work outside the home, and both play active roles in raising children. According to many family-values advocates, children can best thrive in this family structure, amidst love and security. According to Robert H. Knight Jr., a director at the Family Research Council, "There's a wealth of data that shows that the mom-and-dad household is more stable and excels in every measurable social category [including] the accomplishment of the children reared."

Others, however, are quick to argue that alternatives to traditional families—whether single-parent families, nonmarried cohabiting adults, or families headed by same-sex couples—are equally successful in raising children in a safe and loving environment. In the words of Colorado representative Patricia Schroeder, "I applaud the diversity of families. That haven—that place of protection and nurturance and loyalty: that's the foundation . . . whether there are two parents or one."

The welfare of children—whether they live under a traditional or nontraditional family structure—is a main concern of the authors in this chapter as they debate family values.

173

"Sadly, there are few high-profile happy, healthy marriages that can be held up to convince others that this is a lifestyle . . . valuable enough to preserve."

Family Values Should Be the Focus of Attention

Cal Thomas

According to many Americans, the concept of the traditional two-parent family is under siege. In the following viewpoint, Cal Thomas agrees and contends that abortion, divorce, homosexuality, out-of-wedlock births, and a lack of traditional values have combined to erode the foundations of marriage and family. Thomas asserts that former vice president Dan Quayle was correct in 1992 when he praised family values and criticized single-parent families and lack of personal responsibility in society. Thomas maintains that most Americans agree with Quayle that a good marriage improves the odds of having happy, well-adjusted children. Thomas is a syndicated columnist and the author of *The Things That Matter Most*, from which this viewpoint is excerpted.

As you read, consider the following questions:

1. According to Paul Johnson, quoted by the author, what is extraordinary about the revival of marriage?
2. How does Thomas define the two camps in the debate over families and family values?
3. What impact does selfishness have on rights and justice, in Thomas's opinion?

Marriage has taken a beating in the last thirty years. Even *Woman's Day*, once considered a magazine for "homemakers," has published a "marriage contract" that couples can sign before the wedding. It's the type of do-it-yourself prenuptial agreement that offers couples the opportunity to jettison one another if things "don't work out."

"No-fault" divorces, lesbian and gay "marriages," adoption of children by homosexual couples—along with the daily pressures on married life brought on by double-wage earning and decline in cultural support for matrimony—have brought marriages once thought to be made in heaven to the edge of hell, where they are easily torn apart.

Marriage: Nothing Nobler

For three thousand years, marriage was considered one of humanity's most civilized rituals and institutions. In *The Odyssey*, Homer articulated a belief about marriage that was widely shared, if not always practiced, by most civilized human beings: "There is nothing nobler or more admirable than when two people who see eye-to-eye keep house as man and wife, confounding their enemies and delighting their friends."

Until recently, marriage was largely thought of as a noble relationship, not an "institution"—the word used with such glee by comedians. Lately, though, the general cynicism that dilutes and corrupts nearly everything it touches has spoiled even the idea of marriage for many.

Writing in the September 20, 1993, issue of *Time* magazine, essayist Barbara Ehrenreich uses the breakup of the supposedly "picture-perfect" marriage of actors Burt Reynolds and Loni Anderson to say that we expect too much from marriage and ought to revise the system and our expectations of it.

"To put the whole thing in an anthropological perspective," she writes, "what we lack is not 'values' but old-fashioned neighborhood or community. Once people found companionship among their old high school buddies and got help with child raising from granddads and aunts. Marriages lasted because less was expected of them. If you wanted a bridge partner or plumber or confidant, you had a whole village to choose from. Today we don't marry a person—i.e., a flawed and limited human being—we attempt to marry a village."

So far, a pretty fair analysis of how marriage has evolved. But Ehrenreich goes on to offer a perplexing remedy: "The solution is to have separate 'marriages' for separate types of marital functions. For example, a gay man of my acquaintance has entered into a co-parenting arrangement with two lesbian women. He will be a father to their collective child without any expectations that he will be a lover to the child's mothers or, for that matter, a jogging companion or co-mortgage holder. Child raising, in other words, has cleanly been separated from the turbulent realm of sex, which can only be good for the child. Or consider my relationship with the plumber. He dashes over loyally whenever a pipe bursts, but there is no expectation of sex or profound emotional sharing. Consequently, ours is a 'marriage' that works."

A New Dawn for Marriage

Contrary to Barbara Ehrenreich's view, for many there remains something purposeful and energizing about marriage. Writing in the May 15, 1993, issue of the British magazine *The Spectator*, Paul Johnson sees the first light of a new dawn in which marriage may again be affirmed and widely practiced and preserved. Part of that reason, he notes, is the "hard knocks" marriage has recently sustained.

ALL THE IDLE WEEDS THAT GROW... —SHAKESPEARE

Ramirez/Copley News Service. Used with permission.

"First," says Johnson, "there has been that grotesque and hostile parody of marriage which has been enacted in a Manhattan courtroom, as Mia Farrow and Woody Allen, each flanked by platoons of lawyers, shrinks, and counselors, and watched by strings of wide-eyed, silent, reproachful children, both adopted and (as they say) biological, have hurled accusations of cruelty, incest, betrayal, and madness at each other. The case has at-

176

tracted huge interest even over here: Men and women I know have taken sides, often quite violently. In a way, all the modern age and its secularist, faithless, psychiatrist's values have been on trial in the courtroom, and a disgusted world has pronounced a unanimous verdict: Guilty!"

Sadly, there are few high-profile happy, healthy marriages that can be held up to convince others that this is a lifestyle worth entering into and valuable enough to preserve.

Still, what else is there? Despite its sometime problems, most people would prefer the depth of a marital relationship to the comparative superficiality of living together, living alone, or trying to relate to a pet.

Paul Johnson writes that the "extraordinary thing about this revival of marriage is that it runs directly counter to the whole spirit of the age. All the resources and provisions of the welfare state, the injunctions of political correctness, the weight of academic opinion, the advice of tax accountants, the verdicts of the courts, and the direction of new legislation . . . combine to suggest that marriage today is not merely unnecessary, expensive, evidence of heterosexual triumphalism and homophobia, old-fashioned, reactionary, Thatcherite, and suburban, but legally perilous too."

That marriage may be making a comeback in spite of all these obstacles may be due to the growing realization that while a good marriage cannot *guarantee* happy, socially well-adjusted children, it does increase the odds.

Dan Quayle Revisited

Famous family values advocate Vice President Dan Quayle took a lot of flak for linking successful marriages with successful child rearing in what has become known as the "Murphy Brown Speech." Time has since vindicated him. In an April 1993 *Atlantic* cover story, "Dan Quayle Was Right," writer Barbara Dafoe Whitehead states: "According to a growing body of social-scientific evidence, children in families disrupted by divorce and out-of-wedlock birth do worse than children in intact families on several measures of well-being."

And how does Whitehead define "worse"? Worse in terms of family income. Worse in terms of teenage pregnancies and dropping out of school, drug abuse, and crime. Among Whitehead's findings:

- Children in single-parent families are six times as likely to be poor.
- Children in single-parent families are two to three times as likely as children in two-parent families to have emotional and behavioral problems. They are also more likely to drop out of high school, to get pregnant as teenagers, to abuse

drugs, and to be in trouble with the law.

- The out-of-wedlock birthrate in 1990 was 27 percent—a huge jump from the five percent rate in 1960. Altogether, more than one out of every four women who had a child in 1990 was not married.

As the body of evidence grows that the sixties flower children have sown the seeds that produced a breakdown of the family, we hear only a grudging admission, not the apology that is due the country—and certainly not any suggestion that we should turn back on this road that has led to cultural destruction and take another one leading to healing and restoration.

"Coping" remains the key word. Supermarket checkout magazines continue their fiction of the liberated divorced woman with children. Trouble is, most of these "liberated" women (like ABC's Joan Lunden, who has appeared on several magazine covers in articles about her divorce from her producer-husband) are financially well-off. They do not represent most American women, for whom a drastically reduced income and lifestyle, and often poverty, result from the breakup of their marriages.

Increasingly the tactic of apologists from the sixties generation's "if it feels good, do it" approach is to ask, "What are 'family values'?" and "What is a 'family'?"

Two Views of Family

The debate over families and family values generally finds advocates in two camps. One camp says that a family begins when a man and a woman legally marry. (Families also would include widowed or divorced people and extended families that might be made up of grandparents or guardians. But the beginning of the family could be traced back to the marriage of a man and a woman.)

The other camp says that no one should try to define the family because people disagree on a definition and some might be unfairly excluded.

This latter position is just one example of the virus that has caused America's sickness. We have abandoned a standard for objective truth and the process by which it might be discovered.

The idea that a fixed standard cannot be established because some people might disagree does not apply to weights and measures. Imagine the chaos if every supermarket decided for itself what was a pound, a quart, or a liter, and each one came up with different standards according to its own methods of measuring.

The argument that there should be no fixed standards in the family and moral arenas is unevenly applied by those who make it. Logic tells us that if there is no objective standard for one agenda, there can be none for any other. In fact, the Left has universal standards based on "truths" it considers politically correct: from welfare, to universal health care, to high taxes for "the rich"; from civil rights for all—including homosexuals, whom they consider a bona fide minority—to no censorship for pornography, but censorship for religion.

But the possibility of "standards" or "truths" is conveniently forgotten when the situation warrants.

As the late philosopher Francis Schaeffer wrote in his book *How Should We Then Live?*, "Pragmatism, doing what seems to work without regard to fixed principles of right or wrong, is largely in control. In both international and home affairs, expediency—at any price to maintain personal peace and affluence at the moment—is the accepted procedure. Absolute principles have little or no meaning in the place to which the decline of Western thought has come."

Wrongheaded Thinking

If divorce or abortion or any other behavior can be indulged in without people being held accountable to a standard that society deems in the best interests of everyone, why should anyone be concerned about the rights of others, or justice, or equality? If we are all on a grand evolutionary course (as Darwinists assert), then survival of the fittest becomes our creed, not appeals to things "noble," whatever that may mean.

Following this line of wrongheaded thinking, I can go ahead and abort my child or divorce my wife as long as it makes me "happy," even in the short term (no matter how miserable I or others may be in the long term). That is all that should matter.

The debate in our culture in the nineties is whose values, whose philosophy, whose moral vision for America, and whose idea of "family" will prevail. That is what underlies the talk about "family values." The resolution of that debate will determine whether we will have to apologize to our grandparents for our poor stewardship of the nation we must deliver to our grandchildren.

Another Dan, but the Same Conclusion

Another Dan, Senator Daniel Patrick Moynihan, New York Democrat, said nearly thirty years ago some of the same things that Dan Quayle said in 1992. He, too, challenged a domestic social order that had turned the wreckage of family breakups into a major industry. He, too, argued the crucial importance of stable marriages, especially among the poor.

Senator Moynihan said in the sixties, when he was a young assistant in the Lyndon Johnson administration, "From the wild Irish slums of the nineteenth-century Eastern seaboard to the riot-torn suburbs of Los Angeles, there is one unmistakable lesson in American history: A community that allows a large number of young men to grow up in broken families, dominated by women, never acquiring any set of rational expectations about the future—that community asks for and gets chaos."

Moynihan suffered the most extreme form of criticism. He was called a racist by those who used the word to avoid debate on the substance of his remarks. Moynihan challenged the prevailing view among intellectual and social elites that "Negroes" (as blacks, or African-Americans, were then called) had been so affected by the slavery of their ancestors that they bore a type of mark of Cain which would remain with them forever and that it was incumbent upon white America to pay reparations in the form of government checks to all blacks who are poor—thus ensuring they remain so.

Moynihan was right then and so was Dan Quayle in 1992.

In the aforementioned "Murphy Brown Speech," Dan Quayle hit a raw nerve when he said, "I believe the lawless social anarchy which we saw [in the Los Angeles riots following the state trial of the police officers involved in beating Rodney King] is directly related to the breakdown of family structure, personal responsibility, and social order in too many areas of our society."

Liberals' Misrepresentation

How could anyone argue with this? But many do, because to acknowledge the legitimacy of such a diagnosis would require those who unleashed this plague on the country to take responsibility for it. And if the sixties taught these people anything, it was to avoid responsibility and accountability at all costs. For them, as Rush Limbaugh has commented about President Clinton, the buck doesn't stop here; the buck never gets here at all.

In order to avoid discussing Quayle's conclusions (and those of Daniel Patrick Moynihan, for that matter), many liberals misrepresented his comments. They tried to convince the public that Quayle believed a situation comedy, "Murphy Brown," which seemed to advocate single parenthood, had caused the social fabric to unravel.

Yet Quayle's figures, which were ignored in the reporting and editorializing on his speech, were exactly on target. Since 1965, the fastest-growing segment of the poor has been single mothers and their children under age eighteen. Illegitimacy rates in some poverty areas surpass 80 percent. And with so many single mothers having to "cope" by themselves, children are getting far less supervision—a situation that has had tragic consequences.

The irony is that most Americans remain philosophically in accord with the former vice president's assessment of the problem. Trouble is, they do not set the "American Agenda." The elite does.

"An overemphasis on family issues as the primary problem facing America ignores equally pressing nonfamilial social, economic, and ethical concerns."

Family Values Should Not Be the Focus of Attention

Stephanie Coontz

The troubles many families face are rooted in economic stress, gender inequality, irresponsibility, and selfishness—affecting all types of families—and are not the result of a collapse of the traditional family structure or "family values," Stephanie Coontz argues in the following viewpoint. Coontz maintains that an overemphasis on family values not only ignores these problems but leads to moral scapegoating of nontraditional families. Coontz asserts that the traditional family of the 1950s, extolled by the "family values camp," owed its strengths to socioeconomic and political factors rather than family forms and cultural values. The author concludes that politicians should stop promoting this ideal. Coontz teaches history at Evergreen State College in Olympia, Washington.

As you read, consider the following questions:

1. According to Coontz, what is the primary cause of most poverty?
2. How has restructuring of the economy harmed families, according to Coontz?
3. What economic and political supports does the author believe helped families in the 1950s?

From "The Futility of Preaching Family Values" by Stephanie Coontz. This article appeared in the August 1994 issue and is reprinted with permission from *The World & I*, a publication of The Washington Times Corporation, ©1994.

Despite popular rejection of their "family values" platform during the 1992 election, right-wingers have reason to congratulate themselves on the way their general analysis of family issues has prevailed.

Many liberals and conservatives now agree that "the breakdown of the traditional family" is the source of America's social problems. Groups such as the Progressive Policy Institute, a major Clinton administration think tank, have echoed Dan Quayle's assertion, made in the wake of the Los Angeles riots in 1992, that "marriage is the best antipoverty program." Strengthening parental responsibility, we now hear from all sides, is the key to solving America's ills.

As a family historian, I am extremely skeptical of an analysis that romanticizes "traditional" family forms and gender roles, or focuses on family behaviors to the exclusion of socioeconomic factors. But this does not make me that mythical monster—part moral relativist, part adult-centered hedonist, part blind optimist—that right-wingers love to slay.

In Trouble

Only a fool would deny that families and their values are important. And only a fool would deny that many families are in trouble.

There have been sharp increases in child poverty since 1970. Reversing a twenty-five-year trend, the health and nutrition gaps between poor and nonpoor children have widened. At all income levels, many youngsters need more attention and supervision than they are currently getting. Divorce and single parenthood often have painful consequences for children, and too many parents, married or unmarried, have abandoned their responsibilities.

I'm at least as troubled by the exploitative, dehumanized sex and violence in our culture as the "moral majority" crowd, and arguably *more* disturbed by America's me-first individualism, rampant materialism, and "not-in-my-backyard" parochialism. I favor fostering a stronger sense of personal and social obligation, improving child-support collection, removing marriage penalties in tax and welfare laws, helping parents spend more time with their children, and teaching youngsters resistance skills for sex and drugs. But we cannot help contemporary families if we accept a simplistic analysis of where their problems originate or lay down unrealistic blueprints for how all families should look and act.

According to groups such as the Family Research Council, the underlying cause of America's social ills is the collapse of the "traditional" nuclear family. The fundamental source of this collapse has been our culture's willful abandonment of tried-and-true family forms and values. Family breakup, single parenthood, and latchkey children, in this analysis, result from "life-style choices." The many different reasons that people end up with "nontraditional" families or gender roles are lumped together as the product of their selfish pursuit of personal gratification.

No More Preaching

Should we have no more family-values speeches? Yes. Cut out the preaching about how individuals are to reform themselves, and tell us instead how government is to be reformed. Government has profound effects on the American family, from a tax code that penalizes marriage to a welfare system that subsidizes illegitimacy. Enough about family values; let's hear about family policy.

Charles Krauthammer, *Time*, October 17, 1994.

In turn, the argument goes, such irresponsible individual choices have produced an almost-uniform decline in personal well-being, social stability, and economic security. The causal arrow points firmly in one direction. Deterioration of the family is seen as cause, not result, of poverty, inequality, crime, educational failure, and social alienation. Therefore, the main thrust of social policy should be to reestablish family stability, increase parental investment in children, encourage working mothers to take a few years off while their children are young, and combat "antifamily" trends or influences in our culture. . . .

A Simplistic Argument

The argument that the crux of America's problems is deterioration of the family is emotionally appealing but dangerously simplistic. It ignores the complex interactions between families and other social variables, implying that economic, political, racial, and gender inequities will disappear if we just change our values and tax incentives to reward marriage, full-time motherhood, and teenage chastity. It blames individuals for making bad choices, without considering their changing options. And even aside from its gross disregard of the evidence in counting working mothers as part of a "social problem," it makes unwarranted prejudgments about the strengths and weaknesses of individual families.

At best, an overemphasis on family issues as the primary problem facing America ignores equally pressing nonfamilial social, economic, and ethical concerns. At worst, it leads to moralistic scapegoating of "nontraditional" families. In either case, it limits discussion of moral issues to questions of sexual behavior and family relationships, narrowing our political discourse and decision-making options.

When one's definition of morality centers on opposition to divorce, premarital sex, abortion, and parental irresponsibility, then issues of racial, gender, or economic injustice and political or corporate irresponsibility all too easily disappear. Indeed, the notion of the nuclear family as the primary crucible of commitment can easily shade into an antisocial denial of obligation beyond the family. After all, by many definitions of traditional family morality, Mafia families, which condemn premarital sex, abortion, and divorce and value intergenerational loyalty, would score higher than single-parent families or couples with a working mother.

Family Breakdown and Our Social Ills

Let's turn to some specific claims of those who argue that family breakdown lies behind the major social problems facing America today. Take the example of poverty, so often blamed on divorce and unwed motherhood. It is certainly true that single-parent families are more likely to be poor than two-parent ones, due partly to low wages for women and partly to the decline in real wages that has made it more difficult for one earner, of whatever sex, to support a family. Single-parent families may also fall into poverty after divorce because of unfair property division laws or inadequate enforcement of child-support agreements. These are injustices we can and should correct.

But most poverty, contrary to myth, is caused primarily by our earnings structure, not our family structure. The University of Michigan Panel Study of Income Dynamics, which has followed a representative sample of five thousand families since 1968, found that only one-seventh of the childhood transitions into long-term poverty were associated with family breakup, while more than half were linked to changes in labor market participation or pay. A 1991 census study found that the average family that falls into poverty after the father leaves was already in economic distress before his departure, typically because he had recently lost his job.

Family dissolution, moreover, is often result rather than cause of economic and social stress. Poor parents are twice as likely to divorce as more affluent ones, poor jobless individuals are three times less likely to marry in the first place, and teens who live in areas of high unemployment and inferior social services, regardless of their personal values and intentions, are much more likely to become unwed parents than other teens.

This is not to say that the stresses of single parenthood and family instability do not intensify the effects of poverty, nor that the exceptional individuals who can maintain a stable two-parent family in the absence of a stable community or job will

184

not benefit from doing so. But the fact remains that marriage is no solution to the crisis of child well-being in our country. The United States tolerates higher levels of child poverty in *every* family form than any other major industrial democracy. Most of the growth in poverty during the 1980s, as well as in the recession of the 1990s, has taken place among married-couple families. Meanwhile, other two-parent families have avoided poverty only by abandoning "traditional" family arrangements and sending the wife to work: More than one-third of all two-parent families today would be poor if both parents did not work.

Family Stress and Conflict

The restructuring of the economy since the 1970s has multiplied the stresses facing all families, whatever their forms or values. The export of formerly high-paying jobs, and their later reimport in low-wage, nonbenefit forms, has led to unemployment and underemployment for some families, while the tendency of American businesses to increase overtime rather than jobs in periods of increased production has led to overemployment and a time crunch for others. The fact that some parents cannot adequately support their offspring, while many others do not have time for their children, is often a corporate, not a parental, "life-style choice."

Or what about the impact of single parenthood on the psychological well-being of children? There is no denying that children need more than one caring adult in their lives or that divorce is a potent cause of childhood distress. Why, then, ask "profamily" advocates, can we not simply revive the "cultural consensus" that "on the average, an intact, two-parent family is best"? The problem is that such seemingly innocuous generalizations encourage preconceived notions that a particular intact, two-parent family *does* have a responsible, caring mother and father, and that a particular single-parent or reconstituted family does *not* have alternative strengths.

Behind the averages lie critical variations. Of course, divorced families are more likely to have problems: Families with problems are more likely to end in divorce. But when researchers distinguish between frequently coexisting yet analytically and causally separate factors such as financial loss, prior parental conflict, school relocation, and social prejudices, it is those factors, not single parenthood per se, that correlate most closely with personal dysfunction, crime, and educational failure. According to a recent study, for example, persistent poverty during the first five years of life leaves children with an I.Q. deficit averaging more than nine points, regardless of family structure or maternal education. Children whose parents work out separation agreements that minimize parental conflict and provide for continuity in a child's schooling and social networks have very few academic or psychosocial problems. In many cases, they are better off in the long run than children who stay in homes marked by constant fighting, alcohol or substance abuse, or emotional destructiveness. . . .

Reforms, Not Sermons

Pious sermons about restoring family values, which often stigmatize so many families, will do little to repair a social order that has been criminally slow to respond to families' pressing needs. Instead of exhorting or coercing people to enter or remain in unequal, hostile marriages, those who bemoan family decline should be airing legal, economic and social reforms to serve diverse kinds of families and values that cannot be homogenized.

Judith Stacey, *Insight on the News*, November 29, 1993.

Exaggerating the deficits of single parents may scare some couples into staying married, but it is not much help to the millions of children who are already in one-parent families. What is the "pro-family" solution for people who, for better or worse, are already in such families? Should we press mothers to remarry? If so, we are in a classic double bind: The same studies that are used to make blanket generalizations about divorce reveal that the educational failure rates and personal adjustment problems of children in stepfamilies are much higher than those of children in single-mother homes.

I do not want to minimize the importance of cultural trends, nor to imply that all social problems are caused by poverty or economic stress. Self-centeredness, irresponsibility, and callousness can be found at all income levels. But these problems are not confined to "nontraditional" families. . . .

In the 1950s

For the "family values" camp, though, the decisive change has been the breakdown of the traditional family life that used to hold individualistic tendencies in check. In the 1950s, they argue, stable marriages and devoted parenting fostered personal and social security, national prosperity, and a strong work ethic. We can regain those traits if we reverse our cultural course, reviving the traditional family and its moral precepts.

History does not support this hopeful scenario. In fact, the strengths of the 1950s were due less to that decade's family forms and cultural values than to its unique socioeconomic and political climate. Many "traditional" families of the 1950s were hardly idyllic, as thousands of survivors of alcoholic dysfunction, abuse, battering, or incest can testify. Women and African Americans were denied the most fundamental economic, educational, and legal rights. Low rates of divorce and unwed motherhood did not prevent 30 percent of American children from living in poverty, a higher figure than today's. Married-couple black families had a poverty rate of nearly 50 percent.

Of course, there were harmonious families in the 1950s, as well. It takes nothing away from their achievements to point out that economic and political support systems made it much easier to form and sustain families than it is today. High rates of unionization, heavy corporate investment in manufacturing plants and equipment, and generous government assistance in the form of public works projects, veterans' benefits, student loans, and housing subsidies gave people predictable paths out of poverty and led to unprecedented increases in real wages. By the time the average man reached the age of thirty, in both the 1950s and 1960s, he could pay the principal and interest on a median-priced home with only 15 to 18 percent of his income. (By 1983, it took 40 percent.) . . .

Rapid Social Change

In the social environment of the 1950s, even children from dysfunctional families could succeed. When the children of the supposedly ideal 1950s families reached adulthood in the 1970s, however, they faced quite a different economic and political climate. *It was the children of the stable families formed in the 1950s, the recipients of so much parental time and attention, that pioneered the sharp breaks with traditional family arrangements in the 1970s.* This occurred not because their parents read too much [of child development expert] Dr. Benjamin Spock but because these youths were caught in a historical cross fire from which even the most ideal family could not protect them.

First, rapid social change in the 1960s swept away several old family and gender patterns, including many repressive and hypocritical ones, without firmly establishing a solid new value system or set of family roles. Then this generation was hit by economic reverses and political trends in the 1970s that frustrated and in some cases deformed their attempts to carve out workable new patterns. On top of this came the 1980s, an age of sleaze, greed, and economic insecurity that undermined people's confidence in the point of doing anything other than "taking care of number one."

Major causes of the breakdown in social solidarities over the past two decades lie in the acceleration of economic and social inequality since the early 1970s, and the restructuring of the economy to reward financial speculation and capital gains over hard work and sweat equity. Young Americans have been hardest hit by the fall in real wages that has occurred since 1973; indeed, their real incomes are lower today than in 1967. During the late 1980s, the number of people who worked full time year-round but still remained poor increased by more than 50 percent. While incomes fell for most Americans between 1990 and 1991, and capital investment for public works dropped to less than half its 1960 level, the average top pay of corporate CEOs rose by 26 percent. In Japan, the typical chief executive officer of a corporation earns twenty times as much as his typical worker; in America, the average CEO now earns 160 times as much as the average worker. At the same time, respected religious, legal, and political leaders stripped away older sanctions against the unfettered pursuit of self-interest and profit in the market, assuring us that the only place we need to curtail our appetites is in the family.

The Me-First Mentality

The result of these socioeconomic and cultural trends has been collapse of an older belief (or perhaps illusion) that all of us, whatever our differences in income or social status, share long-term interests and solidarities. This breeds a cynical, "me-first" mentality that is as prevalent on Wall Street and Main Street as on the streets of the inner city, even if its expression is typically less violent. Such cynicism deforms personal relations, including family ones. It extends to two-parent families with homemaker moms as well as to single-parent ones, and it should not be construed primarily as a family failure.

In today's socioeconomic climate, it is a mistake to overestimate what parents can do to hold such cultural trends at bay, or to underestimate the dependence of every family on support networks, economic advantage, or just plain luck. It is especially unfair to blame poor families for failing to inculcate proper values and behaviors, since research shows that impoverished parents have far less influence over their children than parents with more rewards and social status to offer. But *all* parents are losing influence today, as economic and political institutions teach our kids that selfishness and callousness *do* pay, while hard work and deferred gratification do not.

There have been many casualties in the rapid, contradictory transformations of economic, social, and personal life that have occurred over the past twenty-five years. But calling for a revival of "traditional" family forms and values will not heal the wounds. In the long run, it will only multiply the guilt and frustration that families feel when they cannot live up to an ideal that continually collides with reality.

"*The weight of evidence is so decisively on one side of the issue: on the whole, for children, two-parent families are preferable to single-parent and stepfamilies.*"

Traditional Families Are Best

Barbara Dafoe Whitehead

The increasing dissolution of intact two-parent families harms large numbers of children, Barbara Dafoe Whitehead argues in the following viewpoint. Whitehead cites studies by several social scientists who tally the toll from broken families: higher rates of child abuse, drug abuse, emotional and behavioral problems, poverty, pregnancy, and trouble in school and with the law—difficulties that often persist into adulthood and affect future relationships, the author contends. Whitehead concludes from such studies that traditional two-parent families offer more socioeconomic advantages, greater security, and better emotional outcomes for children than their fast-growing alternatives: single-parent and stepparent families. Whitehead is a research associate at the Institute for American Values in New York City.

As you read, consider the following questions:

1. What does Whitehead identify as the string of events in family disruption?
2. How does the author compare stepfamilies and single-parent families?
3. Why do many researchers hesitate to use family structure itself to measure family conditions, according to Whitehead?

Abridged from Barbara Dafoe Whitehead, "Dan Quayle Was Right," *The Atlantic Monthly,* April 1993. Reprinted by permission of the author.

Divorce and out-of-wedlock childbirth are transforming the lives of American children. In the postwar generation more than 80 percent of children grew up in a family with two biological parents who were married to each other. By 1980 only 50 percent could expect to spend their entire childhood in an intact family. If current trends continue, less than half of all children born today will live continuously with their own mother and father throughout childhood. Most American children will spend several years in a single-mother family. Some will eventually live in stepparent families, but because stepfamilies are more likely to break up than intact (by which I mean two-biological-parent) families, an increasing number of children will experience family breakup two or even three times during childhood.

Children in Disrupted Families

According to a growing body of social-scientific evidence, children in families disrupted by divorce and out-of-wedlock birth do worse than children in intact families on several measures of well-being. Children in single-parent families are six times as likely to be poor. They are also likely to stay poor longer. Twenty-two percent of children in one-parent families will experience poverty during childhood for seven years or more, as compared with only two percent of children in two-parent families. A 1988 survey by the National Center for Health Statistics found that children in single-parent families are two to three times as likely as children in two-parent families to have emotional and behavioral problems. They are also more likely to drop out of high school, to get pregnant as teenagers, to abuse drugs, and to be in trouble with the law. Compared with children in intact families, children from disrupted families are at a much higher risk for physical or sexual abuse.

Contrary to popular belief, many children do not "bounce back" after divorce or remarriage. Difficulties that are associated with family breakup often persist into adulthood. Children who grow up in single-parent or stepparent families are less successful as adults, particularly in the two domains of life—love and work—that are most essential to happiness. Needless to say, not all children experience such negative effects. However, research shows that many children from disrupted families have a harder time achieving intimacy in a relationship, forming a stable marriage, or even holding a steady job. . . .

The debate about [family structure] is not simply about the social-scientific evidence, although that is surely an important part of the discussion. It is also a debate over deeply held and often conflicting values. How do we begin to reconcile our long-standing belief in equality and diversity with an impressive body of evidence that suggests that not all family structures produce equal outcomes for children? How can we square traditional notions of public support for dependent women and children with a belief in women's right to pursue autonomy and independence in childbearing and child-rearing? How do we uphold the freedom of adults to pursue individual happiness in their private relationships and at the same time respond to the needs of children for stability, security, and permanence in their family lives? What do we do when the interests of adults and children conflict? These are the difficult issues at stake in the debate over family structure. . . .

Family Disruption at Its Peak

In the 1960s the rate of family disruption suddenly began to rise. After inching up over the course of a century, the divorce rate soared. Throughout the 1950s and early 1960s the divorce rate held steady at fewer than ten divorces a year per 1,000 married couples. Then, beginning in about 1965, the rate increased sharply, peaking at twenty-three divorces per 1,000 marriages by 1979. (In 1974 divorce passed death as the leading cause of family breakup.) The rate has leveled off at about twenty-one divorces per 1,000 marriages—the figure for 1991. The out-of-wedlock birth rate also jumped. It went from 5 percent in 1960 to 27 percent in 1990. In 1990 close to 57 percent of births among black mothers were nonmarital, and about 17 percent among white mothers. Altogether, about one out of every four women who had a child in 1990 was not married. With rates of divorce and nonmarital birth so high, family disruption is at its peak. Never before have so many children experienced family breakup caused by events other than death. Each year a million children go through divorce or separation and almost as many more are born out of wedlock.

Half of all marriages now end in divorce. Following divorce, many people enter new relationships. Some begin living together. Nearly half of all cohabiting couples have children in the household. Fifteen percent have new children together. Many cohabiting couples eventually get married. However, both cohabiting and remarried couples are more likely to break up than couples in first marriages. Even social scientists find it hard to keep pace with the complexity and velocity of such patterns. In the revised edition (1992) of his book *Marriage, Divorce, Remarriage*, the sociologist Andrew Cherlin ruefully comments: "If there were a truth-in-labeling law for books, the title of this edition should be something long and unwieldy like *Cohabitation, Marriage, Divorce, More Cohabitation, and Probably Remarriage*."

Under such conditions growing up can be a turbulent experience. In many single-parent families children must come to terms with the parent's love life and romantic partners. Some

191

children live with cohabiting couples, either their own unmarried parents or a biological parent and a live-in partner. Some children born to cohabiting parents see their parents break up. . . . As it affects a significant number of children, family disruption is best understood not as a single event but as a string of disruptive events: separation, divorce, life in a single-parent family, life with a parent and live-in lover, the remarriage of one or both parents, life in one stepparent family combined with visits to another stepparent family; the breakup of one or both stepparent families. And so on. This is one reason why public schools have a hard time knowing whom to call in an emergency.

Marriage and Moral Commitments

Building a marriage will pattern positive behavior. This patterned behavior rebuilds in us moral commitments and shapes the personal capital of the future generation. Those with moral commitments are able to build social capital, through which they attain jobs and their own marriages. Producing illegitimate children pours both down the drain.

David W. Murray, *Policy Review*, Spring 1994.

Given its dramatic impact on children's lives, one might reasonably expect that this historic level of family disruption would be viewed with alarm, even regarded as a national crisis. Yet this has not been the case. In recent years some people have argued that these trends pose a serious threat to children and to the nation as a whole, but they are dismissed as declinists, pessimists, or nostalgists, unwilling or unable to accept the new facts of life. The dominant view is that the changes in family structure are, on balance, positive. . . .

There are several reasons why this is so, but the fundamental reason is that at some point in the 1970s Americans changed their minds about the meaning of these disruptive behaviors. What had once been regarded as hostile to children's best interests was now considered essential to adults' happiness. In the 1950s most Americans believed that parents should stay in an unhappy marriage for the sake of the children. The assumption was that a divorce would damage the children, and the prospect of such damage gave divorce its meaning. By the mid-1970s a majority of Americans rejected that view. . . .

The Bad News About Stepparents

Perhaps the most striking, and potentially disturbing, new research has to do with children in stepparent families. Until quite recently the optimistic assumption was that children saw their lives improve when they became part of a stepfamily. When [psychologist] Nicholas Zill and his colleagues began to study the effects of remarriage on children, their working hypothesis was that stepparent families would make up for the shortcomings of the single-parent family. Clearly, most children are better off economically when they are able to share in the income of two adults. When a second adult joins the household, there may be a reduction in the time and work pressures on the single parent.

The research overturns this optimistic assumption, however. In general the evidence suggests that remarriage neither reproduces nor restores the intact family structure, even when it brings more income and a second adult into the household. Quite the contrary. Indeed, children living with stepparents appear to be even more disadvantaged than children living in a stable single-parent family. Other difficulties seem to offset the advantages of extra income and an extra pair of hands. However much our modern sympathies reject the fairy-tale portrait of stepparents, the latest research confirms that the old stories are anthropologically quite accurate. Stepfamilies disrupt established loyalties, create new uncertainties, provoke deep anxieties, and sometimes threaten a child's physical safety as well as emotional security. . . .

Poverty, Crime, and Education

Family disruption would be a serious problem even if it affected only individual children and families. But its impact is far broader. Indeed, it is not an exaggeration to characterize it as a central cause of many of our most vexing social problems. Consider three problems that most Americans believe rank among the nation's pressing concerns: poverty, crime, and declining school performance.

More than half of the increase in child poverty in the 1980s is attributable to changes in family structure, according to David Eggebeen and Daniel Lichter of Pennsylvania State University. In fact, if family structure in the United States had remained relatively constant since 1960, the rate of child poverty would be a third lower than it is today. This does not bode well for the future. With more than half of today's children likely to live in single-parent families, poverty and associated welfare costs threaten to become even heavier burdens on the nation.

Crime in American cities has increased dramatically and grown more violent over recent decades. Much of this can be attributed to the rise in disrupted families. Nationally, more than 70 percent of all juveniles in state reform institutions come from fatherless homes. A number of scholarly studies find that even after the groups of subjects are controlled for income, boys from single-mother homes are significantly more likely than others to commit crimes and to wind up in the juvenile justice, court, and penitentiary systems. One such study summarizes the relationship between crime and one-parent families in this way: "The relationship is so strong that controlling for family configuration erases the relationship between race and crime and between low income and crime. This conclusion shows up time and again in the literature." The nation's mayors, as well as police officers, social workers, probation officers, and court officials, consistently point to family breakup as the most important source of rising rates of crime.

A Vital Institution

Common sense, the lessons of history and the work of anthropologists actually point to the family as a universal and necessary institution. It is commonly defined as a man and a woman bonded together through a socially approved covenant of marriage to regulate sexuality; to provide mutual care and support; to create a home economy; to bear, raise and protect children; and to maintain continuity between the generations.

Allan Carlson, *Insight on the News*, November 29, 1993.

Terrible as poverty and crime are, they tend to be concentrated in inner cities and isolated from the everyday experience of many Americans. The same cannot be said of the problem of declining school performance. Nowhere has the impact of family breakup been more profound or widespread than in the nation's public schools. There is a strong consensus that the schools are failing in their historic mission to prepare every American child to be a good worker and a good citizen. And nearly everyone agrees that the schools must undergo dramatic reform in order to reach that goal. In pursuit of that goal, moreover, we have suffered no shortage of bright ideas or pilot projects or bold experiments in school reform. But there is little evidence that measures such as curricular reform, school-based management, and school choice will address, let alone solve, the biggest problem schools face: the rising number of children who come from disrupted families. . . .

The Two-Parent Advantage

All this evidence gives rise to an obvious conclusion: growing up in an intact two-parent family is an important source of advantage for American children. Though far from perfect as a social institution, the intact family offers children greater security and better outcomes than its fast-growing alternatives: single-parent and stepparent families. Not only does the intact family protect the child from poverty and economic insecurity; it also provides greater noneconomic investments of parental time, attention, and emotional support over the entire life course. This does not mean that all two-parent families are better for children than all single-parent families. But in the face of the evidence it becomes increasingly difficult to sustain the proposition that all family structures produce equally good outcomes for children.

Curiously, many in the research community are hesitant to say that two-parent families generally promote better outcomes for children than single-parent families. Some argue that we need finer measures of the extent of the family-structure effect. As one scholar has noted, it is possible, by disaggregating the data in certain ways, to make family structure "go away" as an independent variable. Other researchers point to studies that show that children suffer psychological effects as a result of family conflict preceding family breakup. Consequently, they reason, it is the conflict rather than the structure of the family that is responsible for many of the problems associated with family disruption. Others, including [clinical psychologist] Judith Wallerstein, caution against treating children in divorced families and children in intact families as separate populations, because doing so tends to exaggerate the differences between the two groups. "We have to take this family by family," Waller-stein says. . . .

However, the case against the two-parent family is remarkably weak. It is true that disaggregating data can make family struc-ture less significant as a factor, just as disaggregating Hurricane Andrew into wind, rain, and tides can make it disappear as a meteorological phenomenon. Nonetheless, research opinion as well as common sense suggests that the effects of changes in family structure are great enough to cause concern. Nicholas Zill argues that many of the risk factors for children are doubled or more than doubled as the result of family disruption. . . .

Constants of Intact Families

There are some useful rules of thumb to guide our thinking about and policies affecting the family. For example, [Princeton sociologist] Sara McLanahan says, three structural constants are commonly associated with intact families, even intact families who would not win any "Family of the Year" awards. The first is economic. In intact families, children share in the income of two adults. Indeed, as a number of analysts have pointed out, the two-parent family is becoming more rather than less neces-sary, because more and more families need two incomes to sustain a middle-class standard of living.

McLanahan believes that most intact families also provide a stable authority structure. Family breakup commonly upsets the established boundaries of authority in a family. Children are often required to make decisions or accept responsibilities once considered the province of parents. Moreover, children, even very young children, are often expected to behave like mature adults, so that the grown-ups in the family can be free to deal with the emotional fallout of the failed relationship. In some instances family disruption creates a complete vacuum in authority; everyone invents his or her own rules. With lines of authority disrupted or absent, children find it much more difficult to engage in the normal kinds of testing behavior, the trial and error, the failing and succeeding, that define the developmental pathway toward character and competence. McLanahan says, "Children need to be the ones to challenge the rules. The parents need to set the boundaries and let the kids push the boundaries. The children shouldn't have to walk the straight and narrow at all times."

Gaining and Losing Partners

Finally, McLanahan holds that children in intact families benefit from stability in what she neutrally terms "household personnel." Family disruption frequently brings new adults into the family, including stepparents, live-in boyfriends or girlfriends, and casual sexual partners. Like stepfathers, boyfriends can present a real threat to children's, particularly to daughters', security and well-being. But physical or sexual abuse represents only the most extreme such threat. Even the very best of boyfriends can disrupt and undermine a child's sense of peace and security, McLanahan says. "It's not as though you're going from an unhappy marriage to peacefulness. There can be a constant changing until the mother finds a suitable partner."

McLanahan's argument helps explain why children of widows tend to do better than children of divorced or unmarried mothers. Widows differ from other single mothers in all three respects. They are economically more secure, because they receive more public assistance through Survivors Insurance, and possibly private insurance or other kinds of support from family members. Thus widows are less likely to leave the neighborhood in search of a new or better job and a cheaper house or apartment. Moreover, the death of a father is not likely to disrupt the authority structure radically. When a father dies, he is no longer physically present, but his death does not dethrone him as an authority figure in the child's life. On the contrary, his authority may be magnified through death. The mother can draw on the powerful memory of the departed father as a way of intensifying her parental authority: "Your father would have wanted it this way." Finally, since widows tend to be older than divorced mothers, their love life may be less distracting.

Decisive Evidence

Regarding the two-parent family, the sociologist David Popenoe, who has devoted much of his career to the study of families, both in the United States and in Scandinavia, makes this straightforward assertion:

> Social science research is almost never conclusive. There are always methodological difficulties and stones left unturned. Yet in three decades of work as a social scientist, I know of few other bodies of data in which the weight of evidence is so decisively on one side of the issue: on the whole, for children, two-parent families are preferable to single-parent and stepfamilies.

"Our marriage wasn't some flaming disaster—with broken dishes and hitting and strange hotel charges . . . on the MasterCard bill. It was just unhappy."

Traditional Families May Not Be Best

Katha Pollitt

In the following viewpoint, Katha Pollitt argues that traditional families are often plagued by unhappiness, lack of love and support, child and spousal abuse, hostility, and other problems. Pollitt contends that because of these problems, many parents choose to separate or divorce to make better lives for themselves and their children. The author maintains that a child has as good a chance to thrive in a single-parent family as in one having two parents. But Pollitt asserts that single parents—often working women—and poor families need economic justice: pay comparable to men's, decent jobs, and social services. Pollitt is an associate editor of the *Nation*, a weekly magazine.

As you read, consider the following questions:

1. According to Pollitt, why are Western European teens less likely than American teens to have babies?
2. On what basis does Pollitt criticize proposals aimed at preventing divorce?
3. How are money problems related to family dissolution and the demise of marriage, according to the author?

From "Why I Hate 'Family Values' (Let Me Count the Ways)," *The Nation*, July 20-27, 1992.

Unlike many of the commentators who have made Murphy Brown the most famous unmarried mother since Ingrid Bergman ran off with Roberto Rossellini, I actually watched the notorious child-birth episode. After reading my sleep-resistant 4-year-old her entire collection of Berenstain Bears books, television was all I was fit for. And that is how I know that I belong to the cultural elite: Not only can I spell "potato" correctly, and many other vegetables as well, I thought the show was a veritable riot of family values. First of all, Murph is smart, warm, playful, decent and rich: She'll be a great mom. Second, the dad is her ex-husband: The kid is as close to legitimate as the scriptwriters could manage, given that Murph is divorced. Third, her ex spurned *her*, not, as Dan Quayle implies, the other way around. Fourth, she rejected abortion. On TV, women have abortions only in docudramas, usually after being raped, drugged with birth-defect-inducing chemicals or put into a coma. Finally, what does Murph sing to the newborn? "You make me feel like a natural woman"! Even on the most feminist sitcom in TV history (if you take points off *Kate and Allie* for never so much as mentioning the word "gay"), anatomy is destiny.

Murphy Brown's Baby and Traditional Families

That a show as fluffy and genial as *Murphy Brown* has touched off a national debate about "family values" speaks volumes—and not just about the apparent inability of Dan Quayle to distinguish real life from a sitcom. (And since when are TV writers part of the cultural elite, anyway? I thought they were the crowd-pleasing lowbrows, and *intellectuals* were the cultural elite.) The *Murphy Brown* debate, it turns out, isn't really about Murphy Brown; it's about inner-city women, who will be encouraged to produce fatherless babies by Murph's example—the trickle-down theory of values. (Do welfare moms watch *Murphy Brown*? I thought it was supposed to be soap operas, as in "they just sit around all day watching the soaps." Marriage is a major obsession on the soaps—but never mind.) Everybody, it seems, understood this substitution immediately. After all, why get upset about Baby Boy Brown? Is there any doubt that he will be safe, loved, well schooled, taken for checkups, taught to respect the rights and feelings of others and treated to *The Berenstain Bears Visit the Dentist* as often as his little heart desires? Unlike millions of kids who live with both parents, he will never be physically or sexually abused, watch his father beat his mother (domestic assault is the leading cause of injury to women) or cower beneath the blankets while his parents scream at each other. And chances are excellent that he won't sexually assault a retarded girl with a miniature baseball bat, like those high school athletes in posh Glen Ridge, New Jersey; or shoot his lover's spouse, like Amy Fisher; or find himself on trial for rape, like William Kennedy Smith—children of intact and prosperous families every one of them. He'll probably go to Harvard and major in semiotics. Maybe that's the problem. Just think, if Murph were married, like Dan Quayle's mom, he could go to DePauw University and major in golf.

Targets of Blame

That there is something called "the family"—Papa Bear, Mama Bear, Brother Bear and Sister Bear—that is the best setting for raising children, and that it is in trouble because of a decline in "values," are bromides accepted by commentators of all political stripes. The right blames a left-wing cultural conspiracy: obscene rock lyrics, sex ed, abortion, prayerless schools, working mothers, promiscuity, homosexuality, decline of respect for authority and hard work, welfare and, of course, feminism. (On the *Chicago Tribune* Op-Ed page, Allan Carlson, president of the ultraconservative Rockford Institute, found a previously overlooked villain: federal housing subsidies. With all that square footage lying around, singles and unhappy spouses could afford to live on their own.) The left blames the ideology of postindustrial capitalism: consumerism, individualism, selfishness, alienation, lack of social supports for parents and children, atrophied communities, welfare and feminism. The center agonizes over teen sex, welfare moms, crime and divorce, unsure what the causes are beyond some sort of moral failure—probably related to feminism. Interesting how that word keeps coming up.

I used to wonder what family values are. As a matter of fact, I still do. If abortion, according to the right, undermines family values, then single motherhood (as the producers of *Murphy Brown* were quick to point out) must be in accord with them, no? No. Over on the left, if gender equality, love and sexual expressivity are desirable features of contemporary marriage, then isn't marriage bound to be unstable, given how hard those things are to achieve and maintain? Not really.

Just say no, says the right. Try counseling, says the left. Don't be so lazy, says the center. Indeed, in its guilt-mongering cover story "Legacy of Divorce: How the Fear of Failure Haunts the Children of Broken Marriages," *Newsweek* was unable to come up with any explanation for the high American divorce rate except that people just didn't try hard enough to stay married.

"The Family" and Its "Values"

When left, right and center agree, watch out. They probably don't know what they're talking about. And so it is with "the family" and "family values." In the first place, these terms lump together distinct social phenomena that in reality have virtually nothing to do with one another. The handful of fortysomething professionals like Murphy Brown who elect to have a child without a male partner have little in common with the millions of middle- and working-class divorced mothers who find themselves in desperate financial straits because their husbands fail to pay court-awarded child support. And neither category has much in common with inner-city girls like those a teacher friend of mine told me about the other day: a 13-year-old and a 12-year-old, impregnated by boyfriends twice their age and determined to bear and keep the babies—to spite abusive parents, to confirm their parents' low opinion of them, to have someone to love who loves them in return.

It's just as well you have a business trip; we could probably all use a break from each other

Gail Machlis/©Chronicle Features. Used with permission.

Beyond that, appeals to "the family" and its "values" frame the discussion as one about morals instead of consequences. In real life, for example, teen sex—the subject of endless sermons—has little relation with teen childbearing. That sounds counterfactual, but it's true. Western European teens have sex about as early and as often as American ones, but are much less likely to have babies. Partly it's because there are far fewer European girls whose lives are as marked by hopelessness and brutality as those of my friend's students. And partly it's because European youth have much better access to sexual information, birth control and abortion. Or consider divorce. In real life, parents divorce for all kinds of reasons, not because they lack moral fiber and are heedless of their children's needs. Indeed, many divorce because they *do* consider their kids, and the poisonous effects of growing up in a household marked by violence, craziness, open verbal warfare or simple lovelessness.

A Separation

Perhaps this is the place to say that I come to the family-values debate with a personal bias. I am separated myself. I think my husband and I would fall under *Newsweek*'s "didn't try harder" rubric, although we thought about splitting up for years, discussed it for almost a whole additional year and consulted no fewer than four therapists, including a marital counselor who advised us that marriage was one of modern mankind's only means of self-transcendence (religion and psychoanalysis were the others, which should have warned me) and admonished us that we risked a future of shallow relationships if we shirked our spiritual mission, not to mention the damage we would "certainly" inflict on our daughter. I thought he was a jackass—shallow relationships? *moi*? But he got to me. Because our marriage wasn't some flaming disaster—with broken dishes and hitting and strange hotel charges showing up on the MasterCard bill. It was just unhappy, in ways that weren't going to change. Still, I think both of us would have been willing to trudge on to spare our child suffering. That's what couples do in women's magazines; that's what the Clintons say they did. But we saw it wouldn't work: As our daughter got older, she would see right through us, the way kids do. And, worse, no matter how hard I tried to put on a happy face, I would wordlessly communicate to her—whose favorite fairy tale is "Cinderella," and whose favorite game is Wedding, complete with bath-towel bridal veil—my resentment and depression and cynicism about relations between the sexes.

The family-values types would doubtless say that my husband and I made a selfish choice, which society should have impeded or even prevented. There's a growing sentiment in policy land to make divorce more difficult. In *When the Bough Breaks*, Sylvia Ann Hewlett argues that couples should be forced into therapy (funny how ready people are to believe that counseling, which even when voluntary takes years to modify garden-variety neuroses, can work wonders in months with resistant patients who hate each other). Christopher Lasch briefly supported a constitutional amendment forbidding divorce to couples with minor children, as if lack of a separation agreement would keep people living together (he's backed off that position, he told me). The Communitarians, who flood *The Nation*'s mailboxes with self-promoting worryfests, furrow their brows wondering "How can the family be saved without forcing women to stay at home or otherwise violating their rights?" (Good luck.) But I am still waiting for someone to explain why it would be better for my daughter to grow up in a joyless household than for her to live as she does now, with two reasonably cheerful parents living around the corner from each other, both committed to her support and cooperating, as they say on *Sesame Street*, in her care. We may not love each other, but we both love her. Maybe that's as much as parents can do for their children, and all that should be asked of them.

Cooperation Is Difficult

But, of course, civilized cooperation is exactly what many divorced parents find they cannot manage. The statistics on deadbeat and vanishing dads are shocking—less than half pay child support promptly and in full, and around half seldom or never see their kids within a few years of marital breakup. Surely, some of this male abdication can be explained by the very thinness of the traditional paternal role worshiped by the preachers of "values"; it's little more than breadwinning, discipline and fishing trips. How many diapers, after all, has Dan Quayle changed? A large percentage of American fathers have never changed a single one. Maybe the reason so many fathers fade away after divorce is that they were never really there to begin with.

It is true that people's ideas about marriage are not what they were in the 1950s—although those who look back at the fifties nostalgically forget both that many of those marriages were miserable and that the fifties were an atypical decade in more than a century of social change. Married women have been moving steadily into the work force since 1890; beginning even earlier, families have been getting smaller; divorce has been rising; sexual activity has been initiated even earlier and marriage delayed; companionate marriage has been increasingly accepted as desirable by all social classes and both sexes. It may be that these trends have reached a tipping point, at which they come to define a new norm. Few men expect to marry virgins, and children are hardly "stigmatized" by divorce, as they might have been a mere fifteen or twenty years ago. But if people want different things from family life—if women, as Arlie Hochschild pointed out in *The Second Shift*, cite as a major reason for separation the failure of their husbands to share domestic labor; if both sexes are less willing to resign themselves to a marriage devoid of sexual pleasure, intimacy or shared goals; if single women decide they want to be mothers; if teenagers want to sleep together—why shouldn't society adapt? Society is, after all, just us. Nor are these developments unique to the United States. All over the industrialized world, divorce rates are high, single women are having babies by choice, homosexuals are coming out of the closet and infidelity, always much more common than anyone wanted to recognize, is on the rise. Indeed, in some ways America is behind the rest of the West: We still go to church, unlike the British, the French and, now that [dictator] Francisco Franco is out of the way, the Spanish. More religious than Spain! Imagine.

Clinton's Mistake

When Bill Clinton says that because of single motherhood "we are raising a whole generation of kids who aren't sure they're the most important person in the world to anybody," he is saying either that single mothers don't love their kids or that single mothers are nobodies. I hope the ghost of Virginia Kelley [Clinton's long-time single mother] gives him the haunting he so richly deserves.

Katha Pollitt, *The Nation*, October 3, 1994.

I'm not saying that these changes are without cost—in poverty, loneliness, insecurity and stress. The reasons for this suffering, however, lie not in moral collapse but in our failure to acknowledge and adjust to changing social relations.

We still act as if mothers stayed home with children, wives didn't need to work and men earned a "family wage." We'd rather preach about teenage "promiscuity" than teach young people—especially young women—how to negotiate sexual issues responsibly. If my friend's students had been prepared for puberty by schools and discussion groups and health centers, the way Dutch young people are, they might not have ended up pregnant, victims of what is, after all, statutory rape. And if women earned a dollar for every dollar earned by men, divorce and single parenthood would not mean poverty. Nobody worries about single fathers raising children, after all; indeed, paternal custody is the latest legal fad.

What is the point of trying to put the new wine of modern personal relations in the old bottles of the sexual double standard and indissoluble marriage? For that is what most of the current discourse on "family issues" amounts to. No matter how fallacious, the culture greets moralistic approaches to these subjects with instant agreement. Judith Wallerstein's travesty of social science, *Second Chances*, asserts that children are emotionally traumatized by divorce, and the fact that she had no control group is simply ignored by an ecstatic press. As it happens, a study in *Science* did use a control group. By following 17,000 children for four years, and comparing those whose parents split with those whose parents stayed in troubled marriages, the researchers found that the "divorce effect" disappeared entirely for boys and was very small for girls. Not surprisingly, this study attracted absolutely no attention.

Similarly, we are quick to blame poor unmarried mothers for all manner of social problems—crime, unemployment, drops in reading scores, teen suicide. The solution? Cut off all welfare for additional children. Force teen mothers to live with their parents. Push women to marry in order to attach them to a male income. (So much for love—talk about marriage as legalized prostitution!) . . .

A Problem of Money, Not Values

The fact is, the harm connected with the dissolution of "the family" is not a problem of values—at least not individual values—it's a problem of money. When the poor are abandoned to their fates, when there are no jobs, people don't get to display "work ethic," don't feel good about themselves and don't marry or stay married. The girls don't have anything to postpone motherhood for; the boys have no economic prospects that would make them reasonable marriage partners. This was as true in the slums of eighteenth-century London as it is today in the urban slums of Latin America and Africa, as well as the United States. Or take divorce: The real harm of divorce is that it makes lots of women, and their children, poor. One reason, which has got a fair amount of attention recently, is the scandalously low level of child support, plus the tendency of courts to award a disproportionate share of the marital assets to the man. The other reason is that women earn much less than men, thanks to gender discrimination and the failure of the workplace to adapt to the needs of working mothers. Instead of moaning about "family values" we should be thinking about how to provide the poor with decent jobs and social services, and about how to insure economic justice for working women. And let marriage take care of itself.

Family values and the cult of the nuclear family is, at bottom, just another way to bash women, especially poor women. If only they would get married and stay married, society's ills would vanish. Inner-city crime would disappear because fathers would communicate manly values to their sons, which would cause jobs to spring up like mushrooms after rain. Welfare would fade away. Children would do well in school. (Irene Impellizeri, anti-condom vice president of the New York City Board of Education, gave a speech attributing inner-city children's poor grades and high dropout rates to the failure of their families to provide "moral models," the way immigrant parents did in the good old days—a dangerous argument for her, in particular, to make; doesn't she know that Italian-American kids have dropout and failure rates only slightly lower than black and Latino teens?)

Preaching Morality

When pundits preach morality, I often find myself thinking of Samuel Johnson, literature's greatest enemy of cant and fatuity. What would the eighteenth-century moralist make of our current obsession with marriage? "Sir," he replied to [his biographer,] James Boswell, who held that marriage was a natural state, "it is so far from being natural for a man and woman to live in the state of marriage that we find all the motives which they have for remaining in that connection, and the restraints which civilized society imposes to prevent separation, are hardly sufficient to keep them together." Dr. Johnson knew what he was talking about: He and his wife lived apart. And what would he think of our confusion of moral preachments with practical solutions to social problems? Remember his response to Mrs. Thrale's long and flowery speech on the cost of children's clothes. "Nay, madam," he said, "when you are declaiming, declaim; and when you are calculating, calculate."

Which is it going to be? Declamation, which feeds no children, employs no jobless and reduces gender relations to an economic bargain? Or calculation, which accepts the fact that the Berenstain Bears, like Murphy Brown, are fiction. The people seem to be voting with their feet on "the family." It's time for our "values" to catch up.

Periodical Bibliography

The following articles have been selected to supplement the diverse views presented in this chapter.

Robert E. Burns	"Family Values Can Be Relative," *U.S. Catholic*, June 1994.
Allan Carlson	"It's Time to Put Families First," *Insight on the News*, November 29, 1993. Available from 3600 New York Ave. NE, Washington, DC 20002.
Crisis	Special section on strengthening the family, December 1994. Available from PO Box 1006, Notre Dame, IN 46556.
Barbara Ehrenreich	"Oh, Those Family Values," *Time*, July 18, 1994.
Michael Kinsley	"No, Quayle Was Wrong," *Time*, May 23, 1994.
Charles Krauthammer	"Down with 'Family Values,'" *Time*, October 17, 1994.
John Leo	"A New Values Vocabulary," *U.S. News & World Report*, October 3, 1994.
H. Richard McCord Jr.	"Viewing Families from Three Perspectives," *Origins*, October 6, 1994. Available from Catholic News Service, 3211 Fourth St. NE, Washington, DC 20017-1100.
Patrick T. McCormick	"What Kind of Family Did Jesus Value?" *U.S. Catholic*, October 1993.
Charles Murray	"Society Cannot Tolerate Illegitimacy," *The St. Croix Review*, August 1994. Available from PO Box 244, Stillwater, MN 55082.
Katha Pollitt	"Subject to Debate," *The Nation*, October 3, 1994.
Judith Stacey	"The New Family Values Crusaders," *The Nation*, July 25–August 1, 1994.
Barbara Vobejda	"Not Much like Ozzie and Harriet," *The Washington Post National Weekly Edition*, September 5–11, 1994.
Jack Wertheimer	"Family Values and the Jews," *Commentary*, January 1994.
James Q. Wilson	"The Family-Values Debate," *Commentary*, April 1993.
The Wilson Quarterly	"Two Parents, One, or None?" Summer 1993.

How Do Religious Values Influence America?

AMERICAN
VALUE

Chapter Preface

Many election campaigns nationwide focus attention on the Religious Right, a loose-knit coalition consisting primarily of Christian fundamentalists. Perhaps the most influential and scrutinized of these religious groups is the Christian Coalition, a politically active organization with nearly one million members in fifty states. Led by televangelist Pat Robertson, the Christian Coalition has urged parents, politicians (predominantly Republicans), and others to emphasize the importance of traditional two-parent families, and to advocate prayer in public schools and opposition to abortion.

After its founding in 1989, Robertson told members of the Christian Coalition, "We want . . . as soon as possible to see a working majority of the Republican Party in the hands of pro-family Christians by 1996." At the coalition's annual conference in 1994, Texas activist David Barton remarked that William Penn "built [Pennsylvania's] entire constitution on two simple principles. Principle number one: Whatever is Christian is legal. Principle number two: Whatever is not Christian is illegal. This is something that we've got to come back to."

Such beliefs and desires, combined with the election of Religious Right–endorsed candidates, worry many Americans who fear that fundamentalists may infuse their religious beliefs into government and the law. As political analyst Chip Berlet observed in the *Progressive* in October 1994, "The Religious Right seeks to breach the wall of separation between Church and State" by supporting "legislation and policies that take rights away from individuals perceived as sinful." But some fundamentalists such as Christian Coalition director Ralph Reed insist that such is not their goal: "We do not seek to impose our faith on anyone by law. And we do not seek to legislate our theology."

The viewpoints in the following chapter debate the influence of religion and religious values in America.

"Those committed to the Judeo-Christian values have made our country great."

Judeo-Christian Values Make America Great

William P. Barr

A large majority of Americans identify themselves as religious; many also advocate a greater presence of religion in public life. In the following viewpoint, William P. Barr argues that the moral tradition of Judeo-Christian values has been the driving force behind America's greatness. Barr contends that a moral order flows from God's eternal law, which is also reflected in the natural law of right versus wrong. Barr asserts that these moral laws are the foundation of a free society of liberty, self-discipline, and self-government that serves as an example for the rest of the world to follow. Barr served as attorney general of the United States from 1991 to 1993.

As you read, consider the following questions:

1. What does Barr mean by "moral renewal"?
2. What three points does the author make about natural law?
3. In what two ways are secularists using the law as a weapon, in Barr's opinion?

From William P. Barr's speech "The Judeo-Christian Tradition vs. Secularism," delivered at the Catholic League for Religious and Civil Rights, Washington, D.C., October 6, 1992. (Full text available in *Vital Speeches of the Day*, November 1, 1992.)

There are some people who see the year 1492 as a watershed of evil, the onset of an age of brutal imperialism. The critics of Christopher Columbus focus on the cruelty that the Europeans are said to have brought to the Americas.

The truth, of course, is that—in 1492—cruelty, slavery, and injustice were not new to these shores. They have been part and parcel of human history in all times and in all places.

But the Europeans did bring something that was new. They brought a set of beliefs—the Judeo-Christian tradition—a moral culture which provided a critique of injustice and a compelling account of man's true dignity.

Over the centuries, this Judeo-Christian tradition has been the single greatest contributor to the material and moral progress of the human race. And it is this moral tradition—with its notions of human dignity and rights—that has produced and still undergirds our own system of self-government. It is the foundation upon which this great republic rests.

It is good that we reaffirm the greatness of our western tradition, but we must also recognize that this tradition is gravely threatened, and now faces what may be its greatest challenge.

A Moral Crisis

Today, I believe that we are in the midst of a great moral crisis. It is, I think, precisely the moral crisis that our founding fathers foresaw over two hundred years ago—whether a free society can maintain the public morality—and hence, the personal moderation and restraint—necessary for the survival of a free society.

I would like to discuss the nature of this crisis and why I believe that the solution primarily depends on a moral renewal— the reassertion of a moral consensus, around which, and upon which, we can rebuild our public life as a community, and once again pursue the common good.

The heart of the crisis is a conflict—a struggle—between two fundamentally different systems of values. On the one hand, we are seeing the growing ascendancy of secularism and the doctrine of moral relativism. On the other hand, we are seeing the steady erosion of our traditional Judeo-Christian moral system.

What are the hallmarks of the Judeo-Christian moral system that we see in retreat? This tradition holds that there is a real and transcendent moral order—absolute and objective standards of right and wrong that exist independent of man's will. This transcendent moral order flows from God's eternal law—the plan of divine wisdom by which the whole of creation is ordered.

Moreover, this eternal law is impressed upon, and reflected in, nature—in all created things. This is the natural law. And man can know God's law not only through revelation but also through the "natural law," which he can discern by reason and experience.

211

Now, I want to make three brief, but important, points about this concept of natural law.

The first is that natural law—these rules of right and wrong which make up traditional morality and which modern secularists dismiss as other-worldly superstitions—is, in fact, the ultimate practical, utilitarian rule for human conduct.

"First off, secular humanism is out."

They are the rules that are the best for man—not in the by-and-by, but in the here and now. They are the rules that accord with the true nature of man, and therefore, adherence to them promotes what is good for man—maybe not instant gratification, but what is good over time, both for individuals and for human society.

By the same token, violation of these moral laws have [sic] bad practical consequence for man and society. We may not pay the price immediately, but eventually we will.

The second point I want to make about natural law is this. Because human nature is fallen, we will not automatically conform ourselves to God's law.

But because we can know what is good—because we can discern what is right and what is wrong—we are not doomed to be slaves to our passions and wants. We can train and teach ourselves to want what is good or, at least, to adhere to what is good.

A society, because it can know right from wrong, has the ability to set and communicate moral standards which can restrain the bad, and promote the good. Society does this through moral education; through its customs and traditions that reflect the wisdom of ages; and through its formal laws—the application of natural law to the circumstances of the day.

Through these means—law, custom, and moral education—a society forms a moral culture. To the extent a society's moral culture is based on God's law, it will guide men toward the best possible life.

The third point I want to make about natural law is that it is the only secure basis for human rights. A right cannot be secure—cannot be inalienable—unless it exists independent of the will of man. And that means it must be rooted in a transcendent and objectively true moral order.

This, in a nutshell, is the moral vision of the Judeo-Christian tradition. But why should the erosion of this tradition confront us with a crisis? Why should it have any implication for our system of government and our laws?

America's Founders

As I said at the outset, it is because our whole system of government is predicated upon the traditional Judeo-Christian moral system. Those who founded our great republic crafted the most magnificent legal structure in history. Yet they knew that their legal edifice was not a castle in the air.

The founders believed that popular government and its laws necessarily rested upon an underlying moral order that was antecedent to both the state and to man-made law. They referred to this transcendent moral order in the Declaration of Independence as "self-evident truths" and "the laws of nature and of nature's God."

For a republic to work, the founders thought, the people had to be guided by inwardly possessed and commonly shared moral values. Public morality was essential to the success of popular government.

The fate of free government would ultimately depend on the ability of the people to maintain their moral compass. In the words of James Madison, "We have staked our future on the ability of each of us to govern ourselves according to the Ten Commandments of God."

And the greatest threat to free government, the framers believed, was "licentiousness"—abandonment of Judeo-Christian moral restraints in favor of the unbridled pursuit of personal appetites and self-gratification—the sacrifice of the common good for individual pleasure.

As Father John Courtney Murray observed, the American tenet was *not* that "free government is inevitable, only that it is possible, and that its possibility can be realized *only* when the people as a whole are inwardly governed by the recognized imperatives of the universal moral order."

So for the framers the choice was clear: We would govern ourselves through morality or we would lose our liberty. In the words of John Adams:

> We have no government armed with power which is capable of contending with human passions unbridled by morality and religion. Our Constitution was made only for a moral and religious people, it is wholly inadequate for the government of any other.

And so, the framers viewed themselves as launching a great experiment: Could a free people retain a moral culture that would promote the self-discipline and virtues needed to restrain licentiousness? Or, would the moral culture decline, virtues give way to vice, and the people ultimately sacrifice the good of the community to the pursuit of their individual appetites?

Well, the framers' great experiment in self-government has gone on for over 200 years now. We are still, in many ways, "the shining city on the hill" for the rest of the world. What has sustained us over these two centuries has been our commitment to our great moral heritage.

But, today our great experiment in liberty appears threatened. For the last thirty years, a moral crisis has been brewing. It is undeniable that since the mid-60s, there has been a steady assault on traditional values.

We have lived through 25 years of permissiveness, sexual revolution, and the drug culture. People have been encouraged to cast off conventional morality and old-fashioned restraints. Moral tradition has given way to moral relativism.

Under this doctrine, there are no objective standards of right or wrong. Every individual has his own tastes and we simply cannot say whether any choice is good or bad. It is a very short step from the proposition that all morality is relative to the proposition that all morality rests on the assertion of one's own will.

Everybody writes their own rule book. Accordingly, we cannot have a moral consensus or a moral culture. We have only the autonomous individual. And that individual has no ultimate purpose—no end outside himself. And so the object of human life becomes simply the pursuit of individual pleasure. . . .

Society Adrift

In the past, societies—like the human body—seemed to have had a self-healing mechanism—a self-corrective mechanism that gets things back on course if society goes too far adrift.

The opinion of decent people rebels. These people coalesce and rally against the obvious excess. Eternal truths are rediscovered.

This is the idea of the pendulum. We have all thought: "Some-

214

how the pendulum will naturally swing back." But can we be sure?

Today, we face something different that may mean that we cannot count on the pendulum just naturally swinging back. Today, we face the immense power of mass communications and popular culture—the mass media, the entertainment industry, academia.

Today, I fear that the power and pervasiveness of our high-tech popular culture not only fuels the collapse of morality but also drowns out the scattered voices raised against secularization.

Embracing Judeo-Christian Values

I do not believe that a superior system can be developed than that which we have inherited, and to which our founding fathers so faithfully subscribed. I refer to the Judeo-Christian value system, and I believe that we have no choice but to adopt it as the unifying theory of existence for our [the conservative] side of the great American culture war. To some extent, we have little choice, because the other side has already chosen Scripture as the battlefield. They have made the abolition of transcendent value the centerpiece of their struggle. For us to ignore Judeo-Christian thought is to abandon the main battleground of this war to the political enemy. As rejection of the Judeo-Christian value system fuels and unifies Liberalism, so can the embrace of the system do the same for us.

Daniel Lapin, *The Heritage Foundation Lectures*, no. 493, 1994.

When those who seek to restore traditional morality stick their heads up, they suffer what amounts to a saturation bombing at the hands of the mass media. Dissenters from secularist dogma are viciously attacked and held up to ridicule.

In addition to mass popular culture, I am concerned there is another modern phenomenon that makes it harder for society to restore itself. In the past, when societies deviate too far from sound moral principles, they end up paying such a high price that they ultimately recoil and are forced to re-evaluate the path they are on.

As I said earlier, natural law is the ultimate utilitarian rule. It commands what is best for man, and if it is violated society will pay a price.

So, venereal disease is the price we pay, among many others, for sexual license. Violent crime and poverty is a price we pay for the breakdown of the family. So, in the past, societies have been driven back to their senses by the sheer cost of misconduct.

But today, something is new. The state—which no longer sees itself as a moral institution, but as a secular one—takes on the role as the alleviator of bad consequences. The state is called upon to remove the inconvenience and costs of misconduct.

So the reaction to diseases and illegitimacy is not sexual responsibility but handing out condoms. And the reaction to drug addiction is clean needles.

While we think we are solving problems we are actually subsidizing them. And by lowering the cost of misconduct, the government perpetuates it.

The corrosive impact on society continues. And like most solutions that deal with symptoms rather than causes, it only makes matters worse.

Secularists and the Law

A third phenomenon which makes it difficult for the pendulum to swing back is the way the law is being used as a weapon to break down traditional morality and to establish moral relativism as the new orthodoxy. The secularists are using the law as a weapon in at least two ways.

First, either through legislative action or through litigation and judicial interpretation, secularists are continually seeking to eliminate laws that reflect traditional moral norms.

Just 20 years ago we saw the laws against abortion swept away. And today we see a constant chipping away at laws designed to restrain sexual immorality, obscenity or to prohibit euthanasia.

This is serious because over time, the content of the law plays an important part in framing and shaping the moral culture. In other words, morality will follow the law. What is made legal, will ultimately become viewed by the people as "moral."

There is no better example of this than abortion. Prior to *Roe v. Wade*, the vast majority of Americans believed that abortion was a moral evil. It was considered an abomination and a scandal. Since *Roe*, the number of Americans who consider abortion a moral evil has steadily declined.

A second way in which secularists use law as a weapon is to pass laws which affirmatively promote the moral relativist viewpoint. These are laws that seek to ratify, or put on the equal plane, conduct which previously was considered immoral.

For example, you see laws proposed that say you must treat a cohabitating couple just as you would a married couple. A landlord cannot make a distinction; he must rent to the former just as you would to the latter.

This kind of law says, in effect: "We will not allow people, either by themselves or collectively, to make moral distinctions; you cannot say that certain conduct is good and another bad. You must treat them the same."

Another recent example of this kind of law was the one in D.C. that required Georgetown University to treat homosexual activist groups just as it did other student groups. This kind of law dissolves any kind of moral consensus in society. It precludes the development of a moral culture.

There can be no coalescence of opinion based on the moral feelings of the community. There can only be enforced neutrality.

Swinging Back the Pendulum

How, then, in the face of such a pervasive popular culture and a powerful state, which combine to promote moral relativism and suppress opposition, can we be confident that the pendulum will swing back?

Today, 500 years after Columbus's voyage, on the verge of the third millennium, we are also at a defining moment.

We are no longer sure of who we are as a people. We have no shared "public philosophy." We are living in a "post-modern," post-communist, post-ideological world—an age without a name of its own.

How can we, as a society, regain our moral compass? I've painted a bleak picture, but not to suggest that there is no hope. Instead, to suggest that we are not going to reclaim the moral heritage of our society without a fight.

There is a battle going on that will decide who we are as a people and what name this age will ultimately bear. We cannot sit back and just hope that somehow the pendulum is going to swing back toward sanity. We are going to have to struggle to achieve the moral renewal of our country.

Those committed to the Judeo-Christian values have made our country great. We know that the first thing we have to do to renew our country is to ensure that we are putting our principles into practice in our own personal daily lives. We understand that only by transforming ourselves can we transform the world outside ourselves. We must also place the greatest emphasis on the moral education of our children.

There can be no moral renaissance unless we succeed in passing to the next generation our faith and our values in full vigor. If ever there was a time for the resurgence of religious education, it is today. I think we should do all we can to promote and support religious education at all levels.

Finally, we must stand ready to fight for our values, and to defend them vigorously when they come under attack. We must speak out with confidence and authority about what is right and wrong. Those of you who teach; those of you who practice law; those of you in the media—must speak out.

Ours is a time for sober reflection, and as we ponder with our fellow citizens how best to reconstitute our public life, we would

217

do well to recall the words of that great friend of America, Edmund Burke who wrote:

> Men are qualified for civil liberty, in exact proportion to their disposition to put moral chains upon their own appetites—in proportion as their love of justice is above their rapacity—in proportion as their soundness and sobriety is above their vanity and presumption. Society cannot exist unless a controlling power be placed somewhere; and the less of it there is within, the more there must be without. It is ordained in the eternal constitution of things that men of intemperate minds cannot be free. Their passions forge their fetters.

Together we can make a difference. Nothing is written in stone—neither decline nor triumph, neither the rise nor the fall of nations. Together, I believe that we *can* change the world.

*"The great unmentionable evil at the center of
our culture is monotheism."*

Judeo-Christian Values
Deny Freedom in America

Gore Vidal

Gore Vidal is a noted American writer whose novels include
Burr, Lincoln, and *Myra Breckenridge.* In the following viewpoint, Vidal argues that monotheism and its followers have been
the cause of many problems, such as pollution, racism, and sexism. Vidal asserts that because of monotheistic religions' influence—primarily through their hatred, prohibitions, and superstitions—America has become a nation subservient to harmful
laws. These totalitarian religions are intolerant of liberalism,
which stands for democracy and freedom, Vidal maintains.

As you read, consider the following questions:

1. What are the "sky-god" religions and how are they
   patriarchal, in Vidal's opinion?
2. How has religion fostered the exclusion and hatred of blacks,
   according to the author?
3. How does Vidal describe America's two basic, opposing
   political movements?

From Gore Vidal, "Monotheism and Its Discontents," *The Nation,* July 13, 1992. Reprinted
by permission of *The Nation* magazine, © The Nation Company, L.P.

It is very easy to discuss *what* has gone wrong with us. It is not so easy to discuss what should be done to correct what has gone wrong. It is absolutely impossible in our public discourse to discuss *why* so much has gone wrong and, indeed, has been wrong with us since the very beginning of the country, and even before that when our white tribes were living elsewhere. Unfortunately, there are two subjects that we are never permitted to discuss with any seriousness: race and religion, and how our attitudes toward the first are rooted in the second. Thanks to this sternly—correctly?—enforced taboo, we are never able to get to the root of our problems. We are like people born in a cage and unable to visualize any world beyond our familiar bars of prejudice and superstition. That Opinion the Few create in order to control the Many has seen to it that we are kept in permanent ignorance of our actual estate. . . .

Liberals and Isolationists

The word "radical" derives from the Latin word for root. Therefore, if you want to get to the root of *any*thing you must be radical. It is no accident that the word has now been totally demonized by our masters, and no one in politics dares even to use the word favorably, much less track any problem to its root. But then a ruling class that was able to demonize the word "liberal" in the past ten years is a master at controlling—indeed stifling—any criticism of itself. "Liberal" comes from the Latin *liberalis*, which means pertaining to a free man. In politics, to be liberal is to want to extend democracy through change and reform. One can see why that word had to be erased from our political lexicon. . . .

Monotheism: The Greatest Evil

Now to the root of the matter. The great unmentionable evil at the center of our culture is monotheism. From a barbaric Bronze Age text known as the Old Testament, three antihuman religions have evolved—Judaism, Christianity and Islam. These are sky-god religions. They are, literally, patriarchal—God is the omnipotent father—hence the loathing of women for 2,000 years in those countries afflicted by the sky-god and his earthly male delegates. The sky-god is a jealous god, of course. He requires total obedience from everyone on earth, as he is in place not just for one tribe but for all creation. Those who would reject him must be converted or killed for their own good. Ultimately, totalitarianism is the only sort of politics that can truly serve the sky-god's purpose. Any movement of a liberal nature endangers his authority and that of his delegates on earth. One God, one King, one Pope, one master in the factory, one father-leader in the family at home.

The founders of the United States were not enthusiasts of the sky-god. Many, like Thomas Jefferson, rejected him altogether and placed man at the center of the world. The young Abraham Lincoln wrote a pamphlet *against* Christianity, which friends persuaded him to burn. Needless to say, word got around about both Jefferson and Lincoln and each had to cover his tracks. Jefferson said that he was a deist, which could mean anything or nothing, while Lincoln, hand on heart and tongue in cheek, said he could not support for office anyone who "scoffed" at religion.

From the beginning, sky-godders have always exerted great pressure in our secular republic. Also, evangelical Christian groups have traditionally drawn strength from the suppressed. African slaves were allowed to organize heavenly sky-god churches, as a surrogate for earthly freedom. White churches were organized in order to make certain that the rights of property were respected and that the numerous religious taboos in the New and Old Testaments would be enforced, if necessary, by civil law. The ideal to which John Adams subscribed—that we would be a nation of laws, not of men—was quickly subverted when the churches forced upon everyone, through supposedly neutral and just laws, their innumerable taboos on sex, alcohol, gambling. We are now indeed a nation of laws, mostly bad and certainly antihuman.

Imposing Religious Beliefs

Roman Catholic migrations in the last century further reenforced the Puritan sky-god. The Church has also put itself on a collision course with the Bill of Rights when it asserts, as it always has, that "error has no rights." The last correspondence between John Adams and Thomas Jefferson expressed their alarm that the Jesuits were to be allowed into the United States. Although the Jews were sky-god folk, they followed Book One, not Book Two, so they have no mission to convert others; rather the reverse. Also, as they have been systematically demonized by the Christians sky-godders, they tended to be liberal and so turned not to their temple but to the A.C.L.U. [American Civil Liberties Union]. Unfortunately, the recent discovery that the sky-god, in his capacity as realtor, had given them, in perpetuity, some parcels of unattractive land called Judea and Samaria has, to my mind, unhinged many of them. I hope this is temporary.

In the First Amendment to the Constitution the founders made it clear that this was not to be a sky-god nation with a national religion like that of England, from whom we had just separated. It is curious how little understood this amendment is—yes, everyone has a right to worship any god he chooses but he does *not* have the right to impose his beliefs on others who do not happen to share in his superstitions and taboos. This sep-

221

aration was absolute in our original Republic. But the sky-godders do not give up easily. In the 1950s they actually got the phrase "In God We Trust" onto the currency, in direct violation of the First Amendment.

Although many of the Christian evangelists feel it necessary to convert everyone on earth to their primitive religion, they have been prevented—so far—from forcing others to worship as they do, but they *have* forced—most tyrannically and wickedly—their superstitions and hatreds upon all of us through the civil law and through general prohibitions. So it is upon that account that I now favor an all-out war on the monotheists.

Democracy Without Supernatural Authority

Any set of convictions derived either from dogma or personal revelation is, by its nature, beyond discussion—and if there is anything that democracy requires of us, it *is* discussion. . . . Only when we ask, "What is best for the world?" without resorting to supernatural authority to foreclose the question, do we open up the possibility of truly democratic decision-making.

Barbara Ehrenreich, *Vogue*, December 1985.

Let us dwell upon the evils they have wrought. The hatred of blacks comes straight from their Bad Book. As descendants of Ham, blacks are forever accursed, while Saint Paul tells the slaves to obey their masters. Racism is in the marrow of the bone of the true believer. For him, black is forever inferior to white and deserves whatever ill fortune may come his way. The fact that some monotheists can behave charitably means, often, that their prejudice is at so deep a level that they are not aware it is there at all. In the end, this makes any radical change of attitude impossible. Meanwhile, welfare has been the price the sky-godders were willing to pay to exclude blacks from their earthly political system. So we must live—presumably forever—with a highly enervating race war, set in train by the One God and his many hatreds.

Women and Homosexuals

Patriarchal rage at the thought of Woman ever usurping Man's place at the helm, in either home or workplace, is almost as strong now as it ever was. According to the polls at the time of the hearings, most American women took the side of [U.S. Supreme Court nominee] Clarence Thomas against Anita Hill. But then the sky-god's fulminations against women are still very much part the psyche of those in thrall to the Jealous God.

The ongoing psychopathic hatred of same-sexuality has made the United States the laughingstock of the civilized world. In most of the First World, monotheism is weak. Where it is weak or nonexistent, private sexual behavior has nothing at all to do with those not involved, much less with the law. At least when the Emperor Justinian, a sky-god man, decided to outlaw sodomy, he had to come up with a good *practical* reason, which he did. It is well known, Justinian declared, that buggery is a principal cause of earthquakes, and so must be prohibited. But our sky-godders, always eager to hate, still quote Leviticus, as if that loony text had anything useful to say about anything except, perhaps, the inadvisability of eating shellfish in the Jerusalem area.

We are now, slowly, becoming alarmed at the state of the planet. For a century, we have been breeding like a virus under optimum conditions, and now the virus has begun to attack its host, the earth. The lower atmosphere is filled with dust, we have been told from our satellites in space. Climate changes; earth and water are poisoned. Sensible people grow alarmed, but sky-godders are serene, even smug. The planet is just a staging area for heaven. Why bother to clean it up? . . . At Rio [the United Nations Earth Summit, George Bush] refused to commit our government to the great cleanup, partly because it would affect the incomes of the 100 corporate men and women who paid for him but largely because of the sky-god, who told his slaves to "be fruitful and multiply, and replenish the earth, and subdue it, and have dominion . . . over every living thing that moveth upon the earth." Well, we did just like you told us, massa. We've used everything up. We're ready for heaven now. Or maybe Mars will do.

Denying Rights

Ordinarily, as a descendant of the eighteenth-century Enlightenment, which shaped our Republic, I would say live and let live and I would try not to "scoff"—to use Lincoln's verb—at the monotheists. But I am not allowed to ignore them. They won't let me. They are too busy. They have a divine mission to take away our rights as private citizens. We are forbidden abortion here, gambling there, same-sex almost everywhere, drugs, alcohol in a dry county. Our prisons are the most terrible and the most crowded in the First World. Our death row executions are a source of deep disgust in civilized countries, where more and more we are regarded as a primitive, uneducated and dangerous people. Although we are not allowed, under law, to kill ourselves or to take drugs that the good folk think might be bad for us, we are allowed to buy a handgun and shoot as many people as we can get away with.

Of course, as poor Arthur (There Is This Pendulum) Schlesinger Jr. would say, these things come in cycles. Every twenty years liberal gives way to conservative, and back again. But I suggest that what is wrong now is not cyclic but systemic. And our system, like any system, is obeying the second law of thermodynamics. Everything is running down; and we are well advanced along the yellow brick road to entropy. I don't think much of anything can be done to halt this progress under our present political-economic system. We lost poor Arthur's pendulum in 1950 when our original Constitution was secretly replaced with the apparatus of the national security state, which still wastes most of our tax money on war or war-related matters. Hence deteriorating schools, and so on.

Another of our agreed-upon fantasies is that we do not have a class system in the United States. The Few who control the Many through Opinion have simply made themselves invisible. They have convinced us that we are a classless society in which anyone can make it. Ninety percent of the stories in the pop press are about winners of lotteries or poor boys and girls who, despite adenoidal complaints, become overnight millionaire singers. So there is still hope, the press tells the folks, for the 99 percent who will never achieve wealth no matter how hard they work. We are also warned at birth that it is not polite to hurt people's feelings by criticizing their religion, even if that religion may be damaging everyone through the infiltration of our common laws.

Happily, the Few cannot disguise the bad times through which we are all going. Word is spreading that America is now falling behind in the civilization sweepstakes. So isn't it time to discuss what we all really think and feel about our social and economic arrangements?

Racial Conflict

Although we may not discuss race other than to say that Jesus wants each and every one of us for a sunbeam, history is nothing more than the bloody record of the migration of tribes. When the white race broke out of Europe 500 years ago, it did many astounding things all over the globe. Inspired by a raging sky-god, the whites were able to pretend that their conquests were in order to bring the One God to everyone, particularly those with older and subtler religions. Now the tribes are on the move again. Professor Pendulum is having a nervous breakdown because so many different tribes are now being drawn to this sweet land of liberty and, thus far, there is no indication that any of the new arrivals intends ever to read [Schlesinger's] *The Age of Jackson*. I think the taking in of everyone can probably be overdone. There may not be enough jobs for very many more immigrants, though what prosperity we have ever enjoyed in the past was usually based on slave or near-slave labor.

On the other hand, I think Asians, say, are a plus culturally, and their presence tends to refocus, somewhat, the relentless white versus black war. Where I *am* as one with friend Pendulum is that the newcomers must grasp certain principles as expressed in the Declaration of Independence and the Bill of Rights. Otherwise, we shall become a racially divided totalitarian state enjoying a Brazilian economy.

To revert to the unmentionable, religion. It should be noted that religion seemed to be losing its hold in the United States in the second quarter of this century. From the [creationism vs. evolution] Scopes trial in '25 to the repeal of Prohibition in '33, the sky-godders were confined pretty much to the backwoods. Then television was invented and the electronic pulpit was soon occupied by a horde of Elmer Gantrys [a well-known fictional preacher], who took advantage of the tax exemption for religion. Thus, out of greed, a religious revival has been set in motion and the results are predictably poisonous to the body politic.

Judeo-Christian Indoctrination

Whether we like it or not, the United States is saturated with Judeo-Christianity. Its citizens have been deliberately indoctrinated into this religion by government and church coercion from the time of the First World War. Born and reared into homes where religion has been an (or even *the* most) important value of their families, the overwhelming majority of Americans actually believe in life after death, the efficacy of both prayer and oath taking, and the existence of souls. The entire culture is based on the value system projected from Judeo-Christianity.

Jon G. Murray, *American Atheist Newsletter*, February 1994.

It is usual, on the rare occasions when essential problems are addressed, to exhort everyone to be kinder, gentler. To bring us together, O Lord, in our common humanity. Well, we have heard these exhortations for a couple of hundred years and we are further apart than ever. So instead of coming together in order that the many might be one, I say let us separate so that each will know where he stands. From the *one, many*, and each of us free of the sky-god as secular law-giver. I preach, to put it bluntly, confrontation.

Jerry Brown and Pat Buchanan [in the 1992 presidential campaign], whether they knew it or not, were revealing two basic, opposing political movements. Buchanan speaks for the party of

God—the sky-god with his terrible hatred of women, blacks, gays, drugs, abortion, contraception, gambling—you name it, he hates it. Buchanan is a worthy peddler of hate. He is also in harmony not only with the prejudices and superstitions of a good part of the population but, to give him his due, he is a reactionary in the good sense—reacting against the empire in favor of the old Republic, which he mistakenly thinks was Christian.

Brown speaks for the party of man—feminists can find another noun if they like. Thomas Paine, when asked *his* religion, said he subscribed only to the religion of humanity. There now seems to be a polarizing of the country of a sort that has never happened before. The potential fault line has always been there, but whenever a politician got too close to the facts of our case, the famed genius of the system would eliminate him in favor of that mean which is truly golden for the ownership, and no one else. The party of man would like to re-establish a representative government firmly based upon the Bill of Rights. The party of God will have none of this. It wants to establish, through legal prohibitions and enforced taboos, a sky-god totalitarian state. The United States ultimately as prison, with mandatory blood, urine and lie-detector tests and with the sky-godders as the cops, answerable only to God, who may have just sent us his Only Son, H. Ross Perot, as warden.

For once, it's all out there, perfectly visible, perfectly plain for those who can see. That Brown and Buchanan did not figure in the election does not alter the fact that, for the first time in 140 years, we now have, due in part to their efforts, the outline of two parties. Each knows the nature of its opposite, and those who are wise will not try to accommodate or compromise the two but will let them, at last, confront each other.

The famous tree of liberty is all that we have ever really had. Now, for want of nurture, it is dying before our eyes. Of course, the sky-god never liked it. But some of us did—and some of us do. So, perhaps, through facing who and what we are, we may achieve a nation not under God but under man—or should I say our common humanity?

> *"The Religious Right's role [is] in keeping alive moral issues and traditional values important to most Americans."*

The Religious Right's Influence Is Good for America

Fred Barnes

The Religious Right—the political bloc of fundamentalist Christian groups—is duly concerned with social issues that are vital to America, Fred Barnes argues in the following viewpoint. Barnes maintains that there is much support for the inclusion of religious values in public debate and as a source of political values. Barnes asserts that the Religious Right has been misunderstood, and he welcomes an emerging positive view of this faction. Barnes is a senior editor covering politics and the White House for the *New Republic*, a biweekly magazine, and he is a commentator on *The McLaughlin Group*, a public television show.

As you read, consider the following questions:

1. How did the myth of the Religious Right's domination of the Republican Party arise, in Barnes's opinion?
2. According to Barnes, have some Democrats heeded the Religious Right's message?
3. What issues does the Religious Right need to emphasize, according to the author?

Fred Barnes, "Who Needs the Religious Right? We All Do," *Crisis*, September 1994. Reprinted by permission.

Three things about the Religious Right's influence on the 1992 election and in American politics are of particular interest to me. First, a myth that grew out of the 1992 Republican Convention in Houston. Second, the surprising gains that the Religious Right has made, particularly in the media (National Public Radio presented a fair piece on efforts by the Religious Right to expand into the black and Hispanic communities). And third, the Religious Right's role in keeping alive moral issues and traditional values important to most Americans.

The Takeover Myth

I was in Houston when the myth began. The Religious Right was said to have taken over the convention and to have imposed its own religious views on the Republican Party, with the goal of imposing them on the entire nation. The myth created a media consensus on the convention: that it was intolerant, mean-spirited, exclusive, judgmental, narrow-minded, or worse. When Pat Buchanan gave his speech, I happened to be sitting next to another Washington journalist who is a bellwether of press opinion. At first he loved Buchanan's speech, but two days later his view had changed entirely, as had the view of many other press people. Now he felt the convention had turned into a hate-fest because of its domination by the Religious Right. That became the conventional wisdom among reporters in Houston. No, they didn't conspire to reach this conclusion, but as they gathered to trade information and gossip, the consensus emerged that the Religious Right, if not in total control of the convention, at least had a large and pernicious influence there.

The evidence? It was the speeches by Religious Right people, like Pat Buchanan (even though he has little to do with the organized Religious Right). The mainstream press pointed to these speeches more than to the issues of homosexuality and family values. Pat Robertson's speech was cited. So was Marilyn Quayle's, though she didn't dwell on religious issues but talked about feminism and women who don't work.

There were 128 speeches at the convention, only three of which could be considered religious. Just one—Robertson's, which wasn't even given during prime time—could truly be called a Religious Right speech. Yet this was enough for the press to conclude that the Religious Right had dominated the convention.

Traditional Women

A week after the convention, a woman television producer—married, with one child—was still furious about Marilyn Quayle's speech, because she felt it attacked women who work. Here's what Mrs. Quayle, who herself has sometimes worked full-time, actually said: "I sometimes think that the liberals are always so

228

angry because they believe the grandiose promises of the liberation movement. They are disappointed because most women do not want to be liberated from their essential natures as women. Most of us love being mothers and wives, which gives us a richness that few men and women get from professional accomplishments alone." This was hardly a broadside against women with full-time jobs. Nonetheless many women and men in the press took it that way.

In any case, the supposed domination of the GOP by the Religious Right didn't contribute heavily to George Bush's defeat in the November election. I think Bush was defeated because he signed the 1990 budget deal. Without that, he would have been re-elected. But in the media the view lingers that the convention was a critical moment that doomed Bush and his re-election chances.

The myth is not confined to the media. Spencer Abraham, executive director of the 1992 House Republican campaign organization, ran for Republican National Chairman after the election and was defeated by Haley Barbour. Abraham talked to each of the 165 members of the Republican National Committee, because they were the electorate choosing the chairman. Amazingly, he found that a majority believed the press view of what happened at the convention, even though they themselves had been there and should have known better. Abraham was regarded as the Religious Right candidate, even though he wasn't.

Religious Right Gains

My second observation about the Religious Right is the good news that the fog hovering over it is beginning to lift. The hostility toward it has begun to soften. The 1993 races for Virginia governor, lieutenant governor, and attorney general greatly affected press opinion about the Religious Right. Since Virginia is right next door to Washington, D.C., the commercials for the races were on Washington television for national reporters to see. Clearly the Democrats overkilled in their attempts to discredit the Religious Right, trying to make it an issue not only against Michael Farris, a Religious Right favorite who was running for lieutenant governor, but also against George Allen, the Republican gubernatorial candidate. The Democrats cast Allen—who won—as a patsy for Pat Robertson, which he obviously is not.

The backlash in the press, while not sympathetic, was the beginning of a recognition that the Religious Right is a legitimate bloc in the Republican coalition. I don't want to overstate this. But after talking to ten political reporters who followed the Virginia race—Christopher Matthews of the San Francisco *Examiner*, Gloria Borger of *U.S. News*, Brit Hume of ABC, Eleanor Clift of *Newsweek*, Carl Leubsdorf of the Dallas *Morning News*,

Thomas DeFrank of *Newsweek*, syndicated columnist Robert Novak, Morton Kondracke of *Roll Call*, Paul West of the Baltimore *Sun*, and John Mushek of the Boston *Globe*—I found that most agreed the Religious Right is not an evil juggernaut, as they'd previously thought, but rather is a viable element of the Republican Party. They acknowledged that during the campaign the issue of the Religious Right changed from fear of a religious takeover to the unfairness of attacks on people for holding strong religious views. The result is a more positive view of the Religious Right, and that's a gain. The Religious Right has further enhanced its legitimacy with the secular press by tackling non-religious issues, as in the Christian Coalition's decision to air TV ads critical of the Clinton health-care plan.

Right and Radical

It is high time for Christians to stop being shamefaced. Christians should come out of the "closet," and proclaim, "We are out and we are proud!" They have the principles, they are becoming all-round conservatives and libertarians, and they are acquiring the necessary organizational and political savvy. And they should no longer allow their enemies to "define" them, to say that they must not carry religious or moral principles into the political arena, or that they must confine themselves to "conserving," but never take the offensive to return to the old American Republic. Christians should have the courage to be "right" *and* to be "radical," and if the combination is "radical right," let the radical left, or "radical wrong," try to make the most of it.

Murray N. Rothbard, *Rothbard-Rockwell Report*, August 1994.

Moreover, there are other voices now arguing that religious views are a legitimate source of political values and should be included in the public debate. The political left doesn't accept this, insisting that religious people want to impose their views on everyone. But President Clinton dissents from that liberal view, and so does David Wilhelm, the Democratic National Chairman. When Wilhelm spoke to the Christian Coalition, he made a significant concession. He stressed that religious values are fine and legitimate as roots of political views. That's the Religious Right position. It is not the position of most Democrats.

Clinton and Wilhelm declared that people of strong faith should not be ostracized from the public square. Christians, Jews, Muslims, and members of other faiths can properly draw on spiritual teachings to guide their political views. Wilhelm has also noted, "Let us say that while religious motivation is appropriate, it is wrong to use religious authority to coerce support in the public arena."

The Religious Right's Importance

The third thing I find interesting about the Religious Right is the notion that it is driving people away from the GOP, that most Americans want a party based on serious economic and foreign policy issues, not those horrible social issues. Here the real issue is the Republican Party's strong stand against abortion. If you are part of the elite opinion stream—where it is socially unacceptable to be opposed to abortion—you'll get flak from friends and maybe your spouse for being associated with such a party.

Richard Nixon, in an interview with William Safire, gave his opinion on abortion: "The state should stay out—don't subsidize, and don't prohibit." The view that abortion should be kept out of politics is shared by many other Republican politicians. I think this shows they are ignorant as to the party's real base. They don't understand who grassroots Republicans are.

The Republican Party does not stand a chance of becoming a majority party in America or electing another president without the Religious Right. Vast numbers of Americans are alienated from the Democratic Party, yet are leery of the Republican Party. What attracts them to the GOP is not supply-side economics or hawkishness on foreign policy but serious moral and social concerns. I understand the reluctance of millions of former Democrats to become Republicans—the thought of being a Republican makes even me wince. But the Religious Right's cluster of issues attracts many of them.

Abortion is an issue that helped George Bush in 1992 and certainly helped George Allen win the governorship of Virginia. Millions of people were also attracted to Republican candidates because they believe in a role for religion in American life. Others became sympathetic to Republicans because they care about, for instance, the injection of gay values into the mainstream of American opinion, or about moral relativism. Whether it's the kind of multiculturalism that shows up in the Rainbow Curriculum in New York [public schools] or Outcomes-based Education, only the Religious Right keeps all these values issues alive. And the beneficiary is the Republican Party.

There used to be something called the New Right, but it doesn't exist anymore. Its leaders were people like Paul Weyrich (who said in 1985 that the only serious grassroots activity in the Republican Party was religiously based—which is even more true now), Richard Viguerie, and Howard Phillips. But the New Right is now gone, leaving only the Religious Right.

If the Religious Right is driven out of the Republican Party, I think values issues—abortion, the role of religion in public life, gay rights, and moral relativism—will all but vanish. It is religious people who keep them on the table. Their departure would cause the Republican Party's base to shrivel dramatically. Republican elites simply do not understand this. I worry when Ralph Reed says that the Christian Coalition is not going to concentrate on opposing abortion because abortion cannot be blocked; instead, they will talk about parental consent and about other important issues like tax cuts. In truth, the Religious Right needs to emphasize the issues that brought its people into politics in the first place—basically moral issues.

The Religious Right's issues are critical politically not only for the Republican Party but for everybody. They are more important than cutting the capital-gains tax rate or aiding the Bosnian Muslims. They involve the moral upbringing of our children, the character of our citizens and our leaders, the way we regard and treat religious faith and religious believers. If American politicians do not want to grapple with these moral issues, the overarching issues of our era, then what are they in office for?

I do not always agree with the positions of the Religious Right. I am not really concerned, for instance, whether a school-prayer amendment passes. I have also disagreed with their style, although under Ralph Reed it has gotten better. But I give them credit for forcing things onto the national agenda that are critical to the Republican Party and to the rest of us.

In 1989, when Ronald Reagan returned to California on Air Force One, he was asked what his greatest regret was after eight years as president. He said he regretted that he hadn't done more to restrict or end abortion in this country. If an entire party abandons that issue and other moral concerns and ostracizes from the party the people who want to raise those concerns, the regret will ultimately be felt by the entire nation.

"When organizations acting in the name of Christianity seek political power, then religion becomes subordinate to politics. It becomes infected with the darker egoism of group and nation."

The Religious Right's Influence Is Bad for America

John B. Judis

Many Americans fear that the Religious Right will infuse its religious beliefs into politics and government. In the following viewpoint, John B. Judis argues that many Americans fear an assault on their privacy from the Religious Right and its moral opposition to abortion, homosexuality, and pornography. Judis also criticizes Religious Right school board candidates who seek to incorporate their ideology into public school policies, while remaining ignorant of pressing educational concerns. Even more disturbing, Judis maintains, is the Religious Right's lack of compassion toward needy Americans such as the poor and those suffering from AIDS. Judis is a contributing editor for the *New Republic*, a biweekly magazine.

As you read, consider the following questions:

1. How does the Religious Right differ from other religious organizations, according to Judis?
2. What does Judis mean by the Christian Coalition's politics of "stealth"?
3. When is religion most constructive, according to the author?

From John B. Judis, "Crosses to Bear," *The New Republic*, September 12, 1994. Reprinted by permission of *The New Republic*, ©1994, The New Republic, Inc.

The religious right, defined as a fusion of conservative Christianity and political conservatism, goes back at least to the 1930s and the anti–New Deal crusades of Gerald B. Winrod and Gerald L.K. Smith. The movement's current incarnation, however, dates from the late '70s. It was initially organized by Southern evangelical ministers who wanted to prevent the Internal Revenue Service from removing the tax exemption on the segregated Christian academies they had set up in response to *Brown* v. *Board of Education*. More broadly, the religious right coalesced in response to Supreme Court decisions limiting school prayer and liberalizing abortion, and to the dramatic changes in American family life and leisure that spurred feminism, gay rights, teenage sexuality and, of course, MTV.

Two kinds of religious organizations emerged from this crucible. The first, epitomized by the Rev. James Dobson's Focus on the Family, defined itself primarily as an educational organization concerned with family issues that were relevant to evangelical Christians, including sex education and abortion. Focus on the Family lobbies the government, but only on these issues, and it does not back candidates. In political terms, it resembles Jewish, Catholic and mainline Protestant pressure groups.

Mixing Religion and Politics

The second kind of organization, more properly termed the "religious right," is typified by the Rev. Jerry Falwell's Moral Majority and the Rev. Pat Robertson's Freedom Council and Christian Coalition. Of these, the coalition is currently the most important, with nearly 1 million registered members, 900 chapters and a $13 million annual budget. All these groups function like political movements and parties—implicitly or explicitly running and endorsing candidates, and even participating as a political faction within the Republican Party. (Many of these organizations are registered as nonprofit with the IRS and must use artful dodges like grading candidates on issues through "Christian scorecards" to get around restrictions on open political endorsements.)

Initially, this new religious right was divided along denominational lines. Anti-Darwinian fundamentalists, who believed the Bible was literally true, gravitated toward Falwell's Moral Majority; Pentecostals and other charismatic Christians, who believed, in addition, that Jesus granted mortals the power to speak in tongues and perform miracles, joined Robertson's Freedom Council. Through the Christian Coalition, Robertson and [its director] Ralph Reed, to their great credit, have united what Robertson calls "biblical Christians" in a single organization.

Reed tries to portray the coalition as a garden-variety lobby. "We really see ourselves as a kind of faith-based Chamber of

Commerce, a kind of League of Women Voters, if you will, for people of faith," he told National Public Radio in June 1994. But if he's looking for an analogy, he's looking in the wrong place. The new religious right doesn't resemble the Chamber of Commerce or other business interests so much as it does the old Socialist and Communist parties. Its members are united by conviction rather than by function or employment; and its goal is not merely to defend certain discrete interests but to win political power on behalf of a broad agenda. . . .

"I'm Christian, You're Not"

In several states, religious right candidates have been turning school board races into religious contests. In 1994 in a Dallas suburb Christian right candidates, facing two Jewish incumbents, emphasized their church affiliation and religious beliefs at candidate forums. Afterward, Rebecca Morris, one of the defeated incumbents, told an interviewer, "I never know how to deal with the issue 'I'm a Christian and you're not.'" Protestants and Catholics also feel the burden. Said Republican Mary Bennett of the Texas party's elections to choose delegates, "If you didn't say, 'I am a Christian and I attend a certain church,' you were excluded."

In each presidential election since 1980, religious right leaders have argued for supporting the Republicans against the Democrats on religious grounds. In 1992 Operation Rescue founder Randall Terry wrote in his newsletter that "to vote for Bill Clinton is to sin against God." Later, Reed told a conference sponsored by the Center for Ethics and Public Policy that Terry's statement "presented a harsh side of religious belief that is simply inappropriate in a political context." Reed did not say that Terry's views were inappropriate because they imposed a religious test on candidates. They were inappropriate because they were "harsh."

A Threat to Privacy

In building its movement, the religious right has run up against another even more formidable wall than that separating church and state. In 1989 the Gallup Poll asked people to rate whom they would like to have as neighbors. Near the bottom, well behind Catholics, Jews, blacks, Koreans, Hispanics, Vietnamese, Russians and unmarried couples, were "religious fundamentalists." Only members of religious cults were less popular. The poll was about fundamentalists, but the result touches on what bothers many people about the religious right: the suspicion that it is a threat to privacy.

In the last thirty years the Supreme Court has claimed that the right to privacy exists under the "penumbras" of the Bill of Rights. Yet the concept has been a practical part of American life ever since a booming early-twentieth-century economy made it possible for large numbers of citizens to enjoy the kind of education and leisure—including a prolonged period of adolescence—hitherto reserved for the upper classes. This new realm of personal freedom became the basis for new kinds of consumer products, as well as sexual experimentation and novel social arrangements. The religious right arose, however, partly in response to the trends that emerged from this freedom, and its agenda has consisted of seeking to restrict and regulate personal life. The religious right wants to prohibit abortion; allow employers to hire and fire based on a person's sexual practices; maintain criminal statutes against homosexuality and some kinds of heterosexual practices; and force television networks and stations not to show programs that it deems immoral. Jeff Fisher, the director the Texas branch of the American Family Association, boasted to me that his group had succeeded in forcing thirteen of seventeen ABC affiliates to take the acclaimed "NYPD Blue" off the air.

©1994 Sharpnack. Reprinted with permission.

While Americans certainly sympathize with some of the religious right's causes—a majority probably opposes taxpayer financing of abortions and insurance coverage of the "domestic partners" of public employees—it's no surprise that they see the movement's overall agenda as an assault on their privacy. They see in the religious right's obsession with homosexuality and soft-core pornography an unruly intolerance that flows from a repressed discomfort with any kind of sexuality. They see in its attempts to dictate television programming a desire to turn every network into Robertson's Family Channel, which intersperses the televangelist's *700 Club* with *Lassie, Gunsmoke* and *Rin Tin Tin* reruns.

A Politics of Stealth

Reed, Robertson and other savvy religious right leaders recognize that they face a dilemma: namely, that the source of their movement's energy and growth—its sectarian Christian quest to restore a golden age—is also the source of its political weakness. Since its founding in 1989 the Christian Coalition has followed two different strategies for surmounting the problem. First, it has pursued what Reed once imprudently called a politics of "stealth." The coalition focused on low-turnout school board, city council and party organization races where a motivated minority could carry the day, and then mobilized its followers through churches to support coalition-backed candidates, while neutralizing potential opposition by concealing from the public the religious basis of their candidacy. When Election Day came, many of these candidates won simply by gathering 20 percent of the vote in a crowded field.

The strategy, however, had its limits. Take the case of San Diego. In November 1990 religious right candidates captured sixty of eighty-eight local races and took over the Republican Party's central committee. The next fall twenty-four school board candidates won seats—often without revealing what they stood for. But once the new religious right school board and city council members revealed their sectarian priorities—for instance, through demanding that the computer spelling program "Wizards" be removed from the schools and that a Roald Dahl classic be banned from library shelves—moderate Republicans began organizing. In November 1992 moderate Republicans and Democrats won forty-one of forty-two city council and school board races against the right's candidates. . . .

Worthless Solutions

Some conservatives, who are uncomfortable with the religious right's quest for a Christian America, still contend that the movement has served a useful purpose by dramatizing the dissolution of the family and the decline of schools. I'd argue the contrary. Because of its reliance on religious explanations, the Christian right has most often slighted these problems. The solutions it has proffered are either harmful or irrelevant.

Take the schools. The religious right candidates I've observed have stood for the reinstitution of school prayer, the elimination or drastic modification of sex education and the introduction of creation science. These are not issues on which the future of our young rests. School prayers are either blatantly discriminatory or meaningless; sex education is, well, complicated; and creation science is bunkum. At one suburban San Diego school board race that I covered in 1992, none of the three religious right candidates had his children in public schools. These candidates didn't have the faintest idea whether new chemistry labs were needed or what kind of vocational training was being offered. In the 1994 Texas race for the state board of education, four of the six religious right candidates either had their children in private schools or taught them at home.

The Christian Coalition's ventures into broader public policy have also lacked merit. Take fiscal policy. Like other Republican conservatives, the coalition advocates a balanced budget, but it also proposes that the U.S. Treasury raise the tax exemption families receive for each dependent from $2,500 to $10,000. At that rate, no family of four that earns $40,000 or less would pay income taxes. Robert McIntyre, the director of Citizens for Tax Justice, estimated that such a plan would add $200 billion to the 1994 deficit. How does the coalition plan to cut taxes drastically and balance the budget? A call to [economist] Arthur Laffer might be in order.

No Compassion

There is, finally, the even more disturbing question of the religious right's Christianity. Is the movement contributing, however imperfectly, to the spread of virtue and morality? As Reinhold Niebuhr argued in *Moral Man and Immoral Society*, Christianity at its best has leavened the natural egoism of groups and nations. It has contributed a pure love of humankind, a humble recognition of the imperfection of human beings and an ethic of compassion toward the sick and the oppressed. The Christian awakenings, beginning in the 1750s, have played an immensely positive role in shaping America's transition from colony to nation, from agricultural to industrial society—and in lending urgency to the struggle against slavery and racial inequality.

Is today's religious right injecting a Christian spirit of compassion and selflessness into American politics? The only group that seems to elicit its compassion is the unborn; it does not display similar compassion, for instance, toward the poor or the victims of AIDS—two obvious groups for which a modern-day Christian might be expected to express concern. Robertson, who in his youth worked among the poor, now has contempt for their suffering. Asked about the welfare system, he quotes Paul's [biblical] advice on how to deal with disorderly Thessalonians, "If any-one will not work, neither let him eat." And why is the Christian Coalition against community rating of insurance premiums? Reed warns that there will be "massive cross-subsidies from intact, two-parent families with children who lead *healthy* lifestyles to those who do not." Iowa coalition official Steve Sheffler, a former insurance agent, puts it more clearly: families of the healthy will have to pay higher premiums to cover AIDS patients.

It is not a question of what policy government should finally adopt. Perhaps welfare should be eliminated and community rating discouraged. Rather, it is a question of the spirit with which Americans—and Christians—should regard the poor and the ter-minally ill. The Christian right is, in fact, a perfect example of what happens when the founding principles of church and state are violated. What Thomas Jefferson and James Madison under-stood, and what Niebuhr affirmed 150 years later, is that Chris-tianity does not provide a political agenda but rather an underly-ing social conscience with which to approach politics. Religion plays its most constructive role precisely when church and state are separate.

When the two are fused, however, when organizations acting in the name of Christianity seek political power, then religion becomes subordinate to politics. It becomes infected with the darker egoism of group and nation; it no longer softens and counters our ungenerous impulses but clothes them in holy righteousness.

Periodical Bibliography

The following articles have been selected to supplement the diverse views presented in this chapter.

The American Legion Magazine	"How America Devalues Religion," June 1994 An interview with author Stephen Carter.
William L. Anderson	"Onward, Christian Soldiers?" *Reason*, January 1994.
Charles W. Colson	"Can We Be Good Without God?" *USA Today*, May 1994.
Ben A. Franklin	"Evangelists Adopt More Moderate Camouflage for Their Holy War on Democrats," *The Washington Spectator*, October 15, 1994. Available from PO Box 90, Garrett Park, MD 20896.
Free Inquiry	Special section on children and religion, Summer 1994. Available from PO Box 664, Buffalo, NY 14226-0664.
Free Inquiry	"A Statement: In Defense of Secularism," Spring 1994.
Liz Galst	"The Right Fight," *Mother Jones*, March/April 1994.
Leslie Kaufman	"Life Beyond God," *The New York Times Magazine*, October 16, 1994.
Daniel Lapin	"The Severed Flower: Conservatism Without God," *Crisis*, November 1994. Available from PO Box 1006, Notre Dame, IN 46556.
Jon G. Murray	"The Christian Coalition," *American Atheist Newsletter*, October 1994. Available from PO Box 140195, Austin, TX 78714-0195.
Merrill D. Peterson	"Jefferson and Religious Freedom," *The Atlantic Monthly*, December 1994.
The Religion & Society Report	"The Purging of Tradition," November 1994. Available from 2275 Half Day Rd., Suite 350, Deerfield, IL 60015.
Murray N. Rothbard	"Hunting the Christian Right," *Rothbard-Rockwell Report*, August 1994. Available from the Center for Libertarian Studies, PO Box 4091, Burlingame, CA 94011.
John M. Swomley	"Flawed 'Christian Coalition' an International Danger," *The Human Quest*, September/October 1994. Available from Churchman Co., 1074 23rd Ave. N., St. Petersburg, FL 33704.

How Does Materialism Affect America?

**AMERICAN
VALUES**

Chapter Preface

In 1989, Russian president Boris Yeltsin returned to the then-Soviet Union after a tour of America and exclaimed, "Their supermarkets have thirty thousand food items. You can't imagine it." Indeed, Americans are blessed with an abundance of products and services, many of which seem improved every year.

While many American consumers praise the conveniences of faster, smaller, or more powerful personal computers, cellular telephones, and other products, others consider these and varied items such as designer clothing and disposable diapers unnecessary or wasteful. Sociologist Michael Schudson examines this ambivalence toward consumer products:

> How should we weigh the Cadillac or BMW against the subcompact Chevy? The former may use more resources and be less fuel-efficient, but it also may be a better—and safer—car. Some practical and spartan products may not only be aesthetically unappealing but ecologically unsound. Paper plates and towels may be easier to use and dispose of than china and cloth towels that are designed for regular re-use, but they are wasteful.

Yet defining or measuring excess and wastefulness—in all their varying degrees—is difficult. What one group of people considers excess may be viewed by another as necessity, and the two sides may rarely come to agreement. As Schudson writes: "I do not see any likelihood of . . . reach[ing] agreement about whether our own or anyone else's purchases and uses of products are justified." Materialism and related topics—greed, prosperity, and thrift—are analyzed and debated by the authors in this chapter.

242

*"Capitalism is the real enemy of tyranny. It stands
not for accumulated wealth or greed but for
human innovation, imagination, and risk-taking."*

Capitalism Drives
America's Success

Malcolm S. Forbes Jr.

Malcolm S. Forbes Jr. is the president and CEO of Forbes Inc.
and editor in chief of *Forbes*, a biweekly business magazine. In
the following viewpoint, Forbes argues that capitalism is the
driving force behind success in America. Forbes asserts that the
capitalist system gives people the freedom to make their own
choices of goods and services and allows entrepreneurs to seek
and implement innovations in the marketplace. Capitalism,
Forbes contends, is a spur for innovators to learn from their mistakes and try again.

As you read, consider the following questions:

1. According to Forbes, what makes a successful capitalist?
2. Why does Forbes believe that health care needs open
   competition?
3. On what basis does the author criticize "industrial planning"?

Malcolm S. Forbes Jr., "Three Cheers for Capitalism," *Imprimis*, vol. 20, no. 9, September
1993. Reprinted by permission of the author.

Living in the 1990s, we are uniquely able to judge what the American economy has achieved in the 20th century. For this reason, we ought to give three cheers for capitalism. By the term, I mean "democratic capitalism," which is as fundamentally different from the "managed capitalism" of modern-day central planners as it is from the "state capitalism" of old-style fascists, socialists, and communists.

Capitalism works better than any of us can conceive. It is also the only truly *moral* system of exchange. It encourages individuals to freely devote their energies and impulses to peaceful pursuits, to the satisfaction of others' wants and needs, and to constructive action for the welfare of all. The basis for capitalism is not greed. You don't see misers creating Wal-Marts and Microsofts.

Think about it for a moment. Capitalism is truly miraculous. What other system enables us to cooperate with millions of other ordinary people—whom we will never meet but whom we will gladly provide with goods and services—in an incredible, complex web of commercial transactions? And what other system perpetuates itself, working every day, year in, year out, with no single hand guiding it?

Capitalism is a moral system if only because it is based on *trust*. When we turn on a light, we assume that there will be electricity. When we drive into a service station, we assume that there will be fuel. When we walk into a restaurant, we assume that there will be food. If we were to make a list of all the basic things that capitalism provides—things that we take for granted—it would fill an encyclopedia.

How to Become Successful Capitalists

How do we become successful capitalists? The answer sounds simple, but it is often overlooked in places where you would think they would know better. (I am referring, of course, to government, the media, and our most elite business schools and economics departments.) We succeed as capitalists by offering goods and services that others are willing to buy. Many capitalists do not make correct assumptions about what to offer and fail, but that is as it should be. There is no guarantee of success in any area of life, including business—there is always risk. The particular advantage of capitalism is that failed businesses don't necessarily equal a failed economy; they make way for successful businesses.

But even the most successful businesses can't afford to forget about market principles. AT&T is a case in point. In the 1970s, fiber-optic technology was available, but AT&T decided that it would delay fully converting for perhaps 30 to 40 years. It wanted to fully depreciate its old plants and equipment, and, because it enjoyed a virtual monopoly over its customers, it saw no reason to spend a lot of money on a new long distance calling system. But then an upstart company, MCI, raised a couple billion dollars through the much-maligned "junk bonds" market in order to set up its own fiber-optic network. AT&T had no choice but to keep up with its competition, and, as a result, the U.S. experienced an enormous advance in communications that has put it ahead of its foreign competitors and that has benefited hundreds of millions of consumers.

About twenty-five years ago, the federal government filed an antitrust suit against IBM because it had grown so successful that its name had become virtually synonymous with the computer industry. But the would-be trustbusters underestimated the vitality of an open marketplace. IBM's dominance of mainframe computers, microchips, and software did not prevent the rise of rival companies such as Digital Equipment, Apple Computer, Sun Microsystems, and Microsoft. Today, IBM's very existence is in jeopardy.

Capitalism Enhances Life

Sometimes the capitalist is painted as dooming workers to "dehumanizing" toil, monotonous, repetitive work. On the contrary, productivity is so much greater, even in routine work, that workers have far more leisure time to engage in pursuits other than grubbing for a living. Far from dehumanizing mankind, capitalism has enhanced the quality of life.

No matter how you consider the capitalist, he is not the evil person he is portrayed by many to be. Those who presume to malign him by labeling him a capitalist, which he is, should consider what that label really means. A capitalist begins by denying himself consumption he could have enjoyed, undertakes risk, transforms his savings into tools and machines that help to increase production, and so becomes a benefactor of man.

Roger M. Clites, *The Freeman*, September 1994.

Around the same time, John Kenneth Galbraith wrote *The New Industrial State*, in which he argued that though the Ford Motor Company was no longer the biggest of the auto companies (GM had roughly 50 percent of all sales), Ford was so large that it did not have to pay particular attention to its shareholders or its customers. Apparently, Japanese automakers did not read John Kenneth Galbraith, or the reports of countless other "experts" who claimed that it was impossible to compete against Ford, GM, and Chrysler. They even ignored their own early failures to storm the U.S. market in the 1950s and early 1960s.

Finally, after years of trying, Japanese automakers succeeded—and succeeded to an extent that no one could have predicted—in challenging the hegemony of the "giants" in Detroit.

Then there is Sears & Roebuck. What more mundane business could there be than retailing? Yet, around the turn of the century, Sears made retailing truly exciting, reaching out to millions of people with new marketing methods and new products. By the end of the 1940s, it dwarfed all competitors. In the last several decades, however, the company lost its way and became a self-serving, insulated bureaucracy. Now it is closing its doors on numerous stores. Its market share has plunged—and its profits have almost disappeared.

Why, by contrast, has another retail firm, Wal-Mart, achieved its phenomenal success? Not because its founder Sam Walton used to ride around in a pickup truck visiting his stores, though that was good publicity. It was because he recognized the importance of computer technology and had systems devised that help store operators respond to inventory information on a weekly and even daily basis. Sam Walton knew that success, even once it was achieved, was something that couldn't be taken for granted.

What should be clear from each of these examples is that capitalism is not a top-down system—it cannot be mandated or centrally planned. It operates from the bottom up, through individuals—individuals who take risks, who often "don't know any better," who venture into areas where, according to conventional wisdom, they have no business going, who see vast potential where others see nothing.

Often, these individuals literally stumble across ideas that never would have occurred to them if they were forced to work in a top-down system. And they take supposedly "worthless" substances and turn them into infinitely valuable ones. Look at penicillin. Whoever thought that stale bread could be good for anything? The same goes for oil before the invention of the gasoline engine and the automobile and for sand before the invention of glass, fiber optics, and the microchip.

There is another important thing to remember about capitalism: Failure is not a stigma or a permanent obstacle. It is a spur to learn and try again. Edison invented the light bulb on, roughly, his *ten-thousandth* attempt. If we had depended on central planners to direct his experiments, we would all be sitting around in the dark today.

Open vs. Managed Competition

This leads to the next question regarding capitalism: What is the market? Central planners don't like the word; they prefer to say "market forces," as if describing aliens from outer space. But nothing could be further from the truth. The market is *people*. All of us. We decide what to do and what not to do, where to shop and where not to shop, what to buy and what not to buy. So when central planners trash "market forces," they are really trashing us.

Unfortunately, they are the ones who seem to be calling the shots today on a number of issues that should be left up to the market, i.e., up to us. One such issue is the spiraling costs of health care. Not surprisingly, central planners advocate a top-down approach to reform. With unconscious irony, they call it "managed competition."

But we have *already* tried managed competition; in fact, it is managed competition that has caused so many problems in the health care industry in the first place. Specifically, the tax code penalizes individuals who want to buy medical insurance by making them pay for it with after-tax dollars, even if they are self-employed. Only 25 percent of their premiums are deductible. But companies may buy health insurance with pre-tax dollars. So they, instead of their employees, have become the primary purchasers of insurance. This drives a wedge between the real customers and the real providers and obscures the real costs of such features of the system as low deductibles. Imagine if every time you went to the supermarket you gave the cash register receipt to your employer, who then submitted it to the insurance company for a claim. What would happen to food prices? They would sky-rocket, because you wouldn't care whether a bottle of soda cost $10, $100, or $1,000.

Need for Reform

The problem doesn't stop there. Growth in demand and improvements in technology—key ingredients to success in any other business—have instead led to crisis in the health care industry. More people are receiving better treatment than ever before and leading longer, healthier lives, but perversely this has sent costs up rather than down and has overloaded the delivery system.

If we want genuine health care reform we must return to open competition. The tax code must be revised so that individuals can buy health insurance with pre-tax dollars and set up medical IRAs [individual retirement accounts] for their families that can be used to finance routine medical expenses. There is no doubt that a majority of Americans would choose this option. They want to have control over their own health care decisions. Many would choose policies with higher deductibles. Premiums would go down and so would paperwork. Physicians and hospitals would see their patient load come under control and would be induced to offer competitive rates and services. The potential benefits are enormous.

A couple of years ago, Forbes Inc. faced yet another round of steeply rising costs for health care. We wanted to do something that enabled our employees to police those costs in a way we, the employer, were unable to do. So we gave them a stake in the process. We offered them a *bonus:* They could keep the difference between their claims and $500—and we would double the amount. Thus, if they went through a calendar year without filing any health claims on the insurance company, we would pay them as much as $1000, tax free.

What happened? Suddenly, every employee became cost-conscious. On major medical and dental expenses, claims went down 30 percent. These savings financed the bonuses and our total health care costs went up *zero percent* in 1992. This was not because we compelled millions of people to participate in some "managed competition" scheme, but because we let a few hundred individuals make their own health care decisions.

Letting Individuals Decide

Letting individuals make their own decisions is what capitalism is all about, but virtually all central planners (now in their heyday under the Clinton administration) and a good many members of the U.S. Congress (Republicans as well as Democrats) fail to realize it. They do not, for example, realize that it is the decisions of individuals that really decide how much tax revenue the government collects and how well the economy prospers. Between 1982 and 1986, the American private sector created well over 18 million new jobs, including a record number of high-paying positions. Of these, 14 million were created by new businesses. But, in 1987, Congress raised the capital gains tax to one of the highest levels in the industrial world. What happened? New business and job creation declined sharply. The nation was hit with a recession. And tax revenues, which were supposed to rise, went down. All this occurred because individuals made the decision *not* to invest. Today, there is almost *$7 trillion* of unrealized capital gains that is going begging because of high taxes. If Congress lowered the capital gains rate, it would mean *more* not *less* tax revenues. It also would overwhelm any stimulus package Washington could concoct for revitalizing the economy.

Central planners also tend to be big fans of "industrial planning," whereby government picks the "winners" in the marketplace through subsidization of select companies and technologies. They ignore the fact that this will obliterate incentives for companies to remain competitive, breed corruption and special interests, and penalize the small businesses that are the backbone of the economy.

And they want to micromanage the monetary system, knocking

down the value of the dollar against the yen or raising it against some other currency in closed-door meetings with bureaucrats from other industrialized nations. They do not realize that one of the most important functions of money is to serve as a constant, reliable measure. A ruler is supposed to be 12 inches long, but they want to change it to 11 or 13 inches whenever it suits their political strategy. You and I might call this a swindle, but in Washington it is called sophisticated economic management.

Agent of Change

Even such a simple word as "change" takes on a whole new definition in Washington, meaning change directed from above by well-intended central planners and politicians who think that they "know better" than most people when it comes to making decisions. But, in truth, the most revolutionary sweeping agent of change is capitalism. Look at what has happened in Eastern Europe, the Soviet Union, Latin America, and Asia. When people are free to make their own decisions, they have a stake in the economy, and when they have a stake in the economy, they have a stake in serving others, and when they have a stake in serving others, they have a stake in fighting for freedom.

Capitalism is the real enemy of tyranny. It stands not for accumulated wealth or greed but for human innovation, imagination, and risk-taking. It cannot be measured in mathematical models or quantified in statistical terms, which is why central planners and politicians always underestimate it. As I noted at the outset, it is up to us, then, to give three cheers for capitalism. Who knows? If we cheer loud enough, perhaps even they will listen.

"Both liberalism and conservatism are proven failures in preventing the economic and social crackup of capitalism."

Capitalism Is Driving America's Decline

New Unionist

Capitalism is an invidious system that mires America in a morass of selfish greed, violence, and social breakdown, the *New Unionist* argues in the following viewpoint. The paper's editors blame the capitalist scramble for money for promoting the beliefs that greed is good, that nothing should stand in the way of getting rich, and that the poor are deserving losers. Widening gaps between the rich and poor and increases in crime and violence could force the capitalist system to usher in an authoritarian state, the editors conclude. *New Unionist* is a monthly publication of the New Union Party, a socialist political party based in Minneapolis.

As you read, consider the following questions:

1. Why do conservatives like the "dog-eat-dog" quality of capitalism, in the author's opinion?
2. According to the author, what percentage of the population saw their pay fall during the Reagan era?
3. What does the author mean by America's "split personality"?

"America the Violent," *New Unionist*, March 1993. Reprinted with permission of the New Union Party, Minneapolis, Minnesota.

Disgruntled employee kills boss, co-workers.

12-year-old injured by gunshot at area school.

Unemployed man shoots wife, 3 children before turning gun on self.

Angry patient fires at doctors in hospital emergency room.

Headlines such as these that not long ago would have seemed shocking and outrageous are today commonplace. American society is gripped by a passion for violence and death that borders on the pathological.

This deeply disturbing trend has not, of course, gone unnoticed. Editorialists, political commentators, cultural critics, religious leaders—all join in a chorus of anguish over violence in America. And many do accurately identify the reasons for the violence epidemic.

People are working harder and longer just to keep their heads above water, and often they fail to keep up regardless how hard they try.

More and more workers who had the idea their jobs were secure and were used to comfortable incomes suddenly get a layoff notice. Then they find it impossible to get another job in their field or at the same pay level.

The unskilled and semiskilled labor of greater numbers of workers—especially minorities—is no longer needed due to automation and industry's flight to the third world. They become permanently excluded from the regular work force with no hope for a decent standard of life.

A Heavy Toll

These economic pressures take a heavy toll on personal relations. Families break up, which usually only exacerbates the economic problems, especially for the woman.

Frustrated, angry, hopeless, stressed out—people lash out violently at the individuals they imagine are responsible for their distress, or even randomly at people they don't even know.

While identifying these causes of violence, the commentators are nevertheless at a loss to find a solution for it. It's not because no solution exists. It's because they all—liberal and conservative alike—share an allegiance to the profit economy, an allegiance that is a prerequisite for being a recognized "expert." Intellectually chained to the status quo, they are prohibited from acknowledging that the social breakdown they describe is the inevitable product of the competitive system and can only be reversed by building a new economic system.

The liberal idea is that the social problems that arise from the competitive market system can be solved without changing the economic system. The government, liberals say, can and should

251

intervene, not to eliminate the pursuit of profit, but to regulate it and to aid the victims of its social destructiveness. We can preserve capitalism *and* have social justice, they claim; in fact, government must address the needs of the propertyless in order to secure the interests of the propertied.

Sidewalk Bubblegum ©1993 Clay Butler. Used by permission.

Liberalism did succeed in patching over the social conflict and containing the potential violence inherent in the "I-got-mine-you-get-yours" ethos of capitalism. As long as the economy grew fast enough, it could provide both profits for business and money for government social programs. And as long as at least an artificial social concern and national unity could be bought, the tensions and frustrations that lead to violence could be minimized.

Following World War II, U.S. corporations were unchallenged

in world markets, which fostered rapid economic growth in the U.S. The capitalist system, which had been rocked by the Great Depression, was now stabilized, and the prospects of those who questioned the legitimacy of the system waned, as the liberals had predicted.

In these years of liberalism triumphant, the right wing of capitalist opinion was also forced to retreat.

A Dog-Eat-Dog System

The right-wingers—so-called conservatives—acknowledge that capitalism is a dog-eat-dog system. But this is the very thing that makes it so wonderful to them, because it matches what they believe is the pit-bull nature of human beings. The competitive scramble for money is the "survival of the fittest." When some people end up with lots of dough, it just proves they are superior, and, being superior, they therefore deserve their riches.

This thinking leaves a lot to be desired as far as logical reasoning is concerned. But it does serve to justify the right's insistence that the government should not interfere in or restrict in any way the anything-goes pursuit of riches of the free market. Since people get rich as the reward for their superior talents, other people get poverty as the penalty for inferior talent, lack of initiative, laziness, etc. For liberals to reward the laggards with welfare programs or ghastly "quotas" and set-asides is little short of treason to the Constitution. And the fact the system's winners are taxed to pay for the welfare state is a virtual abomination against the Lord!

While the rightists insist on small, weak government when it comes to regulating business and aiding the working class, they simultaneously insist on greatly expanding government powers to police and suppress the workers.

While they consider any infringement on their property interests by government as unconstitutional meddling by a bloated state bureaucracy, they are eager to toss out constitutional freedoms that restrict the police in crushing outbreaks of rebellion in the lower ranks of society. They want aggressive government action when it comes to cracking down on the petty criminals who stick up convenience stores, or on the homeless and beggars who scare customers away.

Pat Buchanan expressed this sentiment in his peculiar froth-mouthed eloquence when he told the 1992 Republican National Convention that the only way to deal with L.A.-style riots is with overwhelming force. Which the new-car-dealer and real-estate-promoter delegates gleefully interpreted to mean killing rampaging darkies in the thousands rather than the tens.

Such outspoken cries for blood were relegated to the backwater political swamp of right-wing fringe groups during the 1950s and '60s heyday of liberalism.

But beginning in the early '70s, the period of capitalist stability came to an end. President Lyndon Johnson's liberal program of defeating "communism" in Asia while expanding the welfare state in the United States strained the economic resources of the system. When the war in Vietnam and the Great Society were then paid for by letting the printing presses roll, the ground was prepared for the debilitating inflation of the '70s.

By the time the 1980 election rolled around, liberalism had been completely discredited. Not only was it held responsible for the economy's malaise, the social peace it claimed the welfare state had bought also seemed to be unraveling.

What the right called "special-interest groups"—women, blacks, gays, seniors, et al.—were demanding more and more from a system that could less and less afford to give. After for years building up the expectations of people, liberalism in the end couldn't deliver. The result was heightened frustration, which produced greater rather than lessened social tension and explosiveness and reopened the possibility that the capitalist system itself might be challenged by a popular uprising.

These developments vindicated the right wing in its own mind. They also opened the door to political power for the right.

The financial and activist base of the right is small- and medium-size business owners and those who aspire to the American dream of business ownership. But given their small number relative to the population as a whole, their votes alone could never win an election. To do that, right-wing candidates have to be able to win working-class votes.

The liberals' hold on the majority of voters stemmed from the fact that their regulated capitalism and social programs were immediate economic gains for the working class. The challenge for conservatives was to win the workers to a 19th-century vision of capitalism unbound, a change backward that would be an immediate economic loss for the majority.

Exploiting Public Fear

Openly stating that the right-wing ideal would have wage earners working harder for less obviously wouldn't do much to win votes. The conservative propagandists therefore had to devise a more clever vote bait to win elections.

While crime and violent acts have become more and more prevalent in American society, most people, of course, conduct their affairs nonviolently. In fact, rather than commit violence, most people live in fear of its being committed on them. And this is especially true of rank-and-file working people, who can't afford expensive security systems in their homes, who have to live and work in high-crime areas, who rely on public transportation to get around.

The right-wingers, in control of the Republican Party with the nomination of Ronald Reagan in 1980, played on these fears, giving their appeal a distinctly racist flavor to inflame what were fact-based fears into irrational hysteria.

The rightists claimed liberal "permissiveness" was the reason people couldn't feel safe in their homes and on the streets. They blamed people on welfare (again with a not-too-subtle racist undertone) for being the economic burden felt by "hardworking Americans." They created dreamy images of a make-believe American past, where happy families raised their children in safety and security, which Ronald Reagan would bring back.

Crisis and Decay

Capitalism is bad enough today. But as time goes by the problems of the people will get worse as capitalism continues to slide deeper into crisis and decay. Capitalism as a socioeconomic system has served its historic purpose. But science, technology and life in general continue to develop. Because capitalism cannot basically change its nature it cannot serve the present, and especially the future needs of society, the people of the United States will be forced to consider socialism as a solution.

Capitalism careens from one crisis to another because it is unplanned, chaotic and anarchistic. Its credo is each dog for himself and dog-eat-dog.

Gus Hall, *People's Weekly World*, October 22, 1994.

So when people voted for Reagan they weren't voting for lower wages and a longer workweek. They were voting for safe streets, personal responsibility and strong families. What they got, however, was lower wages and longer hours—and *more* crime, violence, family breakup and emotional crisis.

The Reaganites unleashed the free market as promised. They also promoted the right-wing ideology to justify the workings of unregulated capitalism: that greed is good; that no one should let moral feelings inhibit their doing whatever necessary to get rich; that losers deserve to be poor and shouldn't be assisted by government.

But at the same time they celebrated the goodness of money, 80% of the population were seeing their pay fall. Workers who had swallowed Reagan's line and now discovered that *they* were the losers had to deal with their sense of failure. Many did so by insisting they were cheated out of their rightful place by blacks or women or other "special interests," who were still receiving special treatment.

Right-Wing Propaganda

To cover up the failures of Reaganism, the right-wing propagandists played to and reinforced the resentments of white male workers. The talk-radio clowns especially sent out the message that discrimination and violence against non-white, non-male Americans was justified.

Using these tactics, they succeeded for a while in holding the Republican voting bloc together. Reagan was reelected in '84 and George Bush, employing the same campaign techniques, got in in '88.

But when Reagan's debt-induced expansion turned into recession under Bush, the economic realities could no longer be ignored. The total failure of the conservative program became obvious, and voters returned to the Democrats in '92.

This doesn't mean that liberalism has been rehabilitated. Bill Clinton insists he's a "new Democrat" rather than an old "tax-and-spend" Democrat. In fact, he hints at further cutbacks in the welfare state (under the guise of welfare "reform") as well as in government benefits that go to middle-income workers. He intends to deal with crime not by ameliorating poverty but with more police.

The Democrats have been conservatized not by the force of any philosophical arguments but by the hard economic reality that the government is essentially busted. Far from growing robustly, the economy is stagnant, incapable of generating the revenue to fund social programs at current levels, much less expand them.

Without the means to buy social peace, and with economic security evaporating for more and more citizens at the same time the traditional support networks of family, church and social-service agencies are crumbling, more violence, not less, is on the agenda for American society.

An Authoritarian Crackdown?

Both liberalism and conservatism are proven failures in preventing the economic and social crackup of capitalism. As the deterioration proceeds, the system may well be forced to play its final political card—an authoritarian police state.

The election loss by Reagan-Bush conservatism has prompted mainstream Republicans to try to steer the party back toward the middle. But the defeat hasn't chastened the hard right. In fact, it has responded by becoming even more hysterical in condemning "out groups" as the cause of social turmoil—gays, minorities, feminists, immigrants. In doing so, it is preparing mainstream America to accept the need for an authoritarian crackdown in the name of "stability."

Right now, the great majority is not prepared to see our political democracy overturned for the sake of "order." And it would be a great mistake for rank-and-file labor activists to become demoralized by the influence of the right or to give up the struggle for economic democracy in the face of right-wing propaganda intended to divide and emasculate the working class.

American culture has a split personality, a product of the nation's origins in a radical democratic revolution and its growth as an expansionary frontier society.

On the one hand, Americans are highly individualistic and committed to the pursuit of self-interest and the accumulation of wealth as life's goal. On the other hand, there is a strong sense of egalitarianism—a belief that no one is better than anyone else, that everyone deserves an equal chance and that everyone should work together for the good of the community.

The unique American ideology holds that these two outlooks are not opposing ones but entirely consistent with one another, that there's no contradiction between property accumulation and equality.

The Scramble for Wealth

That's the belief system. But in the objective world of dollars and cents, the competitive race for wealth does create huge disparities and inequalities in a capitalist society.

The power of ideology is that it enables people to believe contradictory things simultaneously—at least for a while.

For example, early in our history most free Americans saw nothing wrong with slavery in a nation they prided as the most freedom-loving in the world. But as the economies of the North and South developed in opposing ways, it became apparent that the institution of slavery threatened to subvert the freedom of white people as well.

People then understood that the nation couldn't exist "half slave and half free." Virtually overnight the majority recognized that slavery mocked the ideals of freedom, that accumulating wealth on the basis of slave labor was evil and should not be allowed. And they became willing to make great sacrifices in a bloody civil war to destroy it.

The whole history of America is one of periods of individualism, greed, selfishness and inequality alternating with opposite periods of social concern and egalitarianism. In these reactions against the destructiveness of profit making, people struggled to put limits on the scramble for wealth that was disrupting the cohesion and peace of society.

Today there is widespread apprehension and revulsion over

257

the direction the nation is headed. As the extent of the damage wrought by the free market becomes apparent to more and more people, a renewed sense of community solidarity to recapture the American ideal of equality will rapidly emerge.

It is then that the American people will need to finally understand that the ideal and the profit system are incompatible. We will have to choose, once and for all, between the America of equality, democracy and freedom promised by the Revolution of 1776 and the America we know today of inequality, conflict and unrelenting violence.

"Who could have predicted a century ago that the richest civilization in history would be filled with polluted suburban tracts dominated by automobiles, shopping malls and a throwaway economy?"

Americans Consume Too Much

Alan Thein Durning

Americans are often criticized for their overconsumption and wastefulness. In the following viewpoint, Alan Thein Durning argues that advertising, television, and shopping malls are powerful and dangerous forces that compel Americans to buy products they can easily live without and to spend far more than is necessary. Consumerism in America is worthy of rejection, Durning contends, but individual action is not enough. What is required are committed individuals to help steer society away from materialism and excess, he concludes. Durning, author of *How Much Is Enough? The Consumer Society and the Future of the Earth*, is a senior researcher at the Worldwatch Institute, a Washington, D.C., organization concerned with environmental degradation.

As you read, consider the following questions:

1. In Durning's opinion, how does consumerism in America affect the environment?
2. How is a mall unlike a community, according to Durning?
3. According to the author, how did Benjamin Franklin and other historic figures regard materialism and money?

For Sidney Quarrier of Essex, Connecticut, Earth Day 1990 was Judgment Day—a day of ecological reckoning. While tens of millions of people around the world were celebrating in the streets, Sidney was sitting at his kitchen table with a yellow legal pad and a pocket calculator. His self-imposed task was to tally up the burden he and his family had placed on the planet since Earth Day 1970. He began tabulating everything that had gone into their house—oil for heating, nuclear-generated electricity, water for showers and for the lawn, cans of paint, appliances, carpeting, furniture, clothes, food and thousands of other things. Then he turned to everything that had come out—garbage pails of junk mail and packaging, newspapers and magazines by the cubic meter, polluted water, and smoke from the furnace. "I worked on that list most of the day," Sid said. "I dug out wads of old receipts, weighed trash cans and the daily mail, excavated the basement and shed, and used triangulation techniques I hadn't practiced since graduate school to estimate the materials we used in the roofing job."

Incremental Consumption

But Sid knew he wasn't counting everything, such as the re-sources needed to manufacture and deliver each object on his list. National statistics suggested, for example, that he should double the energy used in his house and car to allow for what businesses and government used to provide him with goods and services. He visualized a global industrial network of factories making things for him, freighters and trucks transporting them, stores selling them, and office buildings supervising the process. He wondered how much steel and concrete his state needed for the roads, bridges and parking garages he used. He thought about resources used by the hospital that cared for him, the Air Force jets and police cars that protected him, the television sta-tions that entertained him, and the veterinary office that cured his dog.

As his list grew, Sid imagined a haunting mountain of dis-carded televisions, car parts and barrels of oil—all piling up to-ward the sky on his lot. "It's only when you put together all the years of incremental consumption that you realize the totality." And that totality hit him like the ton of paper packaging he'd hauled out with the trash over the years. "The question is," Sid said, "Can the Earth survive the impact of Sid, and can the Sids of the future change?"

That *is* the question. Sidney Quarrier and his family are no gluttons. "During those years, we lived in a three bedroom house on two and a half acres in the country, about 35 miles from my job in Hartford," he recounts. "But we have never been rich," he insists. "What frightened me was that our consumption was typical of the people here in Connecticut."

Sid's class—the American middle class—is the group that, more than any other, defines the contemporary international vision of the good life. Yet the way the Quarriers lived for two decades is among the world's premier environmental problems, and may be the most difficult to solve. Only population growth rivals high consumption as a cause of ecological decline, and at least population is seen as a problem by many governments and citizens of the world. Consumption, in contrast, is almost universally seen as good.

The Consumer Society

The consumer society was born in the U.S. in the 1920s, when brand names became household words; when packaged, processed foods made their widespread debut; and when the automobile took over the center of American culture. . . .

Since its birth, the consumer society has moved far beyond American borders, yet its most visible symbols remain American. Coca-Cola products are distributed in over 170 countries. The techniques of mass marketing perfected in the U.S. now appear on every continent, teaching former East Germans, for example, to "Taste the West. Marlboro."

Unfortunately, the furnishings of the American lifestyle—such as automobiles, throwaway goods and packaging, a high-fat diet and air conditioning—are provided at great environmental cost. We depend on enormous inputs of the very commodities that are most damaging to the Earth: energy, chemicals, metals and paper. In the U.S., these industries dominate the most-wanted lists for energy use, toxic emissions and polluting the air with sulfur and nitrogen oxides, particulates and volatile organic compounds.

The natural systems that sustain our consumer society are fraying badly. If all the world's people produced as much carbon dioxide as we do, global emissions of this greenhouse gas would multiply threefold. If everyone used as much metal, lumber and paper as we do, mining and logging—rather than tapering off as ecological health necessitates—would jump more than threefold.

Our high consumption levels are not the inevitable results of economic success; they are partly produced by institutions in our society that intentionally prompt our acquisitive impulses. Advertising, commercial TV and shopping malls, for example, are so omnipresent that they have become centerpieces of our culture.

A Barrage of Advertising

Advertising is everywhere, bombarding us with some 3,000 messages a day, according to *Business Week*. Ads are broadcast by thousands of TV and radio stations, towed behind airplanes, plastered on billboards and in sports stadiums, and bounced around the planet from satellites. They are posted on ski lifts, hung on banners at televised parades and festivals, piped into classrooms and doctors' offices, woven into the plots of feature films, and stitched onto Boy Scout merit badges and professional athletes' jerseys. The Viskase company of Chicago prints edible slogans on hot dogs, and Eggverts International is using a similar technique to advertise on thousands of eggs in Israel.

Reprinted with special permission of King Features Syndicate.

Entire industries have manufactured a need for themselves. One advertising executive writes that ads can "make [people] self-conscious about matter-of-course things such as enlarged nose pores [and] bad breath." Advertisers especially like to play on the personal insecurities of women. As B. Earl Puckett, then head of the Allied Stores Corporation, said 40 years ago, "It is our job to make women unhappy with what they have."

The cultivation of needs is a mammoth global enterprise. For four decades, advertising has been one of the world's fastest-growing industries. In the U.S., ad expenditures rose from about $200 per capita in 1950 to almost $500 in 1990, while total global advertising expenditures rose from an estimated $39 billion in 1950 to a whopping $247 billion in 1988, growing far more rapidly than economic output.

Marketers increasingly target the young. One specialist told *The Wall Street Journal*, "Even two-year-olds are concerned about their brand of clothes, and by the age of six are full-out consumers." The children's market in the U.S. is so valuable—over $75 billion in 1990—that our companies spent $500 million marketing to it in 1990, five times more than a decade earlier. They started cartoons centered on toys, and began direct-mail sales to youngsters enrolled in their company-sponsored "clubs." Such saturation advertising has let some firms stake huge claims in the children's market. Mattel vice president Meryl Friedman brags, "Mattel has achieved a stunning 95 percent penetration with Barbie [dolls] among girls age three to eleven in the U.S." Major retailers have opened Barbie departments to compete for the loyalty of doll-doting future consumers, and Barbies now come equipped with Reebok shoes and Benetton clothes.

Advertising promotes consumerism, but it also uses lots of paper. Ads pack the daily mail—14 billion catalogs plus 38 billion other pieces of junk mail clog the post each year in the U.S. They fill periodicals: a typical American newspaper is 65 percent advertising, up from 40 percent half a century ago. Every year, Canada cuts 17,000 hectares of its primeval forests—an area the size of the District of Columbia—just to provide American dailies with newsprint for ads. As Colleen McCrory, one of a growing cadre of Canadians trying to protect their forests, says, "Basically, we're turning the whole nation into pulp."

TV and the Malling of America

TV is a fixture of life in the consumer society. Almost every home has a set—or two or three—operating seven hours a day in the U.S. on average, issuing a stream of soap operas, situation comedies, music videos and sales spiels. All that TV would not be worrisome for the environment were it not for the message of most programs, since the technology itself—like most communications media—uses comparatively little energy and materials. But commercial TV promotes the restless craving for more by portraying the high consumption lifestyle as a model to be emulated. And as commercial TV advances around the world, it has proved exceptionally effective at stimulating buying urges. As Anthony J.F. Reilly, chief executive of the food conglomerate H.J. Heinz, told *Fortune* magazine, "Once television is there, people of whatever shade, culture or origin want roughly the same things."

The shift in U.S. retailing from neighborhood and downtown shops to huge suburban shopping malls has encouraged the consumer lifestyle. Our almost 35,000 shopping centers surpassed high schools in number in 1987. Over the past three decades, shopping center space has grown twelvefold: 2,000 new centers opened each year from 1986 to 1989. With so many competing malls, new ones may go to extremes to draw shoppers. The Mall of America, which opened in Bloomington, Minnesota, in August, 1992, expects to attract more visitors each year than Mecca or the Vatican. Along with four department stores and more than 300 specialty shops, it offers a seven-acre Camp Snoopy theme park, a giant walk-through aquarium, a two-story miniature golf course, countless cinemas and restaurants, plus some 13,000 parking spaces.

These malls suck commerce from downtown and neighborhood merchants. In Denver, Colorado, each of six suburban malls takes in more dollars from sales than does the entire downtown commercial district. Shopping by public transit or on foot becomes difficult, auto traffic increases, and sprawl accelerates. In the end, noncommercial public places such as town squares and city streets lose their vitality, leaving us fewer attractive places to go, besides the malls that set the whole process in motion.

The Cult of Growth

The way market societies make a fetish of economic growth is a clue to the failure of consumption to truly nourish. The cult of growth is a sign of the triumph of hope over satisfaction, of the life of promise over the life of fulfillment.

So the culture of mass consumption develops around a core of unfulfilled longing, in which advertising promises that the goods we can buy carry with them the states of consciousness we desire and in which the broken promise of each purchase leads to new yearnings.

People become addicts, willing participants in an economy based on the premise of growth without limit.

Andrew Bard Schmookler, *The Futurist*, July/August 1991.

Perhaps by default, malls have taken over some of the traditional functions of public spaces. They offer entertainment in the forms of video arcades, multi-screen theaters and exercise centers. Avia, a top sports footwear manufacturer, even has a shoe especially designed for mall walking. William Kowinski writes in *The Malling of America:* "Someday it may be possible to be born, go from pre-school through college, get a job, date, marry, have children . . . get a divorce, advance through a career or two, receive your medical care, even get arrested, tried and jailed; live a relatively full life of culture and entertainment, and eventually die and be given funeral rites without ever leaving a particular mall complex—because every one of those possibilities exists now in some shopping center somewhere."

Shopping has become our primary cultural activity. Americans go to shopping centers on average once a week—more often than to church or synagogue. We spend six hours a week shopping—more than the Soviets did in the late 1980s, when their shopping queues were world-famous. Our teenagers spend more time in malls than anywhere besides school or home. The time we spend shopping is second only to that spent watching TV when it comes to categories of time use that have grown fastest since mid-century.

Yet a mall is not a community. It is a commercial enterprise, designed in minute detail to prompt impulse buying. It artificially isolates people from the cycles of nature, from the time of day and from changes of weather. It excludes those who cannot afford to spend as much as the rest of the consumer class. And rather than grounding people in attachments to their neighbors and their community, it fosters a sort of care-free anonymity.

Consumerism or Sufficiency

The forces that manufacture desire—ads, TV, shopping centers—are so familiar as to go virtually unnoticed in today's consumer society. Yet the conscious and widespread cultivation of needs is relatively recent in human history, tracing its roots back scarcely a century. There is no reason these forces cannot be fundamentally redirected—constraining advertising to its appropriate role of informing buyers, turning TV to conserving ends, and replacing shopping malls with real communities. Indeed, there is every reason to do so, for the sake of the planet and our own peace of mind. . . .

Consumerism has shallow historical roots. To reject it is not to jettison anything of lasting significance from our cultural inheritance; it is to reaffirm ancient teachings rooted in the philosophy of sufficiency. Materialism was denounced by all the sages, from Buddha to Muhammad, and every world religion is rife with warnings against the evils of excess. "These religious founders," observed historian Arnold Toynbee, "disagreed with each other in the pictures of what is the nature of the universe, the nature of the spiritual life, the nature of ultimate reality. But they all agreed in their ethical precepts. . . . They all said with one voice that if we made material wealth our paramount aim, this would lead to disaster."

Even in the U.S., arguably the most wasteful society in human history, thrift and frugality are buried touchstones of our national character. None other than Benjamin Franklin wrote, "Money never made a man happy, yet nor will it. There is nothing in its nature to produce happiness. The more a man has, the more he wants. Instead of filling a vacuum, it makes one." Only in this century has consumption rather than thrift gained acceptance as a way to live. In 1907, economist Simon Nelson Patten was still considered a heretic when he declared, "The new morality does not consist in saving but in expanding consumption."

Consumerism's roots may be shallow and vulnerable, but individual action and voluntary simplicity alone do not appear capable of uprooting it. We must combine the political and the personal. To rejuvenate the ethic of sufficiency, a critical mass of committed individuals must emerge. But they must balance their efforts to change themselves with a bold agenda to challenge the laws, institutions and interests that profit from profligacy. They must target not only the perennial environmental foes—industrial polluters and resource extractors—but the advertisers and mall developers who fan the flames of consumerism.

The future of life on Earth depends on whether we among the richest fifth of the world's people, having fully met our material needs, can find other sources of fulfillment. Having invented the automobile and airplane, can we return to bicycles, buses and trains? Having pioneered sprawl and malls, can we recreate human-scale settlements where commerce is an adjunct to civic life rather than its purpose? Having introduced the high fat, junk-food diet, can we instead nourish ourselves on wholesome, locally produced fare? Having devised disposable plastics, endless packaging and instant obsolescence, can we make objects that endure? If we can, we might be happier, for our affluence has brought us to a strange pass. Who could have predicted a century ago that the richest civilization in history would be filled with polluted suburban tracts dominated by automobiles, shopping malls and a throwaway economy? Surely, this is not the ultimate fulfillment of our destiny.

Living by sufficiency rather than excess lets us return, culturally speaking, to the human home: the ancient order of family, community, good work and a good life. Perhaps Henry David Thoreau was right when he scribbled in his notebook beside Walden Pond, "A man is rich in proportion to the things he can afford to let alone."

"The era of conspicuous consumption is dead. Long live the age of conspicuous thrift."

Americans Are Becoming Thrifty

Walecia Konrad

In contrast to the free-spending lifestyles of many Americans in the 1980s, the leitmotif of the 1990s is thriftiness and savings, Walecia Konrad asserts in the following viewpoint. Konrad describes the attitudes of prosperous individuals who, like many others, have made frugality a daily part of their lives. Konrad maintains that these diligent savers have taken to heart the value of spending less, seeking out bargains, and making thrift a virtue. Konrad is a senior writer for *Smart Money*, a monthly magazine of personal business published by the *Wall Street Journal*.

As you read, consider the following questions:

1. What is the personal savings rate in America compared to other nations, according to Konrad?
2. According to the author, how do some people stretch their dollars?
3. How are some individuals planning for retirement, according to Konrad?

At a trendy New York City lunch spot one afternoon, Malinda Banash, a public relations executive from Boston, is catching up with two friends. As long as the topics are work and current events, the conversation is pleasant enough, but hardly what you'd call vivacious. But when talk turns to bargain-hunting, it's as if the entire table has been wired into a 220-volt socket. "You won't believe what I found," Banash says in a can-you-top-this tone. "See these pantyhose? One buck a pair from the hosiery catalog. It sure beats paying $7 for Calvin Kleins, and they fit just as well."

Yes, the era of conspicuous consumption is dead. Long live the age of conspicuous thrift. Formerly free-spending yuppies have discovered the virtues of saving money, and they're bragging about it to anyone within earshot. At cocktail parties and around water coolers, the one-upmanship of the upwardly mobile no longer focuses on sleek new BMWs or $100 silk ties. Instead, friends, neighbors and coworkers compete fiercely to hunt down the best bargains and bank the most money.

Make no mistake: Keeping up with the Joneses is still as much a part of the American character as, say, acquisitiveness. It's just that the definition of keeping up has changed. These days it means clipping coupons, stocking up on gallon jugs of laundry detergent at the warehouse club and fattening up that 401(k) [retirement plan]. Winners in the 1990s version of this game aren't the ones who spend the most, they're the ones who will go to any lengths to save.

Take Joan Gmora, a New York attorney. In the '80s, if your secretary had admired your perfectly tailored, three-piece Michael Kors silk outfit, you might have allowed, modestly, that it cost a pretty penny. Actually, though, Gmora fielded that compliment just the other day. And because we're in the '90s now, Gmora replied: "Only 75 bucks at the sample sale." These days, it's not what you've spent, it's what you've saved.

It's amazing what people can adapt to if they have to. If times are tight, no problem: Just make saving a contact sport. Much to the delight of Gmora and other dedicated shoppers, saving can be just as much fun as spending—as long as you get to crow about your bargains later. "I'm known as the quintessential bargain hunter," Gmora says, "and I'm not embarrassed to brag about it. When you walk into a party wearing a fantastic dress, the best thing you can tell someone is, '$100 in the back room at Loehmann's.'"

Oh, all right, bargain mania isn't all frivolity and friendly rivalry. Demographers and economists can point to a host of dreary, perfectly rational reasons for this new era of competitive saving, most notably the recent recession, persistently high unemployment numbers and the ever-escalating cost of retirement. "This generation of American workers is the first that will be responsible for funding their own retirement," says Barry Bosworth, an economist at the Brookings Institution.

The upshot: a rage for saving. And if it's any consolation, saving doesn't just feel good, it's good for you. Geoffrey Greene, a senior associate at DRI/McGraw Hill, predicts the personal savings rate will climb from last year's 4.8 percent of disposable income to around 8 percent by the year 2010, a level that hasn't been reached since the early 1970s. Granted, that's still pretty puny compared with other countries. The Japanese, for instance, sock away 15 percent of their disposable income, while Germans save 12.6 percent of theirs. But it's a start, and at least we Americans don't need anything but peer pressure to get us motivated. In China, where banks are on a drive to open new savings accounts, people have to put up with dorky slogans like "Save with Enthusiasm."

New Stinginess

Why the new stinginess? It's the economy, stupid. The 1980s and the days of easy money are over. As candidate Bill Clinton endlessly intoned, people are working harder for less money. Naturally, they recognize the virtue and utility of holding on to as much of it as possible. "In the 1980s, we believed that everybody could have everything," says Amy Dacyzyn, founder and editor of the (very real) *Tightwad Gazette*. "Now we're making choices."

The four-year-old *Gazette* provides tips on how to get through life without spending money unnecessarily—one recent article was entitled "I'm Dreaming of a Tight Christmas"—and has attracted 55,000 subscribers and a slew of zeitgeist-riding imitators, including the *Tightwad Newsletter*, *Tightwad Times*, the *Smart Skinflint* and the *Penny Pincher*.

Daniel Gross, *The Washington Post National Weekly Edition*, April 25-May 1, 1994.

Still, for most of us, retirement is a long way off, and worries about the future simply aren't sufficient explanation for this newfound passion for parsimony. No, the most compelling reason is right here, right now. It's over there in the corner, red-faced and making an ungodly racket about the lamentable state of its diaper.

Yep, you guessed it: bambinos. Few things will catapult former spendthrifts into the savings era faster than a new baby. "Face it," says Sheila Gormley, a circulation manager from Harper Woods, Mich., "kids are expensive."

She ought to know. After she and her husband had their first child last year, their lives changed dramatically. Gone are the dinners out and fancy new clothes. Now that Gormley is pregnant again—this time with twins—she has become a master at the competitive savings game.

Let's watch Gormley and some of her fellow Savings All-Stars show how the game is played. The scene: a Detroit suburb. The time: about 7:00 one recent Saturday morning. Gormley and three other moms are staking out the neighborhood garage sales. They've carefully combed the classifieds to find the sales with the best potential deals. One mom is on the lookout for a Little Tikes Cozy Coupe. So in demand are these ubiquitous red and yellow scooter cars that the ads often mention them in the headline. After painstakingly plotting their course, the women hit their first sale, where a dandy, nearly new Cozy Coupe is on offer. Make that *was* on offer. Another early riser has beat them to the punch, bidding $15 for the toy.

Undaunted, Gormley & Co. continue their quest. A few sales down the road, Sheila bags a barely worn windbreaker for her son. The cost: two bucks. It's a little roomy, but it will keep until he grows into it. "You can't help feeling like you won a contest when you find something like that," says Gormley.

The office offers no respite from zealous bargain hunters. One weekday this summer Gormley walked into the office and found a stack of Sunday newspaper coupon inserts sitting in a box. One of her co-workers had managed to get her hands on the inserts a few days early and brought them in for her colleagues to leaf through, looking for favorite brands. Now clipping coupons has become a regular office event. Better get there early, though, or the best deals will be gone.

Every once in a while, the competition gives way to a brief interlude of generosity. When Gormley's son was born, one of the best-received gifts at the baby shower was an inch-thick stack of coupons for Pampers and other baby necessities. "Believe me, I used each and every one of them," says Gormley.

Ron Willis, chief operating officer at Initial Contract Services in Atlanta, no longer needs diapers for his two kids, aged 20 and 11. That doesn't mean the pressure to save is off, though. If anything, it's escalating. You see, if the 44-year-old Willis wants to retire by age 55—and he does—he's got a mountain-size job ahead of him, despite his healthy salary.

In the past, Willis rarely thought twice about saving. But some of his buddies hipped him to the new game in town. "We all went through a period during the eighties where we all were having a big time," says Willis. "We felt that our jobs were secure and that we didn't have to worry about our performance or the future. But then the floor started dropping out and we realized we had to start making sure we were taking care of ourselves and our families."

Now, instead of spending his salary and banking only his bonus, Willis assiduously pursues his early-retirement goal by investing 15 percent of his monthly paycheck in mutual funds, stocks and bonds. So strong is Willis's newfound zeal for saving that he was willing to disappoint his wife by refusing to consider a move to a larger home. Their compromise: a fresh paint job and some new landscaping.

He's also cut back on his quest for status: He gave up his favorite toy, a $44,000 Jaguar, and bought a Ford Explorer. "Like everyone in my age group, I'm rethinking my priorities," he says, with just a hint of resignation.

What's really wild about savings chic is that even folks who don't need to watch their nickels and dimes are doing it anyway—and claiming to enjoy it. Case in point: Kenneth L. Wyse, a vice president at Van Heusen in New York. Until recently, Wyse was well-known among his friends for his designer suits and spacious East Hampton vacation home, not for his sense of thrift. But last year Wyse waited until the end of the season to install a swimming pool at the house in the Hamptons. He figures it was worth the wait: The $9,500 price tag was $3,000 cheaper than it would have been at the start of the summer. Wyse continued bargain-hunting well into the next summer. "I went to buy urns for flowers for this $9,500 pool," he explains (and notice, please, that he makes sure to remind you that the pool cost only $9,500), "and I shopped around four different stores for the best price. A couple of years ago I would have just made a telephone call and ordered them—no matter what the cost."

Clearly, Wyse doesn't have to watch his many, many nickels and dimes. But like the rest of us, he reads the papers and watches CNN. "You're constantly battered by bad news," he says, "so you can't help but think about how much things cost and how much you're spending." He thinks enough about it to supplement his well-stocked 401(k) and company pension plan with a brokerage-house retirement account. He feeds it to the tune of more than $10,000 a year. So when his friends ask him what he's doing about retirement, he has a ready answer.

If someone as well-off as Wyse isn't immune to the zeitgeist, who is? Not Helen Varty, a 38-year-old fundraiser who lives and works in Houston. She sounds like a cat with a mouthful of canary when she describes how she won a recent round of the savings game. Just as she did in the go-go '80s, she meets a group of friends for dinner at least once a week. But instead of vying to find the trendiest new hot spot, she and her friends now challenge one another to come up with the cheapest eats. Varty currently reigns as queen on the strength of a vegetarian Indian hole-in-the-wall, featuring $3.50 entrees, which she recently ferreted out. "I've told everybody and their brother about this place," says Varty.

For Varty, bargain-hunting has become a form of entertainment. But there's also a more serious motivation. Although she's making more money than ever before, Varty has seen enough friends lose their jobs to know that the ax could fall on her, too. That's why she'll be camping in the Grand Canyon this year instead of taking her usual overseas vacation. And when she's not noshing on vegetable curry and papadams with her pals, she's cooking at home instead of ordering out.

Not everyone has adapted so easily to the sport of paupers. Despite his enviable income, New York City dentist Bruce M. Bieber and his wife, Aimee, have had trouble in the past disciplining themselves to put enough money away for retirement and tuition for their two young children. Well, there's nothing like a little peer pressure to stiffen your backbone. As Bieber and his friends started raising families, their talk seemed to drift away from cars and stereos and skiing trips toward the seemingly less sexy subject of household thrift. "Most of my friends with children get pleasure out of saving money," he says. With everyone in his crowd feeling so good about their big bank accounts, Bieber felt compelled to visit a fee-only financial planner for advice on saving and investing.

With the planner's help, Bieber figured that each year he needs to put $30,000 into his Keogh retirement plan and $17,000 into the tuition fund for his son and daughter. Even on Bieber's salary, that's quite a challenge. But his planner has him intoning the mantra of all the best savers—pay yourself first. Every week, says Bieber, before he tackles any other bills, "I write myself a check and put it in a separate passbook account at the same bank I keep my business account. That way I won't spend the money." At the end of each quarter Bieber and his financial planner meet to decide where to invest the funds. At the same time they review Bieber's savings to make sure they're mounting according to plan.

There's a certain breed of saver who would dismiss Bieber as a Bruce-come-lately. They were saving, they'll tell you, long before it was cool (you know the type: they knew all about the Beatles when they were just a rumor to the rest of us). Pat Wigman, from Berkley, Mich., has been penny-pinching ever since she went back to college five years ago. In that time she adopted a baby, quit her job at General Motors and started a day care center in her home. With the help of a computerized budget, Wigman figures to the penny how much she'll spend on household expenses each month and how much she can afford to transfer into savings. The money she socks away goes toward near-term goals such as vacations, Christmas presents and toys and clothing for her three children. Saving for retirement is under the purview of her husband, who is still employed at GM.

Like other diligent savers, Wigman clips coupons and then buys household basics in bulk when they're on sale. And she scored a notable triumph at Winkelman's, a local department store. Besides getting a sizable markdown on the dress she found, Wigman got an additional 15 percent off by taking advantage of a special discount the store offered to new charge-account customers. "I've never used the card since," she says, a little smugly.

To initiates, all this thrift can get old after a while. "If I hear about one more person buying a deep freeze so they can buy a side of beef to save money, I'm going to scream," says Malinda Banash. "What's wrong with the grocery store?" Careful, Malinda. These days, that kind of talk is heresy.

But for every skeptic who questions the true faith, there are dozens of new converts. "It's time for me to get more scientific about savings," says Rich Marx, who runs his family's computer products company in Philadelphia. "Everyone around me is socking it away." That goes for you, too. It might hurt at first, but you'll grow to like it. And besides, if you don't save, you don't get to brag.

"Instead of reviving traditional values, . . . the 1980s have ironically yielded a populace that is suspicious of the common good and addicted to narrow pleasures."

The 1980s Caused Cultural and Economic Decline

Cornel West

Many Americans and much of the media consider the 1980s a decade of rampant greed—an era when corporate raiders and financiers enjoyed enormous profits while the poor and middle classes suffered the loss of jobs and income. In the following viewpoint, Cornel West agrees and argues that the 1980s produced considerable malaise in America: income and wealth inequality, spiritual impoverishment, narcissism, pessimism, and public apathy and fear. For America to recover and succeed, West writes, it must address issues of race and poverty, rights and responsibilities, and violence and despair. West is a professor of religion at Princeton University in New Jersey and the author of *Race Matters*.

As you read, consider the following questions:

1. What were the economic and cultural consequences of Ronald Reagan's economic program, in West's opinion?
2. According to the author, what was the major paradox of the 1980s?
3. What does West mean by "civic terrorism"?

The 1980s were not simply a decade of glitz and greed. More important, they ushered in a new era of American history—the triumphant conservatism of Ronald Reagan, Rambo and retrenchment. The Reagan revolution was a full-blown ideological response to the anemic liberalism of the Jimmy Carter presidency that faltered in the face of runaway inflation, sluggish economic growth, the Iranian hostage crisis and the relative erosion of America's place in the global economy. The Rambo mentality harked back to a gunfighter readiness to do battle with an "evil" empire at nearly any cost. And the unapologetic retrenchment took the form of making people more comfortable with their prejudices and reducing public focus on the disadvantaged. The '80s discouraged a serious national conversation on the deep problems confronting us.

Laissez-Faire Capitalism

For the first time since the 1920s, the political Right—along with highly organized conservative corporate and bank elites—boldly attempted to reform American society. The aim of Reaganomics—couched in the diverse languages of supply-siders (Arthur Laffer), single-minded monetarists (Paul Volcker) and budget balancers (Alan Greenspan)—was to give new life to the utopian ideology of laissez-faire capitalism. This ideology cast high taxes, regulation and welfare assistance to the poor as the major impediments to economic growth and prosperity. Low taxes, deregulation and cutbacks in liberal social programs were viewed as a means to curtail inflation and generate an economic boom.

The decade brought us the largest peacetime military buildup in American history (about 28 percent of the federal budget in 1988!); it brought us the shortsighted choices of highly compensated corporate executives to consume, acquire and merge rather than invest, research and innovate. Together these developments caused high levels of public and private debt and the starvation of the public sector. There was little money for roads, railways. community development, housing, education, neighborhood improvement and, above all, decent-paying jobs for those displaced by industrial flight.

In the 1980s, the expansion of unfettered markets produced great wealth for the top 1 percent of the population, impressive income for the top 20 percent and significant decline in real wages for the bottom 40 percent. For example, the top 1 percent owned 44 percent of the household net wealth in 1929 and 36 percent in 1989 (in 1976, it dropped to 20 percent). By 1989, the top 1 percent of families owned 48 percent of the total financial wealth in the country. Of course, income inequality is less extreme than wealth inequality—yet the significant increase of both in the 1980s reveals the fundamental virtues and vices of unbridled capitalist markets. These markets yield *efficiency* and *ingenuity* in regard to what consumers desire and what products cost. At the same time they increase *inequality* and *isolation* in regard to what the most vulnerable people need and which basic social goods are available to them.

The major *economic* legacy of Reaganomics was to increase the disparity between rich and poor and to downsize the American middle class. Our social structure began to look less like a diamond and more like an hourglass. More hours of work were required to sustain a decent standard of living even as an undeniable decline in the quality of life set in—with increased crime, violence, disease (e.g., AIDS), tensions over race, gender and sexual orientation, decrepit public schools, ecological abuse and a faltering physical infrastructure. In short, Reaganomics resulted in waves of economic recovery, including millions of new jobs (many part-time), alongside a relative drop in the well-being of a majority of Americans.

Downward Mobility in the 1980s

During the 1970s, only a fifth of prime-age adults and their families suffered real income losses. In the decade ending in 1989, the proportion of those who lost income during their prime earning years jumped to a third, and half of that group experienced income losses exceeding 25%. About 42% of both blacks and high school dropouts saw their incomes shrink.

[Economist Stephen J.] Rose notes that those achieving very large income increases of more than 70% over 10 years lost ground, too. In the previous decade, some 35%, or more than a third of prime-age adults and their families, enjoyed such outsize real income gains. During the 1980s, the big winners fell to less than one in four.

Gene Koretz, *Business Week*, January 17, 1994.

The unintended *cultural* consequence of this economic legacy was a spiritual impoverishment in which the dominant conception of the good life consists of gaining access to power, pleasure and property, sometimes by any means. In other words, a fully crystallized market culture appeared in which civic institutions such as families, neighborhoods, unions, churches, synagogues, mosques held less and less sway, especially among young people. Is it a mere accident that nonmarket values like loyalty, commitment, service, care, concern—even tenderness—can hardly gain a secure foothold in such a market culture? Or that more and more of our children believe that life is a thoroughly hedonistic and narcissistic affair?

One of the telling moments of the '80s came when a member of the Federal Communications Commission boasted that when television was deregulated, "the marketplace will take care of children." And, to a significant degree, this unintentionally sad and sobering prophecy has come true. The entertainment industry, with its huge doses of sex and violence, has a disproportionate and often disgusting influence over us and our children. A creeping Zeitgeist of coldheartedness and mean-spiritedness accompanies this full-blown market culture. Everything revolves around buying and selling, promoting and advertising. This logic leads ultimately to the gangsterization of culture—the collapse of moral fabric and the shunning of personal responsibility in both vanilla suburbs and chocolate cities. Instead of reviving traditional values, the strong patriotism and social conservatism of the 1980s have ironically yielded a populace that is suspicious of the common good and addicted to narrow pleasures.

Culture Wars

The 1980s came to a close with the end of the cold war—yet the culture wars of a racially torn and market-driven American society loom large. A strategy of "positive polarization" (especially playing the racial card) has realigned the electorate into a predominantly white conservative Republican Party and a thoroughly bewildered centrist Democratic Party. This has helped produce a disgruntled citizenry that slouches toward cynicism, pessimism and even fatalism. Nearly half of all black children and 20 percent of all American children grow up in poverty, trapped in a cycle of despair and distrust.

The major paradox of the 1980s is that the decade ended with the collapse of moribund communist regimes of repression and regimentation—as well as the advent of more than 40 new social experiments in democracy around the world—just as American democracy is quietly threatened by internal decay. In other words, the far-reaching insights of Adam Smith's defense of the role of markets loom large in the eyes of former communist societies just as the cultural inanities of capitalism pointed out by Karl Marx become clearer in rich capitalist democracies—especially in the United States.

The market magic of the triumphant conservatism of the 1980s did help squeeze out fat and make American business more competitive in the brutal global economy. But we have yet to come to terms with the social costs. Confused citizens now oscillate between tragic resignation and vigorous attempts to hold at bay their feelings of impotence and powerlessness. Public life seems barren and vacuous. And gallant efforts to reconstruct public-mindedness in a Balkanized society of proliferating identities and constituencies seem farfetched, if not futile. Even the very art of public conversation—the precious activity of communicating with fellow citizens in a spirit of mutual respect and civility—appears to fade amid the noisy backdrop of name-calling and finger-pointing in flat sound bites.

Hope and Fear

The new decade of the 1990s begins with Americans hungry to make connections, to communicate their rage, anger, fury and hope. The new popularity of radio and TV talk shows is one symptom of this populist urge. Rap—the major form of popular music among young people—is another. The great American novel of the 1980s, the Nobel Prize laureate Toni Morrison's "Beloved," yearns to tell a "story not to be passed on"—a story of a great yet flawed American civilization afraid to confront its tragic past and fearful of its frightening future.

This fear now permeates much of America—fear of violent attack or vicious assault, fear of indecent exposure or malicious insult. Out of the '80s came a new kind of civic terrorism—physical and psychic—that haunts the public streets and private minds of America.

Race sits at the center of this terrifying moment. Although a small number of black men—who resemble myself or my son in appearance—commit a disproportionate number of violent crimes, the unfair stereotype of all black men as criminals persists. And despite the fact that most of these crimes are committed against black people, the national focus highlights primarily white victims.

Yet we all must assume our share of responsibility for the despair and degradation. The generational layers of social misery that afflict poor communities were rendered invisible in the 1980s not just by our government but by ourselves. Economic desperation coupled with social breakdown now threatens the very existence of impoverished communities in urban areas—with growing signs of the same forces at work in rural and suburban America. The drug and gun cultures among youth are the most visible symptoms of this nihilism. If we are to survive as a nation, the 1990s must be a decade in which candid and critical conversation takes place about race and poverty, rights and responsibilities, violence and despair.

The great comeback pop singer of the 1980s—Tina Turner—tragically croons, "What's Love Got to Do With It?" In a decade of glitz and greed, "who needs a heart when a heart can be broken?" And the most talented songwriting team in American popular music of the 1980s, Babyface and L. A. Reid, nod in their classic song, "My, My, My." Maybe in the '90s we can bring back some love, justice, humor and community.

"In the '80s, capitalism won its ideological battle with socialism and unleashed an epoch-making burst of creative energy."

The 1980s Generated Economic Prosperity

David Kelley and Jeff Scott

That the 1980s were a decade of greed is a myth perpetuated by the media, David Kelley and Jeff Scott argue in the following viewpoint. Kelley and Scott describe four cultural premises they say filtered out the real successes of the 1980s, including the belief that financial transactions create no value and that accumulation of wealth and pursuit of self-interest are unseemly. David Kelley is executive director of the Institute for Objectivist Studies, a research organization in Poughkeepsie, New York, that promotes capitalism and individualism. Jeff Scott is senior financial analyst, assistant vice president, at Wells Fargo Bank in San Francisco.

As you read, consider the following questions:

1. What made criticism of multimillion-dollar incomes invalid, according to Kelley and Scott?
2. How do the authors define greed?
3. According to the authors, what is lacking in reported statistics on income distribution?

From "Gekko Echo" by David Kelley and Jeff Scott. Reprinted, with permission, from the February 1993 issue of *Reason* magazine. Copyright 1993 by the Reason Foundation, 3415 S. Sepulveda Blvd., Suite 400, Los Angeles, CA 90034. For a sample issue, please call (310) 391-2245.

One of the most memorable scenes in Oliver Stone's 1986 movie *Wall Street* takes place at a shareholders' meeting of Teldar Paper Corp. Gordon Gekko, the oily financier, is defending his bid to take over the company. "The point is, ladies and gentlemen, that greed, for lack of a better word, is good. Greed is right. Greed works. . . . And greed, you mark my words, will not only save Teldar Paper, but that other malfunctioning corporation called the USA."

The Decade of "Greed"

Long before they ended, the 1980s were tagged as the decade of greed. That epithet has been repeated in dozens of books and movies, in hundreds of articles, editorials, and sound bites—repeated so often that it no longer seems controversial. In a single phrase, it represents that tumultuous decade as a melodrama peopled by greedy financiers obsessed with short-term profits, yuppies engaged in an escalating spiral of conspicuous consumption, and the long-suffering working and middle classes, who played by the rules but had to pay for the party. . . .

It is true that there was greed on the Street. Greed has always existed and always will. Though no one has yet found a way to measure these things, it may be that the flame of avarice burned brighter in the '80s than at other times. There was easy money to be made for a while, and easy money always draws people of easy virtue. But in every fundamental respect, the story being sold under the title "Decade of Greed" is the exact opposite of the truth.

In the '80s, capitalism won its long political conflict with socialism. Nations in the former Soviet bloc abandoned their commitment to command economies, as the rest of the world rushed to embrace private property, free markets, and limited government. Meanwhile, an unprecedented wave of innovation swept over the capitalist West.

Those who watched the collapse of the Berlin Wall may have taped it (on an '80s VCR) as it was broadcast live on CNN (the '80s news network). Or they could have called the airlines (on an '80s cordless phone) or faxed a travel agent (on an '80s facsimile machine) and reserved a flight to Germany (on an '80s computerized reservation system, at '80s prices for international flights). On the flight back, they could call their friends (from '80s airplane phones), leaving a message if necessary (on '80s voicemail). Then they could put their chunk of the wall next to their PCs and laser printers.

Accompanying these innovations in consumer products and services—and making them possible—was an equally profound wave of innovation in financial markets. The financial innovations were intangible, but they were just as real—and just as valuable—as the new consumer products. . . .

These innovations made a great deal of money for those who invented, developed, and took advantage of them, with the greatest profits typically going to those with the vision and courage to get in early. The profits were a fair return for the creation of value: The innovations lowered costs, improved efficiency, saved time. . . .

A Lasting Illusion

Whatever misdeeds were done, whatever speculative excesses were committed in financial markets, innovations in those markets created tremendous value, and the returns that innovators reaped were justly earned. The real question is: Why has this escaped the notice of the media, which continue to present the '80s as a melodrama of greed? Harvard's Michael Jensen observes, "I know of no area in economics today where the divergence between popular belief and the evidence from scholarly research is so great." Why does the illusion have such a grip on popular belief?

One reason, surely, is the disruptive and unsettling character of innovation. Corporate CEOs were unnerved by the "sharks" circling their companies. Old-line investment bankers had to compete with the brash upstarts from Drexel. Regulators couldn't keep up with the new investment vehicles that sprawled across their categories. And all of them found a sympathetic ear in the press. Despite their self-image as an adversarial class, journalists depend on those in power for access and visibility; they enjoyed their seats in a boat that was being violently rocked.

Average Household Income
(In 1990 Dollars)

	Lowest Fifth	Second Fifth	Third Fifth	Fourth Fifth	Highest Fifth	Top 5%
1989	7,372	18,341	30,488	46,177	90,150	145,651
1980	6,836	17,015	28,077	41,364	73,752	110,213

Bureau of the Census, *Money Income of Households, Families & Persons: 1990.*

But these sociological factors cannot be the full explanation. The establishment's desire to preserve its power could not be put forward publicly and explicitly as a reason for attacking the innovators. The cause of the vested interests is a cause that dare not speak its name; it needs a plausible rationalization. And the standards of plausibility are set by deep-seated cultural premises.

One such premise was stated by Gordon Gekko: "It's a zero-sum game. Somebody wins, somebody loses. Money itself isn't lost or made, it's simply transferred. . . . I create nothing. I own." Unlike the production of tangible goods and services, it is often assumed, financial transactions do nothing but shuffle ownership from one set of hands to another, without creating anything. The clearest manifestation of this premise is the popular response to breathtaking incomes. People were scandalized by the multimillion-dollar earnings of LBO [leveraged buyout] entrepreneurs like Henry Kravis and George Roberts of KKR [Kohlberg Kravis Roberts]. Yet for all that has been written about the "decade of greed," virtually no one has complained about the income of entertainers like Bill Cosby, who earned some $58 million in 1992. Nor are the accusations directed against entrepreneurs like Bill Gates of Microsoft or Sam Walton of Wal-Mart, who earned fortunes by creating new products and services. In 1987, the year that Michael Milken earned $550 million, no eyebrows were raised when Sam Walton gained $4 billion from the increase in the value of his stock.

This invidious distinction is invalid; innovations in the financial sector create value in the same way as innovations in the so-called real sector. In the one case, scientific knowledge about nature leads to inventions that exploit that knowledge, and the inventions are then developed and marketed by high-tech firms like Microsoft, which create benefits far in excess of the profits they retain. In the same way, theoretical insights about the economic and mathematical properties of financial structures lead to the invention of new financial technology that exploits those insights; the technology is then developed and marketed by firms like Drexel and KKR, which create much more value than they ever take back. As Milken said, "Walton used retailing technology to create value; Drexel used financial technology to create value . . . by enabling entrepreneurs to raise money far more efficiently than they could have done without us."

Antimaterialism

A second important cultural premise is a more general and elusive kind of antimaterialism—the attitude that material production is a low and degrading value by comparison with art, knowledge, love, or military glory. This pre-industrial attitude was the source of aristocratic disdain for the merchants and factory owners of 200 years ago. And of course it is a central theme of any deeply religious culture. In the highly secular societies of the West, this premise no longer has the power it once did. But it survives in a number of specific forms, including the tendency of journalists and literati to believe the worst of businessmen. In *Den of Thieves*, for example, [author] James Stewart refers casually to "corporate America's own willingness to dissemble," a sweeping generalization about an entire class of people on the basis of a few specific cases.

The antimaterialist outlook is embodied in the conventional concept of greed. For centuries, religious authorities taught that any concern with material wealth beyond the subsistence level was greedy, just as any sexual desire not connected with the needs of reproduction was lustful. In effect, economic ambition and sexual enjoyment—the two most powerful this-worldly motives—were put on the list of mortal sins. Today most people would not consider it sinful to strive for material comforts beyond the level of a medieval monk. But a vestige of the old view survives in the notion that it is greedy to want too much. Indeed, some dictionaries define greed as an excessive desire for material possessions. Notice that we do not have comparable concepts for those who want too much knowledge, too much beauty, too much love. Why is wealth singled out for special concern, if not for a lingering bias against material success? . . .

The Reagan Boom Years

The raw economic facts of the Reagan years are clear. From 1982 to 1990 the United States experienced 96 straight months of economic growth, the longest peacetime expansion in its history. Almost 20 million brand-new jobs, most of them high-paying jobs, were created. Inflation fell dramatically to low levels and stayed there as the American dollar once again became sound. Interest rates also fell dramatically and stayed down. The stock market soared, nearly tripling in value. Government revenues—at the federal, state, and local levels—nearly doubled.

Martin Anderson, *National Review*, August 31, 1992.

The concept of greed can properly be applied only when the desire for money is divorced from any concern with achievement. Some people want money without having to earn it—a life of luxury without the effort of producing. Some people want the prestige and social status that come with wealth. Some want power over others. In motive, greed is a desire for wealth without regard for achievement or creation. In action, greed is the unprincipled pursuit of wealth. This includes the use of force, fraud, and other coercive means. It also includes the violation of ethical norms, both the universal standards of honesty and fairness, and the specialized standards that apply to particular professions.

Many of those convicted of insider trading fit this description. As far as one can tell from what has appeared in print, for example, Ivan Boesky's motives had more to do with gaining prestige and power than with any concern for creating economic value. And his practice relied on the theft of information; he regularly bribed his informants at law firms and investment banks to violate their fiduciary responsibilities.

So there is such a thing as greed, and it is, as another common definition says, a reprehensible form of the desire for money. But what makes the desire reprehensible is not a matter of degree. If our standard is human life and happiness, we cannot set any arbitrary upper limit on permissible levels of material comfort—any more than there can be too much knowledge or beauty in our lives. It is not greed for a person with expensive tastes to work hard for the wherewithal to satisfy them. It is not greed for an entrepreneur to seek the capital he needs to make his vision real—even if the sums involved are huge.

Income Equality

A third factor that supports the view of the '80s as a decade of greed is an implicit sense of fairness about the distribution of income. Although egalitarians are guilty of considerable statistical subterfuge on this issue, there is no question that the income gap between rich and poor has widened recently. According to the standard Census Bureau measures, the share of aggregate income received by households in the upper fifth of the income scale increased from 44.2 percent in 1979 to nearly 47 percent in 1989. Gains by the upper tenth and the upper 1 percent were even more pronounced. The broadest measure of inequality, an index known as the Gini coefficient, began rising slowly in the mid-'70s and then rose more steeply in the last decade.

Press reports rarely bother to mention what ought to be obvious—that the poorest fifth in 1979 and the poorest fifth in 1989 are not the same class of individuals. Census figures indicate that real income in a given quintile changes by no more than 1 percent from one year to the next, whereas annual turnover in the composition of the quintiles is 20 percent to 40 percent. Thus the commonly reported statistics on income distribution do not measure the economic fate of individuals over time. They measure changes in the value that the market places on various productive functions—various "offices" in the economy that are occupied by different people at different times.

The real question of fairness is whether individuals are free to exploit the opportunities available to them in the effort to improve their condition. A mixed economy like ours places many constraints on such freedom, from the income tax to the regulations that control entry into many businesses and professions.

But longitudinal studies that follow individuals over time show there is still a great deal of social mobility. The Treasury Department's Office of Tax Analysis analyzed a random sample of people who filed tax returns during the decade from 1979 to 1989. Only 14 percent of those in the bottom quintile in 1979 remained there 10 years later; everyone else had moved up the income ladder as they got older. Indeed, more of them (15 percent) made it all the way to the highest quintile than remained at the bottom.

A similar study by the Urban Institute covered two 10-year periods: 1967-77 and 1977-87. In each case, those in the bottom quintile at the beginning of the decade increased their incomes by an average of 75 percent over the next 10 years. Those in the top quintile at the outset had an average increase of 5 percent. . . .

The Pursuit of Self-Interest

The last and the deepest of the cultural premises we need to consider pertains to self-interest. A market is a system of exchange among individuals pursuing their own purposes, largely for their own gain. But moralists have always looked askance at the motive of self-interest. In the 18th century, when an understanding of the market system began to emerge, writers like Bernard Mandeville felt they were asserting a moral paradox: that private vices could produce public benefits. Ever since, the pursuit of self-interest has carried the burden of proving that it serves the public good.

Yet as [social critic] Ayn Rand has observed, this attitude is incompatible with the liberal principle that individuals are ends in themselves—the principle that lies behind the legal system of individual rights. If the individual is an end in himself, he is morally as well as legally entitled to be an end *for* himself. He has the right to the pursuit of happiness, which includes the right to regard his own happiness as a self-sufficient end, requiring no further justification in the form of service to God, society, the biosphere, or whatever. . . .

These four premises—that financial activity is noncreative, that production in general is materialistic, that income should be distributed as equally as possible, and that the pursuit of self-interest is unseemly—served as filters blocking out the real story of the '80s. The successes of that era remain invisible because they violate these popular assumptions. . . .

In the '80s, capitalism won its ideological battle with socialism and unleashed an epoch-making burst of creative energy. But unless we reexamine our ethical assumptions, the history of the decade will be written by those who never liked capitalism and do not wish it well.

Periodical Bibliography

The following articles have been selected to supplement the diverse views presented in this chapter.

Jonathan Alter	"The '80s: A Final Reckoning," *Newsweek*, March 1, 1993.
Janice Castro	"The Simple Life," *Time*, April 8, 1991.
Susan Dentzer	"A Wealth of Difference: New Evidence Reveals Who Really Got Rich During the 1980s—and Why," *U.S. News & World Report*, June 1, 1992.
Peter F. Eder	"The Future of Advertising: Consumption in the Information Age," *The Futurist*, July/August 1993.
Joseph Epstein	"Culture and Capitalism," *Commentary*, November 1993.
Richard A. Falk	"The Free Marketeers," *The Progressive*, January 1994.
Jeanette Gardner	"When Less Equals More," *Moody*, December 1994. Available from Moody Bible Institute, 820 N. La Salle Blvd., Chicago, IL 60610.
Daniel Gross	"No, Brother, I Can't Spare a Dime," *The Washington Post National Weekly Edition*, April 25–May 1, 1994.
Thomas A. Hemphill	"The Two Faces of Capitalism," *Business and Society Review*, Winter 1994. Available from 200 W. 57th St., New York, NY 10019.
Donald McCloskey	"Bourgeois Blues," *Reason*, May 1993.
William Murchison	"Campaign to Smear the 80's Is False and Futile," *Conservative Chronicle*, November 2, 1994. Available from PO Box 11297, Des Moines, IA 50340-1297.
National Review	Special issue on Ronald Reagan and the 1980s, August 31, 1992.
Lynne Nugent	"Notes from an Iron Age: Humanism and the Commodity Fetish," *The Humanist*, January/February 1994.
Andrew Bard Schmookler	"The Insatiable Society," *The Futurist*, July/August 1991.
Michael Schudson	"Delectable Materialism: Were the Critics of Consumer Culture Wrong All Along?" *The American Prospect*, Spring 1991.

For Further Discussion

Chapter 1

1. According to Nelson Hultberg, the philosophy of individualism has been the foundation of freedom and laissez-faire capitalism. In what other areas of society do you see the influence of individualism? Do you agree with the author that individualism cannot be modernized? Why or why not?

2. Amitai Etzioni writes about the influence of both the community voice and the inner, personal voice on the individual. Describe how these two voices have influenced decisions you have made or actions you have taken. In what cases did your personal voice override the community voice? In what case did it submit to the community voice?

Chapter 2

1. Authors Charles Colson and Jack Eckerd argue that families, churches, and schools need to strengthen the work ethic of children. Identify various ways these institutions can accomplish that task. What advantages or disadvantages do these institutions hold regarding their influence on children, in your opinion?

2. According to sources cited by Robert W. Lee, drug and sex education programs in public schools are encouraging drug use and premarital sex rather than discouraging these activities. Do you agree with this assessment? Should these programs educate children by using moral messages? Explain.

3. James E. Wood Jr. contends that the Moral Majority opposes secular humanism in public schools as undermining Judeo-Christian beliefs. Can you find an adequate definition of secular humanism in the viewpoint? What is it? What do these critics believe public schools are doing to promote secular humanism? Do you agree that this is occurring in public schools? Why or why not?

Chapter 3

1. Nina J. Easton argues that cruelty and hostility permeate the entertainment media. According to Easton, why is the relationship between such negative behavior and the media's reflection of it so complex? Do you believe that cruelty in the media is an accurate reflection of your community or society as a whole? Why or why not?

2. In the *American Enterprise* viewpoint on popular culture, Todd Gitlin, Reinhold Wagnleitner, and others describe the success of American popular culture abroad. In your opinion, how are youths in other countries mimicking America's popular culture? Do you believe that this phenomenon is good or bad for these youths? Explain.

3. In their viewpoint, Barbara Ehrenreich and Todd Gitlin contend that many so-called "crises" in America are exaggerated by the media. The authors cite several examples of this, such as terrorism and drug abuse. Make a list of other examples you believe fit this category and explain why you chose them.

Chapter 4

1. Cal Thomas writes that there should be a fixed standard used to define what a family is. Do you agree that there should be only one definition of family? If so, what definition? If not, explain why not.

2. Stephanie Coontz cites studies on poverty to highlight how much economic hardship affects poor families. Barbara Dafoe Whitehead cites studies on the negative behavior of children of nontraditional families in her defense of traditional, two-parent families. Do you consider one type of study more convincing than the other in supporting the author's thesis? Explain.

Chapter 5

1. William P. Barr praises Judeo-Christian morality and God's law as standards for human behavior. Do you agree or disagree with Barr that America's government and laws must be rooted in Judeo-Christian precepts? Does Barr's position conflict with the concept of separation of church and state? Explain your answer.

2. Gore Vidal makes many strong assertions criticizing monotheistic religions. Identify what you consider to be the most valid and the most invalid statements in the viewpoint. Why do you believe they are valid or invalid?

Chapter 6

1. Malcolm S. Forbes Jr. describes the success and failure of several large corporations. What market principles should these corporations heed, according to Forbes? What mistakes did some of these corporations make? What advantages or disadvantages do you find in the open competition that capitalism fosters? Support your answer with examples.

2. The editors of the *New Unionist* maintain that individualism and egalitarianism are consistent with each other in America's belief system. According to the editors, what makes the two inconsistent in the real economic world?

3. Cornel West disagrees with David Kelley and Jeff Scott about the residual effects of the 1980s on American society. West believes that the 1980s levied much damage to social values; Kelley and Scott point out the economic gains of the decade. Which viewpoint makes the more persuasive argument? Why?

Organizations to Contact

The editors have compiled the following list of organizations concerned with the issues debated in this book. The descriptions are derived from materials provided by the organizations. All have publications or information available for interested readers. The list was compiled on the date of publication of the present volume; names, addresses, and phone numbers may change. Be aware that many organizations take several weeks or longer to respond to inquiries, so allow as much time as possible.

American Alliance for Rights and Responsibilities (AARR)
1725 K St. NW, Suite 1112
Washington, DC 20006
(202) 785-7844
fax: (202) 785-4370

AARR believes that democracy can work only if the defense of individual rights is matched by a commitment to individual and social responsibility. It is dedicated to restoring the balance between rights and responsibilities in American life. It publishes the bimonthly newsletter *Re: Rights and Responsibilities*.

American Atheists
PO Box 140195
Austin, TX 78714-0195
(512) 458-1244
fax: (512) 467-9525

American Atheists is an educational organization dedicated to the complete and absolute separation of church and state. It opposes religious involvement such as prayer and religious clubs in public schools. The organization's purpose is to stimulate freedom of thought and inquiry concerning religious beliefs and practices. It publishes the monthly *American Atheist Newsletter*.

American Vision
PO Box 724088
Atlanta, GA 31139
(404) 988-0555

American Vision is a Christian educational organization working to build a Christian civilization. It believes the Bible ought to be applied to every area of life, including government. American Vision publishes a monthly newsletter, *Biblical Worldview*.

Americans for Religious Liberty (ARL)
PO Box 6656
Silver Spring, MD 20906
(301) 598-2447

ARL is an educational organization that works to preserve religious, intellectual, and personal freedom in a secular democracy. It advocates the strict separation of church and state. ARL publishes numerous pamphlets on church/state issues and the quarterly newsletter *Voice of Reason*.

Center for Media and Public Affairs (CMPA)
2101 L St. NW, Suite 405
Washington, DC 20037
(202) 223-2942
fax: (202) 872-4014

CMPA is a research organization that studies the media treatment of social and political affairs. It uses surveys to measure the media's influence on public opinion. it publishes the monthly *Media Monitor*, the monograph *A Day of Television Violence*, and various other books, articles, and monographs.

Center for Media Literacy
1962 S. Shenandoah St.
Los Angeles, CA 90034
(310) 559-2944

The center is a media education organization. It seeks to give the public power over the media by fostering media literacy. It publishes the quarterly *Media & Values*.

Children's Defense Fund (CDF)
122 C St. NW
Washington, DC 20001
(202) 628-8787 / (800) CDF-1200
fax: (202) 662-3530

CDF works to promote the interests of children, especially the needs of poor, minority, and disabled children. It supports government funding of education as well as health care policies that benefit children. The fund publishes many books, articles, and other literature promoting children's interests, including the monthly newsletter *CDF Reports*.

Christian Coalition (CC)
1801 Sarah Dr., Suite L
Chesapeake, VA 23320
(804) 424-2630
fax: (804) 434-9068

Founded by evangelist Pat Robertson, the coalition is a grassroots political organization of Christian fundamentalists working to stop what it believes is the moral decay of government. The coalition seeks to elect moral legislators and opposes extramarital sex and comprehensive drug and sex education. Its publications include the monthly newsletter *The Religious Right Watch* and the monthly tabloid *Christian American*.

Coalition on Human Needs
1000 Wisconsin Ave. NW
Washington, DC 20007
(202) 342-0726
fax: (202) 342-1132

The coalition is a federal advocacy organization concerned with federal budget and tax policy, housing, education, health care, and public assistance. It lobbies for adequate federal funding for welfare, Medicaid, and other social services. Its publications include *How the Poor Would Remedy Poverty* and the bimonthly newsletter *Insight/Action*.

Common Cause
2030 M St. NW
Washington, DC 20036-3380
(202) 833-1200
fax: (202) 659-3716

Common Cause is a liberal lobbying organization that works to improve the ethical standards of Congress and government in general. Its priorities include campaign reform, making government officials accountable for their actions, and promoting civil rights for all citizens. Common Cause publishes the quarterly *Common Cause Magazine* as well as position papers and reports.

Eagle Forum
PO Box 618
Alton, IL 62002
(618) 462-5415
fax: (618) 462-8909

Eagle Forum is a Christian group that promotes morality and traditional family values as revealed through the Bible. It opposes many facets of public education and liberal government. The forum publishes the monthly *Phyllis Schlafly Report* and a periodic newsletter.

Family Research Council (FRC)
700 13th St. NW, Suite 500
Washington, DC 20005
(202) 393-2100
fax: (202) 393-2134

The council is a research, resource, and education organization that promotes the traditional family, which it defines as a group of people bound by marriage, blood, or adoption. It opposes schools' tolerance of homosexuality and school condom distribution programs. The council publishes numerous reports from a conservative perspective. These publications include the monthly newsletter *Washington Watch*, the bimonthly journal *Family Policy*, and *Free to Be Family*, a report that focuses on children and families.

Foundation for Economic Education (FEE)
Irvington-on-Hudson, NY 10533
(914) 591-7230
fax: (914) 591-8910

FEE publishes information and commentary in support of private property, the free market, and limited government. It frequently publishes articles on capitalism and conservatism in its monthly magazine the *Freeman*.

Heritage Foundation
214 Massachusetts Ave. NE
Washington, DC 20002
(202) 546-4400

The Heritage Foundation is a conservative public policy research institute that advocates free-market economics and limited government. Its publications include the monthly *Policy Review*, the *Backgrounder* series of occasional papers, and the *Heritage Lectures* series.

Josephson Institute for the Advancement of Ethics
4640 Admiralty Way, Room 1001
Marina del Rey, CA 90292
(213) 306-1868
fax: (213) 827-1864

The institute is a nonprofit membership organization founded to improve the ethical quality of society by teaching and advocating principled reasoning and ethical decision making. Its Government Ethics Center has conducted programs and workshops for more than twenty thousand influential leaders. Its publications include the periodic newsletter *Ethics in Action*; the quarterly *Ethics: Easier Said Than Done*; course materials; and reports such as *Ethics of American Youth: A Warning and a Call to Action*.

Morality in Media (MIM)
475 Riverside Dr.
New York, NY 10115
(212) 870-3222

MIM opposes what it considers to be indecency in broadcasting—especially the broadcasting of pornography. It works to educate and organize the public in support of strict decency laws, and it has launched an annual "turn off TV day" to protest offensive television programming. The group publishes the *Morality in Media Newsletter* and the handbook *TV: The World's Greatest Mind-Bender*.

National Coalition Against Censorship (NCAC)
2 W. 64th St.
New York, NY 10023
(212) 724-1500

NCAC is an alliance of organizations committed to defending freedom of thought, inquiry, and expression by engaging in public education and advocacy on national and local levels. It publishes periodic reports and the monthly *Censorship News*.

National Organization for Women (NOW)
1000 16th St. NW, Suite 700
Washington, DC 20036
(202) 331-0066
fax: (202) 785-8576

NOW is one of the largest and most influential feminist organizations in the United States. It seeks to end prejudice and discrimination against women in all areas of life. It lobbies legislatures to make more equitable laws and works to educate and inform the public on women's issues. NOW publishes the bimonthly tabloid *NOW Times*, policy statements, and articles.

People for the American Way (PAW)
2000 M St. NW, Suite 400
Washington, DC 20036
(202) 467-4999
fax: (202) 293-2672

PAW works to increase tolerance and respect for America's diverse cultures, religions, and values such as freedom of expression. It distributes educational materials, leaflets, and brochures and publishes the quarterly *Press Clips*, a collection of newspaper articles concerning censorship.

The Rockford Institute
934 N. Main St.
Rockford, IL 61103-7061
(815) 964-5811
fax: (815) 965-1826

The institute works to return America to Judeo-Christian values and supports traditional roles for men and women. It stresses the advantages of two-parent families as the best way to raise children. Its Center on Religion and Society advocates a more public role for religion and religious values in American life. The institute's publications include the monthly periodical *Family in America*, the monthly *Religion & Society Report*, and the quarterly newsletter *Main Street Memorandum*.

Sex Information and Education Council of the U.S. (SIECUS)
130 W. 42nd St., Suite 2500
New York, NY 10036-7901
(212) 819-9770
fax: (212) 819-8776

SIECUS is an organization of educators, physicians, social workers, and others who support the individual's right to acquire knowledge of sexuality and who encourage responsible sexual behavior. The council promotes comprehensive sex education for all children that includes AIDS education, teaching about homosexuality, and instruction about contraceptives and sexually transmitted diseases. Its publications include fact sheets, annotated bibliographies by topic, the booklet *Talking About Sex*, and the bimonthly *SIECUS Report*.

Single Parent Resource Center (SPRC)
141 W. 28th St., Suite 302
New York, NY 10001
(212) 947-0221

The center is a clearinghouse for information about and for single parents. It maintains that as a growing number of children are raised in single-parent families, more aid will be needed to help single parents make good decisions for themselves and their children. SPRC publishes pamphlets on single-parent issues.

Bibliography of Books

Henry J. Aaron,
Thomas E. Mann, and
Timothy Taylor, eds.
Values and Public Policy. Washington, DC: Brookings Institution, 1994.

Michel Albert
Capitalism vs. Capitalism: How America's Obsession with Individual Achievement and Short-Term Profit Has Led It to the Brink of Collapse. New York: Four Walls Eight Windows, 1993.

Robert L. Bartley
The Seven Fat Years: And How to Do It Again. New York: Free Press, 1992.

William J. Bennett, ed.
The Book of Virtues: A Treasury of Great Moral Stories. New York: Simon and Schuster, 1993.

Stephen L. Carter
The Culture of Disbelief: How American Law and Politics Trivialize Religious Devotion. New York: Basic Books, 1993.

James Lincoln Collier
The Rise of Selfishness in America. New York: Oxford University Press, 1991.

Charles Colson and
Jack Eckerd
Why America Doesn't Work. Dallas: Word Publishing, 1991.

James R. Cooper
Twilight's Last Gleaming: The Price of Happiness in America. Buffalo: Prometheus Books, 1992.

William Dunn
The Baby Bust: A Generation Comes of Age. Ithaca, NY: American Demographics, 1993.

Amitai Etzioni
The Spirit of Community: Rights, Responsibilities, and the Communitarian Agenda. New York: Crown, 1993.

Jerry Falwell
The New American Family. Dallas: Word Publishing, 1992.

George P. Fletcher
Loyalty: An Essay on the Morality of Relationships. New York: Oxford University Press, 1993.

John Kenneth
Galbraith
The Culture of Contentment. Boston: Houghton Mifflin, 1992.

William Greider
Who Will Tell the People: The Betrayal of American Democracy. New York: Simon and Schuster, 1992.

Os Guinness
The American Hour: A Time of Reckoning and the Once and Future Role of Faith. New York: Free Press, 1993.

296

Lawrence E. Harrison *Who Prospers: How Cultural Values Shape Economic and Political Success*. New York: Basic Books, 1992.

Nat Hentoff *Free Speech for Me—but Not for Thee: How the American Left and Right Relentlessly Censor Each Other*. New York: HarperCollins, 1992.

James Davison Hunter *Before the Shooting Begins: Searching for Democracy in America's Culture War*. New York: Free Press, 1994.

Russell Kirk *America's British Culture*. New Brunswick, NJ: Transaction Publishers, 1992.

Russell Kirk *The Conservative Constitution*. Washington, DC: Regnery Gateway, 1990.

S. Robert Lichter, Linda S. Lichter, and Stanley Rothman *Watching America: What Television Tells Us About Our Lives*. Englewood Cliffs, NJ: Prentice-Hall, 1991.

Luther S. Luedtke *Making America: The Society and Culture of the United States*. Chapel Hill: University of North Carolina Press, 1992.

Myron Magnet *The Dream and the Nightmare: The Sixties' Legacy to the Underclass*. New York: William Morrow, 1993.

Richard B. McKenzie *What Went Right in the 1980s*. San Francisco: Pacific Research Institute for Public Policy, 1994.

Michael Medved *Hollywood vs. America: Popular Culture and the War on Traditional Values*. New York: HarperCollins, 1992.

Michael J. Meyer and William A. Parent, eds. *The Constitution of Rights: Human Dignity and American Values*. Ithaca, NY: Cornell University Press, 1992.

Art Must Jr. *Why We Still Need Public Schools: Church/State Relations and Visions of Democracy*. Buffalo: Prometheus Books, 1992.

Richard John Neuhaus *America Against Itself: Moral Vision and the Public Order*. Notre Dame, IN: University of Notre Dame Press, 1992.

Katherine Newman *Declining Fortunes: The Withering of the American Dream*. New York: HarperCollins, 1993.

Wallace C. Peterson *Silent Depression: The Fate of the American Dream*. New York: Norton, 1994.

Pat Robertson *The Turning Tide: The Fall of Liberalism and the Rise of Common Sense*. Dallas: Word Publishing, 1993.

Wade Clark Roof	*A Generation of Seekers: The Spiritual Journeys of the Baby Boom Generation.* New York: Harper-Collins, 1993.
Cheryl Russell	*The Master Trend: How the Baby Boom Generation Is Remaking America.* New York: Plenum, 1993.
Arthur M. Schlesinger Jr.	*The Disuniting of America.* New York: Norton, 1991.
Andrew B. Schmookler	*Fool's Gold: The Fate of Values in a World of Goods.* New York: HarperCollins, 1993.
Juliet B. Schor	*The Overworked American: The Unexpected Decline of Leisure.* New York: Basic Books, 1991.
Charles J. Sykes	*A Nation of Victims: The Decay of the American Character.* New York: St. Martin's Press, 1992.
Cal Thomas	*The Things That Matter Most.* New York: Harper-Collins, 1994.
Bob Welch	*More to Life Than Having It All: Living a Life You Won't Regret.* Eugene, OR: Harvest House, 1992.
Gary Wills	*Under God: Religion and American Politics.* New York: Simon and Schuster, 1990.

Index

301